W9-CRH-309

McDougal Littell

World History

Medieval and Early Modern Times

McDougal Littell
A DIVISION OF HOUGHTON MIFFLIN COMPANY

Note *to the* Teacher

The *California Standards Planner and Lesson Plans* is a clear and easy guide that helps teachers use McDougal Littell's *World History: Medieval and Early Modern Times* to teach the History-Social Science Content Standards for the State of California. By using the information in this ancillary, you will be able to teach, assess, and reteach the materials required by state standards, and to do so with enhanced clarity and efficiency.

Whether you are planning your course of instruction, reviewing material, or looking for new and exciting ways to present American history to your students, this ancillary will prove indispensable. Here the correlations between textbook materials and state standards are always at your fingertips. With the help of the Standards Pacing Guide (an entirely new feature), McDougal Littell provides an easy and disciplined way to cover the state standards for California in both standard scheduling and block scheduling. The Lesson Plans provide clear resources to teach the material in *World History: Medieval and Early Modern Times*, allowing you to tailor the text to meet the needs of all your students, to integrate technology into your classroom, and to assess your students in formal and informal ways.

The *California Standards Planner and Lesson Plans* features three main tools:

- **Correlation to California History-Social Science Standards.**
  For ready reference, the California History-Social Science Standards are indexed to page numbers in *World History: Medieval and Early Modern Times*.

- **California Standards Pacing Guide.**
  An entirely new feature, the California Standards Pacing Guide provides a realistic and easy-to-use guide for day-by-day use of *World History: Medieval and Early Modern Times*. This feature ensures that California state standards are thoroughly taught, assessed, and retaught. Presented in both Standard and Block Schedule formats, the entire school year is divided into weekly instructional segments. For each week, standards covered in that week are listed. For each section in the textbook, the relevant state standards are listed, with time provided for assessment and the use of transparencies and technological tools.

- **California Lesson Plans.**
  Provides daily lesson plans, keyed to California standards, for complete help in effective instruction. The relevant California standards are listed at the top of every lesson plan, clear lesson objectives are listed, and a range of instructional materials are referenced, covering Struggling Readers and English Learners, as well as On-Level and Above Level students.

Table *of* Contents

Correlations to California History–Social Science Content Standards and Analysis Skills

Standards Map - Basic Comprehensive Program
Grade Seven - History Social Science
World History and Geography: Medieval and Early Modern Times

Students in grade seven study the social, cultural, and technological changes that occurred in Europe, Africa, and Asia in the years A.D. 500-1789. After reviewing the ancient world and the ways in which archaeologists and historians uncover the past, students study the history and geography of great civilizations that were developing concurrently throughout the world during medieval and early modern times. They examine the growing economic interaction among civilizations as well as the exchange of ideas, beliefs, technologies, and commodities. They learn about the resulting growth of Enlightenment philosophy and the new examination of the concepts of reason and authority, the natural rights of human beings and the divine right of kings, experimentalism in science, and the dogma of belief. Finally, students assess the political forces let loose by the Enlightenment, particularly the rise of democratic ideas, and they learn about the continuing influence of these ideas in the world today.

Standard		Primary Citations	Supporting Citations
7.1	Students analyze the causes and effects of the vast expansion and ultimate disintegration of the Roman Empire.	**PUPIL & TEACHER & eEDITION** Common Pages: **42–43**, 46, **47–51**, 52, **53–56, 57**, 58, **59–63**, 64–65, 66–71, 72–73, 74–75, 236 **PRINT COMPONENT(S)** CA Standards Enrichment Wrkbk: 31–32, 33–34, 35–36 **TRANSPARENCIES/TECHNOLOGY** CA Daily Standards Practice Transparencies: 5–6, 7, 8.	**PRINT COMPONENT(S)** In-Depth Resources Unit 1: 21–22, 24, 26–28, 33–34, 35, 36 In-Depth Resources in Spanish Unit 1: 12, 13, 14, 15, 17, 19–20 History Makers: 3–4 CA Standards Planner & Lesson Plans: L9, L11, L13, L15 **TRANSPARENCIES/TECHNOLOGY** Humanities Transparencies: 3, 4 Map Transparencies: 3, 4 Critical Thinking Transparencies: 7, 8, 9 Benchmark Tests: 2.1, 2.2, 2.3, 2.4 Power Presentations: 2.1, 2.2, 2.3, 2.4

Correlations to California History–Social Science Content Standards and Analysis Skills

Standard	Primary Citations	Supporting Citations
7.1.1 Study the early strengths and lasting contributions of Rome (e.g., significance of Roman citizenship; rights under Roman law; Roman art, architecture, engineering, and philosophy; preservation and transmission of Christianity) and its ultimate internal weaknesses (e.g., rise of autonomous military powers within the empire, undermining of citizenship by the growth of corruption and slavery, lack of education, and distribution of news).	**PUPIL & TEACHER & eEDITION** Common Pages: 42–43, 46, 47–51, 52, **53–56, 57, 66–71, 72–73, 74–75**, 236, R36 **PRINT COMPONENT(S)** CA Standards Enrichment Wrkbk: 31–32 **TRANSPARENCIES/TECHNOLOGY** CA Daily Standards Practice Transparencies: 5–6, 8	**PRINT COMPONENT(S)** In-Depth Resources Unit 1: 21–22, 26–28, 33–34, 36 In-Depth Resources in Spanish Unit 1: 14, 15, 17, 19–20 CA Reading Toolkit: L5, L8 CA Modified Lesson Plans for English Learners: 13, 15, 19 CA Standards Planner & Lesson Plans: L9, L11, L15 **TRANSPARENCIES/TECHNOLOGY** Map Transparencies: 4 Critical Thinking Transparencies: 9 Benchmark Tests: 2.1, 2.2, 2.4 Power Presentations: 2.1, 2.2, 2.4
7.1.2 Discuss the geographic borders of the empire at its height and the factors that threatened its territorial cohesion.	**PUPIL & TEACHER & eEDITION** Common Pages: **42–43**, 52, **49**, 53, 54, **55**, 56, **75** **PRINT COMPONENT(S)** CA Standards Enrichment Wrkbk: 33–34 **TRANSPARENCIES/TECHNOLOGY** CA Daily Standards Practice Transparencies: 6	**PRINT COMPONENT(S)** In-Depth Resources Unit 1: 24 In-Depth Resources in Spanish Unit 1: 12 CA Reading Toolkit: L6 CA Modified Lesson Plans for English Learners: 13, 15 CA Standards Planner & Lesson Plans: L9, L11 **TRANSPARENCIES/TECHNOLOGY** Critical Thinking Transparencies: 7 Benchmark Tests: 2.1, 2.2 Power Presentations: 2.1, 2.2

Standard		Primary Citations	Supporting Citations
7.1.3	Describe the establishment by Constantine of the new capital in Constantinople and the development of the Byzantine Empire, with an emphasis on the consequences of the development of two distinct European civilizations, Eastern Orthodox and Roman Catholic, and their two distinct views on church-state relations.	**PUPIL & TEACHER & eEDITION** Common Pages: **54–55**, 56, **58**, **59–63**, **64–65**, **74**, 75 **PRINT COMPONENT(S)** CA Standards Enrichment Wrkbk: 35–36 **TRANSPARENCIES/TECHNOLOGY** CA Daily Standards Practice Transparencies: 5, 7	**PRINT COMPONENT(S)** In-Depth Resources Unit 1: 21–22, 24, 27, 35 In-Depth Resources in Spanish Unit 1: 13, 15 History Makers: 3–4 CA Reading Toolkit: L7 CA Modified Lesson Plans for English Learners: 17 CA Standards Planner & Lesson Plans: L13 **TRANSPARENCIES/TECHNOLOGY** Critical Thinking Transparencies: 8 Humanities Transparencies: 4 Benchmark Tests: 2.3 Power Presentations: 2.3
7.2	**Students analyze the geographic, political, economic, religious, and social structures of the civilizations of Islam in the Middle Ages.**	**PUPIL & TEACHER & eEDITION** Common Pages: 78–79, 80–81, 82–83, 84, 85–89, 90–91, 92, 93–96, 98, **99–103**, 104–105, 106–107, 108–109, 110–111, 112, **113–116**, 117, 118, **119–125**, 126–129, 130, **131–137**, 138–139, 140–141, **350**, 351–354, R35, R36, R68–R69, R76 Add'l Teacher's Edition: 78, 100, 135 **PRINT COMPONENT(S)** CA Standards Enrichment Wrkbk: 37–38, 39–40, 41–42, 43–44, 45–46, 47–48 **TRANSPARENCIES/TECHNOLOGY** CA Daily Standards Practice Transparencies: 9, 10, 11, 12, 13, 14, 18	**PRINT COMPONENT(S)** In-Depth Resources Unit 2: 11–12, 13, 20, 21, 29–30, 31; Unit 3: 18–19, 20 In-Depth Resources in Spanish Unit 2: 29–30, 31, 32, 37–38, 49 History Makers: 5–6, 7–8 CA Standards Planner & Lesson Plans: L17, L19, L21, L23, L25, L27, L31, L33, L35, L37 **TRANSPARENCIES/TECHNOLOGY** Humanities Transparencies: 5, 6, 7, 8 Map Transparencies: 5, 6, 7, 8, 11 Critical Thinking Transparencies: 11, 12, 13, 14, 15, 16, 23 Benchmark Tests: 3.1, 3.2, 3.3, 4.1, 4.2, 4.3, 5.2, 5.3, 6.1, 6.2 Power Presentations: 3.1, 3.2, 3.3, 4.1, 4.2, 4.3, 5.2, 5.3, 6.1, 6.2

Correlations to California History–Social Science Content Standards and Analysis Skills

Standard	Primary Citations	Supporting Citations
7.2.1 Identify the physical features and describe the climate of the Arabian peninsula, its relationship to surrounding bodies of land and water, and nomadic and sedentary ways of life.	**PUPIL & TEACHER & eEDITION** Common Pages: 78–79, 80–81, 82–83, **85–86**, 87–88, 89, **90–91**, 106, **117** **PRINT COMPONENT(S)** CA Standards Enrichment Wrkbk: 37–38 **TRANSPARENCIES/TECHNOLOGY** CA Daily Standards Practice Transparencies: 9	**PRINT COMPONENT(S)** In-Depth Resources Unit 2: 11–12 In-Depth Resources in Spanish Unit 2: 29–30 CA Reading Toolkit: L9, L36 CA Modified Lesson Plans for English Learners: 21 CA Standards Planner & Lesson Plans: L17, L31, L33 **TRANSPARENCIES/TECHNOLOGY** Critical Thinking Transparencies: 11, 14 Benchmark Tests: 3.1, 5.2, 5.3 Power Presentations: 3.1, 5.2, 5.3
7.2.2 Trace the origins of Islam and the life and teachings of Muhammad, including Islamic teachings on the connection with Judaism and Christianity.	**PUPIL & TEACHER & eEDITION** Common Pages: 78–79, 80–81, 82–83, 84, **88–89**, 92, **93–96**, 98, **99–103**, 104–105, 106–107, **121**, 130, 136, **R68–R69**, R76 Add'l Teacher's Edition: 135 **PRINT COMPONENT(S)** CA Standards Enrichment Wrkbk: 39–40	**PRINT COMPONENT(S)** CA Reading Toolkit: L10, L36 CA Modified Lesson Plans for English Learners: 21, 23, 25 CA Standards Planner & Lesson Plans: L17, L19, L21 **TRANSPARENCIES/TECHNOLOGY** Humanities Transparencies: 5 Map Transparencies: 5 Critical Thinking Transparencies: 12, 14 Benchmark Tests: 3.1, 3.2, 3.3 Power Presentations: 3.1, 3.2, 3.3
7.2.3 Explain the significance of the Qur'an and the Sunnah as the primary sources of Islamic beliefs, practice, and law, and their influence in Muslims' daily life.	**PUPIL & TEACHER & eEDITION** Common Pages: 80, 92, 96, **94–95**, 101, **102**, 103, 106, **107**, R37, R38 Add'l Teacher's Edition: 100 **PRINT COMPONENT(S)** CA Standards Enrichment Wrkbk: 41–42 **TRANSPARENCIES/TECHNOLOGY** CA Daily Standards Practice Transparencies: 10	**PRINT COMPONENT(S)** In-Depth Resources Unit 2: 13 History Makers: 5–6, 7–8 CA Reading Toolkit: L11 CA Modified Lesson Plans for English Learners: 23 CA Standards Planner & Lesson Plans: L19 **TRANSPARENCIES/TECHNOLOGY** Humanities Transparencies: 5 Critical Thinking Transparencies: 14 Benchmark Tests: 3.2 Power Presentations: 3.2

Standard		Primary Citations	Supporting Citations
7.2.4	Discuss the expansion of Muslim rule through military conquests and treaties, emphasizing the cultural blending within Muslim civilization and the spread and acceptance of Islam and the Arabic language.	**PUPIL & TEACHER & eEDITION** Common Pages: 80–81, 98, **99–103, 104–105,** 106–107, 108–109, 110–111, 112, **113–116,** 117, 118, **119–125,** 130, **131–137,** 140–141, 350, 351–354 Add'l Teacher's Edition: 78 **PRINT COMPONENT(S)** CA Standards Enrichment Wrkbk: 43–44 **TRANSPARENCIES/TECHNOLOGY** CA Daily Standards Practice Transparencies: 11, 12, 18	**PRINT COMPONENT(S)** In-Depth Resources Unit 2: 20; Unit 3: 20 In-Depth Resources in Spanish Unit 2: 31; Unit 3: 49 CA Reading Toolkit: L12, L14 CA Modified Lesson Plans for English Learners: 23, 25, 27, 29, 31, 39 CA Standards Planner & Lesson Plans: L19, L21, L23, L25, L27, L35 **TRANSPARENCIES/TECHNOLOGY** Humanities Transparencies: 7 Map Transparencies: 6, 7, 8 Critical Thinking Transparencies: 13, 14, 15, 23 Benchmark Tests: 3.2, 3.3, 4.1, 4.2, 4.3, 6.1 Power Presentations: 3.2, 3.3, 4.1, 4.2, 4.3, 6.1
7.2.5	Describe the growth of cities and the establishment of trade routes among Asia, Africa, and Europe, the products and inventions that traveled along these routes (e.g., spices, textiles, paper, steel, new crops), and the role of merchants in Arab society.	**PUPIL & TEACHER & eEDITION** Common Pages: 78–79, **84,** 87–88, 89, **90–91,** 106, 110–111, 115, **120–121,** 126–129, **133** **PRINT COMPONENT(S)** CA Standards Enrichment Wrkbk: 45–46	**PRINT COMPONENT(S)** In-Depth Resources Unit 2: 29–30; Unit 3: 18–19 In-Depth Resources in Spanish Unit 3: 37–38 CA Reading Toolkit: L13 CA Modified Lesson Plans for English Learners: 21, 29, 31, 39, 41 CA Standards Planner & Lesson Plans: L17, L25, L27, L35, L37 **TRANSPARENCIES/TECHNOLOGY** Humanities Transparencies: 6, 8 Map Transparencies: 11 Critical Thinking Transparencies: 11, 14 Benchmark Tests: 3.1, 4.2, 4.3, 6.1, 6.2 Power Presentations: 3.1, 4.2, 4.3, 6.1, 6.2

Correlations to California History–Social Science Content Standards and Analysis Skills

Standard	Primary Citations	Supporting Citations
7.2.6 Understand the intellectual exchanges among Muslim scholars of Eurasia and Africa and the contributions Muslim scholars made to later civilizations in the areas of science, geography, mathematics, philosophy, medicine, art, and literature.	**PUPIL & TEACHER & eEDITION** Common Pages: **95–96, 103**, 107, 115, **121–123**, 125, 126–129, 130, **132–137, 138–139**, 140–141, R40 Add'l Teacher's Edition: 78, 100 **PRINT COMPONENT(S)** CA Standards Enrichment Wrkbk: 47–48 **TRANSPARENCIES/TECHNOLOGY** CA Daily Standards Practice Transparencies: 13, 14	**PRINT COMPONENT(S)** In-Depth Resources Unit 2: 21, 32 In-Depth Resources in Spanish Unit 2: 32 CA Reading Toolkit: L13, L14 CA Modified Lesson Plans for English Learners: 29 CA Standards Planner & Lesson Plans: L25 **TRANSPARENCIES/TECHNOLOGY** Critical Thinking Transparencies: 16 Benchmark Tests: 4.2 Power Presentations: 4.2
7.3 **Students analyze the geographic, political, economic, religious, and social structures of the civilizations of China in the Middle Ages.**	**PUPIL & TEACHER & eEDITION** Common Pages: **23, 34**, 206–207, **208–209**, 210–211, 212, **213–219**, 220–221, 222, **223–229**, 230–231, 232, **233–237**, 238, **239–242**, 243, 244–245, 276, R72–R73, R76 Add'l Teacher's Edition: 206, 207B **PRINT COMPONENT(S)** CA Standards Enrichment Wrkbk: 49–50, 51–52, 53–54, 55–56, 57–48, 59–60 **TRANSPARENCIES/TECHNOLOGY** CA Daily Standards Practice Transparencies: 21, 22, 23, 24	**PRINT COMPONENT(S)** In-Depth Resources Unit 4: 3, 4, 6, 8, 15, 16 In-Depth Resources in Spanish Unit 4: 58, 59, 61, 63 History Makers: 13–14 CA Standards Planner & Lesson Plans: L41, L43, L45, L47, L55 **TRANSPARENCIES/TECHNOLOGY** Humanities Transparencies: 13, 14 Map Transparencies: 13 Critical Thinking Transparencies: 27, 28, 30, 33, 36 Benchmark Tests: 7.1, 7.2, 7.3, 7.4, 8.4 Power Presentations: 7.1, 7.2, 7.3, 7.4, 8.4
7.3.1 Describe the reunification of China under the Tang Dynasty and reasons for the spread of Buddhism in Tang China, Korea, and Japan.	**PUPIL & TEACHER & eEDITION** Common Pages: 22, 34, 208, **214–215**, 216–217, **218–219, 220–221**, 222, **223–224**, 225–226, 228–229, 244–245 **PRINT COMPONENT(S)** CA Standards Enrichment Wrkbk: 49–50 **TRANSPARENCIES/TECHNOLOGY** CA Daily Standards Practice Transparencies: 21	**PRINT COMPONENT(S)** In-Depth Resources Unit 4: 3 In-Depth Resources in Spanish Unit 4: 58 CA Reading Toolkit: L21 CA Modified Lesson Plans for English Learners: 45 CA Standards Planner & Lesson Plans: L41, L55 **TRANSPARENCIES/TECHNOLOGY** Critical Thinking Transparencies: 27, 33, 36 Benchmark Tests: 7.1, 8.4 Power Presentations: 7.1, 8.4

Standard	Primary Citations	Supporting Citations
7.3.2 Describe agricultural, technological, and commercial developments during the Tang and Sung periods.	**PUPIL & TEACHER & eEDITION** Common Pages: **214–215**, 220–221, 222, 223–224, **225–226**, 228–229, 230–231, **244–245** **PRINT COMPONENT(S)** CA Standards Enrichment Wrkbk: 51–52	**PRINT COMPONENT(S)** In-Depth Resources Unit 4: 4 In-Depth Resources in Spanish Unit 4: 59 CA Reading Toolkit: L22 CA Modified Lesson Plans for English Learners: 47 CA Standards Planner & Lesson Plans: L41, L43 **TRANSPARENCIES/TECHNOLOGY** Map Transparencies: 13 Critical Thinking Transparencies: 28 Benchmark Tests: 7.1, 7.2 Power Presentations: 7.1, 7.2
7.3.3 Analyze the influences of Confucianism and changes in Confucian thought during the Sung and Mongol periods.	**PUPIL & TEACHER & eEDITION** Common Pages: 208, **214–216**, 217, **219**, **220–221**, 224, 227, 235, 276, R72–R73, R76 **PRINT COMPONENT(S)** CA Standards Enrichment Wrkbk: 53–54	**PRINT COMPONENT(S)** CA Modified Lesson Plans for English Learners: 45 CA Standards Planner & Lesson Plans: L41, L45 **TRANSPARENCIES/TECHNOLOGY** Benchmark Tests: 7.1, 7.3 Power Presentations: 7.1, 7.3
7.3.4 Understand the importance of both overland trade and maritime expeditions between China and other civilizations in the Mongol Ascendancy and Ming Dynasty.	**PUPIL & TEACHER & eEDITION** Common Pages: 232, **235–237**, **238**, **239**, **240**, **241–242**, 243, 244–245 Add'l Teacher's Edition: 206 **PRINT COMPONENT(S)** CA Standards Enrichment Wrkbk: 55–56 **TRANSPARENCIES/TECHNOLOGY** CA Daily Standards Practice Transparencies: 23, 24	**PRINT COMPONENT(S)** In-Depth Resources Unit 4: 6, 8 In-Depth Resources in Spanish Unit 4: 61, 63 CA Reading Toolkit: L23 CA Modified Lesson Plans for English Learners: 49, 51 CA Standards Planner & Lesson Plans: L45, L47 **TRANSPARENCIES/TECHNOLOGY** Critical Thinking Transparencies: 30 Benchmark Tests: 7.3, 7.4 Power Presentations: 7.3, 7.4

Correlations to California History–Social Science Content Standards and Analysis Skills

Standard	Primary Citations	Supporting Citations
7.3.5 Trace the historic influence of such discoveries as tea, the manufacture of paper, woodblock printing, the compass, and gunpowder.	**PUPIL & TEACHER & eEDITION** Common Pages: 207, 222, 223, **227–229, 230–231**, 236, 241, **243**, 244–245 **PRINT COMPONENT(S)** CA Standards Enrichment Wrkbk: 57–58 **TRANSPARENCIES/TECHNOLOGY** CA Daily Standards Practice Transparencies: 22	**PRINT COMPONENT(S)** CA Reading Toolkit: L22 CA Modified Lesson Plans for English Learners: 47, 51 CA Standards Planner & Lesson Plans: L43, L47 **TRANSPARENCIES/TECHNOLOGY** Benchmark Tests: 7.2, 7.4 Power Presentations: 7.2, 7.4
7.3.6 Describe the development of the imperial state and the scholar-official class.	**PUPIL & TEACHER & eEDITION** Common Pages: 214, 217–218, 219, 222, **223–224**, 225–227, **228**, 229, 230–231, 235, 244–245 Add'l Teacher's Edition: 207B **PRINT COMPONENT(S)** CA Standards Enrichment Wrkbk: 59–60	**PRINT COMPONENT(S)** CA Modified Lesson Plans for English Learners: 47 CA Standards Planner & Lesson Plans: L43 **TRANSPARENCIES/TECHNOLOGY** Benchmark Tests: 7.2 Power Presentations: 7.2
7.4 Students analyze the geographic, political, economic, religious, and social structures of the sub-Saharan civilizations of Ghana and Mali in Medieval Africa.	**PUPIL & TEACHER & eEDITION** Common Pages: **146–147**, 148–149, 150, 151–154, 156, **157–161**, 162–163, 164, **165–167**, 168, 169, **170–173, 174–175** Add'l Teacher's Edition: 144 **PRINT COMPONENT(S)** CA Standards Enrichment Wrkbk: 55–56, 61–62, 63–64, 65–66, 67–68, 69–70 **TRANSPARENCIES/TECHNOLOGY** CA Daily Standards Practice Transparencies: 15, 16, 17, 19	**PRINT COMPONENT(S)** In-Depth Resources Unit 3: 7, 11–12, 13–14, 24, 29–30 In-Depth Resources in Spanish Unit 3: 45, 47–48 History Makers: 9–10 CA Standards Planner & Lesson Plans: L29, L31, L33, L37, L47 **TRANSPARENCIES/TECHNOLOGY** Humanities Transparencies: 9, 10 Map Transparencies: 9 Critical Thinking Transparencies: 19, 20, 21, 22 Benchmark Tests: 5.1, 5.2, 5.3, 6.2, 7.4 Power Presentations: 5.1, 5.2, 5.3, 6.2, 7.4

Standard		Primary Citations	Supporting Citations
7.4.1	Study the Niger River and the relationship of vegetation zones of forest, savannah, and desert to trade in gold, salt, food, and slaves; and the growth of the Ghana and Mali empires.	**PUPIL & TEACHER & eEDITION** Common Pages: **157–158**, 159, 161, **162–163**, **165**, **174**, **175** Add'l Teacher's Edition: 144 **PRINT COMPONENT(S)** CA Standards Enrichment Wrkbk: 61–62 **TRANSPARENCIES/TECHNOLOGY** CA Daily Standards Practice Transparencies: 16	**PRINT COMPONENT(S)** In-Depth Resources Unit 3: 7, 11–12, 29–30 In-Depth Resources in Spanish Unit 3: 45, 47–48 CA Reading Toolkit: L15 CA Modified Lesson Plans for English Learners: 33, 35, 37 CA Standards Planner & Lesson Plans: L29, L31, L33 **TRANSPARENCIES/TECHNOLOGY** Humanities Transparencies: 10 Critical Thinking Transparencies: 19, 20, 21, 22 Benchmark Tests: 5.1, 5.2, 5.3 Power Presentations: 5.1, 5.2, 5.3
7.4.2	Analyze the importance of family, labor specialization, and regional commerce in the development of states and cities in West Africa.	**PUPIL & TEACHER & eEDITION** Common Pages: **148–149**, **150**, **151–154**, 156, **158–159**, **162–163**, 174–175 Add'l Teacher's Edition: 144 **PRINT COMPONENT(S)** CA Standards Enrichment Wrkbk: 63–64 **TRANSPARENCIES/TECHNOLOGY** CA Daily Standards Practice Transparencies: 15	**PRINT COMPONENT(S)** CA Reading Toolkit: L15 CA Modified Lesson Plans for English Learners: 33 CA Standards Planner & Lesson Plans: L29 **TRANSPARENCIES/TECHNOLOGY** Critical Thinking Transparencies: 19, 22 Benchmark Tests: 5.1 Power Presentations: 5.1
7.4.3	Describe the role of the trans-Saharan caravan trade in the changing religious and cultural characteristics of West Africa and the influence of Islamic beliefs, ethics, and law.	**PUPIL & TEACHER & eEDITION** Common Pages: 147, 148–149, 150, **152–153**, 156, 157–159, 161, 165, **167**, **174**, R41 Add'l Teacher's Edition: 144 **PRINT COMPONENT(S)** CA Standards Enrichment Wrkbk: 65–66 **TRANSPARENCIES/TECHNOLOGY** CA Daily Standards Practice Transparencies: 17	**PRINT COMPONENT(S)** CA Reading Toolkit: L16, L17 CA Modified Lesson Plans for English Learners: 35, 37 CA Standards Planner & Lesson Plans: L31, L33 **TRANSPARENCIES/TECHNOLOGY** Map Transparencies: 9 Critical Thinking Transparencies: 20, 21, 22 Benchmark Tests: 5.2, 5.3 Power Presentations: 5.2, 5.3

Copyright © by McDougal Littell, a division of Houghton Mifflin Company

Correlations to California History–Social Science Content Standards and Analysis Skills

Standard		Primary Citations	Supporting Citations
7.4.4	Trace the growth of the Arabic language in government, trade, and Islamic scholarship in West Africa.	**PUPIL & TEACHER & eEDITION** Common Pages: **159, 160, 165, 166, 168** **PRINT COMPONENT(S)** CA Standards Enrichment Wrkbk: 67–68	**PRINT COMPONENT(S)** CA Reading Toolkit: L17 CA Modified Lesson Plans for English Learners: 35, 37 CA Standards Planner & Lesson Plans: L31, L33 **TRANSPARENCIES/TECHNOLOGY** Critical Thinking Transparencies: 20, 21, 22 Benchmark Tests: 5.2, 5.3 Power Presentations: 5.2, 5.3
7.4.5	Describe the importance of written and oral traditions in the transmission of African history and culture.	**PUPIL & TEACHER & eEDITION** Common Pages: **153–154, 160, 165, 166**, 167, 168, **170–173** **PRINT COMPONENT(S)** CA Standards Enrichment Wrkbk: 69–70 **TRANSPARENCIES/TECHNOLOGY** CA Daily Standards Practice Transparencies: 19	**PRINT COMPONENT(S)** In-Depth Resources Unit 3: 24 History Makers: 9–10 CA Modified Lesson Plans for English Learners: 33, 41 CA Standards Planner & Lesson Plans: L29, L37 **TRANSPARENCIES/TECHNOLOGY** Critical Thinking Transparencies: 19, 22 Benchmark Tests: 5.1, 6.2 Power Presentations: 5.1, 6.2
7.5	Students analyze the geographic, political, economic, religious, and social structures of the civilizations of Medieval Japan.	**PUPIL & TEACHER & eEDITION** Common Pages: 215, **246–247**, 248–249, 250, **251–254**, 255, 256, **257–261**, **262–265**, 266, **267–271**, 272–273, 276, 280–281 Add'l Teacher's Edition: 246 **PRINT COMPONENT(S)** CA Standards Enrichment Wrkbk: 71–72, 73–74, 75–76, 77–78, 79–80, 81–82 **TRANSPARENCIES/TECHNOLOGY** CA Daily Standards Practice Transparencies: 25, 26, 27	**PRINT COMPONENT(S)** In-Depth Resources Unit 4: 28, 35 In-Depth Resources in Spanish Unit 4: 73 History Makers: 15–16 CA Standards Planner & Lesson Plans: L49, L51, L53 **TRANSPARENCIES/TECHNOLOGY** Humanities Transparencies: 15 Map Transparencies: 15 Critical Thinking Transparencies: 32, 33, 34, 36 Benchmark Tests: 8.1, 8.2, 8.3 Power Presentations: 8.1, 8.2, 8.3

Standard		Primary Citations	Supporting Citations
7.5.1	Describe the significance of Japan's proximity to China and Korea and the intellectual, linguistic, religious, and philosophical influence of those countries on Japan.	**PUPIL & TEACHER & eEDITION** Common Pages: **215**, **250**, **252**, **253–254**, **257–258**, 259, 260, **276**, 280–281 **PRINT COMPONENT(S)** CA Standards Enrichment Wrkbk: 71–72 **TRANSPARENCIES/TECHNOLOGY** CA Daily Standards Practice Transparencies: 25, 26	**PRINT COMPONENT(S)** CA Reading Toolkit: L25, L26, L28 CA Modified Lesson Plans for English Learners: 53 CA Standards Planner & Lesson Plans: L49 **TRANSPARENCIES/TECHNOLOGY** Map Transparencies: 15 Critical Thinking Transparencies: 32, 33 Benchmark Tests: 8.1 Power Presentations: 8.1
7.5.2	Discuss the reign of Prince Shotoku of Japan and the characteristics of Japanese society and family life during his reign.	**PUPIL & TEACHER & eEDITION** Common Pages: **250**, **253–254**, **257**, **267**, 280 Add'l Teacher's Edition: 246 **PRINT COMPONENT(S)** CA Standards Enrichment Wrkbk: 73–74	**PRINT COMPONENT(S)** History Makers: 15–16 CA Reading Toolkit: L26 CA Modified Lesson Plans for English Learners: 53 CA Standards Planner & Lesson Plans: L49 **TRANSPARENCIES/TECHNOLOGY** Critical Thinking Transparencies: 32, 33 Benchmark Tests: 8.1 Power Presentations: 8.1
7.5.3	Describe the values, social customs, and traditions prescribed by the lord-vassal system consisting of shogun, daimyo, and samurai and the lasting influence of the warrior code in the twentieth century.	**PUPIL & TEACHER & eEDITION** Common Pages: **248–249**, **266**, **267–271**, **272–273**, 280 Add'l Teacher's Edition: 246 **PRINT COMPONENT(S)** CA Standards Enrichment Wrkbk: 75–76 **TRANSPARENCIES/TECHNOLOGY** CA Daily Standards Practice Transparencies: 27	**PRINT COMPONENT(S)** CA Reading Toolkit: L27 CA Modified Lesson Plans for English Learners: 57 CA Standards Planner & Lesson Plans: L53 **TRANSPARENCIES/TECHNOLOGY** Benchmark Tests: 8.3 Power Presentations: 8.3

Correlations to California History–Social Science Content Standards and Analysis Skills

Standard	Primary Citations	Supporting Citations
7.5.4 Trace the development of distinctive forms of Japanese Buddhism.	**PUPIL & TEACHER & eEDITION** Common Pages: **215, 254, 256, 257–258, 266, 280** **PRINT COMPONENT(S)** CA Standards Enrichment Wrkbk: 77–78 **TRANSPARENCIES/TECHNOLOGY** CA Daily Standards Practice Transparencies: 25, 26	**PRINT COMPONENT(S)** In-Depth Resources Unit 4: 35 CA Reading Toolkit: L26 CA Modified Lesson Plans for English Learners: 55 CA Standards Planner & Lesson Plans: L51 **TRANSPARENCIES/TECHNOLOGY** Critical Thinking Transparencies: 33 Benchmark Tests: 8.2 Power Presentations: 8.2
7.5.5 Study the ninth and tenth centuries' golden age of literature, art, and drama and its lasting effects on culture today, including Murasaki Shikibu's Tale of Genji.	**PUPIL & TEACHER & eEDITION** Common Pages: **256, 258–261, 281** **PRINT COMPONENT(S)** CA Standards Enrichment Wrkbk: 79–80	**PRINT COMPONENT(S)** CA Modified Lesson Plans for English Learners: 55 CA Standards Planner & Lesson Plans: L51 **TRANSPARENCIES/TECHNOLOGY** Humanities Transparencies: 15 Critical Thinking Transparencies: 33 Benchmark Tests: 8.2 Power Presentations: 8.2
7.5.6 Analyze the rise of a military society in the late twelfth century and the role of the samurai in that society.	**PUPIL & TEACHER & eEDITION** Common Pages: **246–247, 248–249, 262–265, 266, 267–271, 272–273, 280** Add'l Teacher's Edition: 246 **PRINT COMPONENT(S)** CA Standards Enrichment Wrkbk: 81–82 **TRANSPARENCIES/TECHNOLOGY** CA Daily Standards Practice Transparencies: 27	**PRINT COMPONENT(S)** In-Depth Resources Unit 4: 28 In-Depth Resources in Spanish Unit 4: 73 CA Reading Toolkit: L27 CA Modified Lesson Plans for English Learners: 57 CA Standards Planner & Lesson Plans: L53 **TRANSPARENCIES/TECHNOLOGY** Critical Thinking Transparencies: 34 Benchmark Tests: 8.3 Power Presentations: 8.3

Standard		Primary Citations	Supporting Citations
7.6	Students analyze the geographic, political, economic, religious, and social structures of the civilizations of Medieval Europe.	**PUPIL & TEACHER & eEDITION** Common Pages: 62–63, 137, 284–285, 286–287, 288–289, 290, **291–297**, 298, **299–302**, 303, 304–305, 306, **307–311**, 312–313, 314–315, 316–317, 318–319, 320, **321–325**, 326, 327–331, 332, **333–337**, 338–339, 340, 341–345, 346–349, 356–357, 458–459, 460, 461–465, 470, 471–475, 479–483, 486, 487, 499, R45 Add'l Teacher's Edition: 284, 285, 316, 324 **PRINT COMPONENT(S)** CA Standards Enrichment Wrkbk: 83–84, 85–86, 87–88, 89–90, 91–92, 93–94, 95–96, 97–98, 99–100 **TRANSPARENCIES/TECHNOLOGY** CA Daily Standards Practice Transparencies: 30–31, 32, 33, 34, 35	**PRINT COMPONENT(S)** In-Depth Resources Unit 5: 1–4, 6–7, 11–14, 26, 31–32, 33, 34 In-Depth Resources in Spanish Unit 5: 78–79, 81, 85–86, 93, 95–96 History Makers: 17–18, 19–20 CA Standards Planner & Lesson Plans: L57, L59, L63, L65, L67, L69 **TRANSPARENCIES/TECHNOLOGY** Humanities Transparencies: 17–18, 19 Map Transparencies: 14, 17 Critical Thinking Transparencies: 37–39, 41, 42, 43, 44 Benchmark Tests: 9.1, 9.2, 10.1, 10.2, 10.3, 10.4 Power Presentations: 9.1, 9.2, 10.1, 10.2, 10.3, 10.4
7.6.1	Study the geography of Europe and the Eurasian land mass, including its location, topography, waterways, vegetation, and climate and their relationship to ways of life in Medieval Europe.	**PUPIL & TEACHER & eEDITION** Common Pages: **291–293, 318–319, 334** **PRINT COMPONENT(S)** CA Standards Enrichment Wrkbk: 83–84	**PRINT COMPONENT(S)** In-Depth Resources Unit 5: 6, 11–12, In-Depth Resources in Spanish Unit 5: 81, 85–86 CA Reading Toolkit: L30, L31 CA Modified Lesson Plans for English Learners: 61 CA Standards Planner & Lesson Plans: L57, L59 **TRANSPARENCIES/TECHNOLOGY** Map Transparencies: 17 Benchmark Tests: 9.1, 9.2 Power Presentations: 9.1, 9.2

Correlations to California History–Social Science Content Standards and Analysis Skills

Standard		Primary Citations	Supporting Citations
7.6.2	Describe the spread of Christianity north of the Alps and the roles played by the early church and by monasteries in its diffusion after the fall of the western half of the Roman Empire.	**PUPIL & TEACHER & eEDITION** Common Pages: **293–295, 296, 308, 314** Add'l Teacher's Edition: 324 **PRINT COMPONENT(S)** CA Standards Enrichment Wrkbk: 85–86	**PRINT COMPONENT(S)** In-Depth Resources Unit 5: 1–4, 6–7, 11–14 In-Depth Resources in Spanish Unit 5: 78–79, 81, 85–86 CA Reading Toolkit: L29, L30 CA Modified Lesson Plans for English Learners: 61, 63, 65 CA Standards Planner & Lesson Plans: L57 **TRANSPARENCIES/TECHNOLOGY** Humanities Transparencies: 17, 18 Map Transparencies: 14 Critical Thinking Transparencies: 37–39 Benchmark Tests: 9.1 Power Presentations: 9.1
7.6.3	Understand the development of feudalism, its role in the medieval European economy, the way in which it was influenced by physical geography (the role of the manor and the growth of towns), and how feudal relationships provided the foundation of political order.	**PUPIL & TEACHER & eEDITION** Common Pages: 286–287, 288–289, 290, **291–293, 295–297**, 298, 299–302, 303, 304–305, 306, **307–311, 312–313,** 314–315 Add'l Teacher's Edition: 284, 285 **PRINT COMPONENT(S)** CA Standards Enrichment Wrkbk: 87–88 **TRANSPARENCIES/TECHNOLOGY** CA Daily Standards Practice Transparencies: 30–31	**PRINT COMPONENT(S)** In-Depth Resources Unit 5: 1–4, 6–7, 11–14 In-Depth Resources in Spanish Unit 5: 78–79, 81, 85–86 CA Reading Toolkit: L29, L30 CA Modified Lesson Plans for English Learners: 61, 63, 65 CA Standards Planner & Lesson Plans: L57 **TRANSPARENCIES/TECHNOLOGY** Humanities Transparencies: 17, 18 Map Transparencies: 14 Critical Thinking Transparencies: 37–39 Benchmark Tests: 9.1 Power Presentations: 9.1
7.6.4	Demonstrate an understanding of the conflict and cooperation between the Papacy and European monarchs (e.g., Charlemagne, Gregory VII, Emperor Henry IV).	**PUPIL & TEACHER & eEDITION** Common Pages: **320, 321–325** **PRINT COMPONENT(S)** CA Standards Enrichment Wrkbk: 89–90 **TRANSPARENCIES/TECHNOLOGY** CA Daily Standards Practice Transparencies: 32	**PRINT COMPONENT(S)** In-Depth Resources Unit 5: 33 CA Reading Toolkit: L29, L32 CA Modified Lesson Plans for English Learners: 67 CA Standards Planner & Lesson Plans: L63 **TRANSPARENCIES/TECHNOLOGY** Critical Thinking Transparencies: 41 Benchmark Tests: 10.1 Power Presentations: 10.1

Standard	Primary Citations	Supporting Citations
7.6.5 Know the significance of developments in medieval English legal and constitutional practices and their importance in the rise of modern democratic thought and representative institutions (e.g., Magna Carta, parliament, development of habeas corpus, an independent judiciary in England).	**PUPIL & TEACHER & eEDITION** Common Pages: **340, 341–345,** 346–349, 356, R46 **PRINT COMPONENT(S)** CA Standards Enrichment Wrkbk: 91–92 **TRANSPARENCIES/TECHNOLOGY** CA Daily Standards Practice Transparencies: 35	**PRINT COMPONENT(S)** CA Reading Toolkit: L35 CA Modified Lesson Plans for English Learners: 73 CA Standards Planner & Lesson Plans: L69 **TRANSPARENCIES/TECHNOLOGY** Critical Thinking Transparencies: 44 Benchmark Tests: 10.4 Power Presentations: 10.4
7.6.6 Discuss the causes and course of the religious Crusades and their effects on the Christian, Muslim, and Jewish populations in Europe, with emphasis on the increasing contact by Europeans with cultures of the Eastern Mediterranean world.	**PUPIL & TEACHER & eEDITION** Common Pages: 326, **327–331,** 356 **PRINT COMPONENT(S)** CA Standards Enrichment Wrkbk: 93–94 **TRANSPARENCIES/TECHNOLOGY** CA Daily Standards Practice Transparencies: 33	**PRINT COMPONENT(S)** CA Reading Toolkit: L33 CA Modified Lesson Plans for English Learners: 69 CA Standards Planner & Lesson Plans: L65 **TRANSPARENCIES/TECHNOLOGY** Critical Thinking Transparencies: 42, 43 Benchmark Tests: 10.2 Power Presentations: 10.2
7.6.7 Map the spread of the bubonic plague from Central Asia to China, the Middle East, and Europe and describe its impact on global population.	**PUPIL & TEACHER & eEDITION** Common Pages: **318–319, 333–334, 337,** 356, 357 Add'l Teacher's Edition: 316 **PRINT COMPONENT(S)** CA Standards Enrichment Wrkbk: 95–96 **TRANSPARENCIES/TECHNOLOGY** CA Daily Standards Practice Transparencies: 34	**PRINT COMPONENT(S)** In-Depth Resources Unit 5: 34 CA Reading Toolkit: L34 CA Modified Lesson Plans for English Learners: 71 CA Standards Planner & Lesson Plans: L67 **TRANSPARENCIES/TECHNOLOGY** Benchmark Tests: 10.3 Power Presentations: 10.3

Correlations to California History–Social Science Content Standards and Analysis Skills

Standard	Primary Citations	Supporting Citations
7.6.8 Understand the importance of the Catholic church as a political, intellectual, and aesthetic institution (e.g., founding of universities, political and spiritual roles of the clergy, creation of monastic and mendicant religious orders, preservation of the Latin language and religious texts, St. Thomas Aquinas's synthesis of classical philosophy with Christian theology, and the concept of "natural law").	**PUPIL & TEACHER & eEDITION** Common Pages: 62–63, **320, 321–325,** 458–459, 460, **461–465,** 470, **471–475, 479–483,** 486–487, 499 **PRINT COMPONENT(S)** CA Standards Enrichment Wrkbk: 97–98	**PRINT COMPONENT(S)** CA Modified Lesson Plans for English Learners: 67 CA Standards Planner & Lesson Plans: L63 **TRANSPARENCIES/TECHNOLOGY** Humanities Transparencies: 19 Critical Thinking Transparencies: 41 Benchmark Tests: 10.1 Power Presentations: 10.1
7.6.9 Know the history of the decline of Muslim rule in the Iberian Peninsula that culminated in the Reconquista and the rise of Spanish and Portuguese kingdoms.	**PUPIL & TEACHER & eEDITION** Common Pages: 137, **330–331** **PRINT COMPONENT(S)** CA Standards Enrichment Wrkbk: 99–100	**PRINT COMPONENT(S)** CA Modified Lesson Plans for English Learners: 69 CA Standards Planner & Lesson Plans: L65 **TRANSPARENCIES/TECHNOLOGY** Critical Thinking Transparencies: 42 Benchmark Tests: 10.2 Power Presentations: 10.2
7.7 Students compare and contrast the geographic, political, economic, religious, and social structures of the Meso-American and Andean civilizations.	**PUPIL & TEACHER & eEDITION** Common Pages: 360–361, **362–363,** 364–365, 366, **367–371,** 372, **373–377,** 378–379, 380, 381–386, 387, 388–389, 390–391, 392–393, 394–395, 396, **397–402,** 403, 404–407, 408, **409–415,** 416–417, 418–419 Add'l Teacher's Edition: 360, 361, 366, 374 **PRINT COMPONENT(S)** CA Standards Enrichment Wrkbk: 1–16, 101–102, 103–104, 105–106, 107–108, 109–110 **TRANSPARENCIES/TECHNOLOGY** CA Daily Standards Practice Transparencies: 37, 38, 39, 40, 41	**PRINT COMPONENT(S)** In-Depth Resources Unit 6: 3, 4, 5, 7, 13, 14, 23, 27–28, 29, 30 In-Depth Resources in Spanish Unit 6: 98, 99, 100, 103, 113–114 History Makers: 21–22, 23–24 CA Standards Planner & Lesson Plans: L61, L73, L75, L77, L79, L81 **TRANSPARENCIES/TECHNOLOGY** Humanities Transparencies: 21, 22, 23, 24 Map Transparencies: 21, 22, 23, 24 Critical Thinking Transparencies: 47, 49, 51, 52, 53 Benchmark Tests: 9.3, 11.1, 11.3, 12.1, 12.2, 12.3 Power Presentations: 9.3, 11.1, 11.3, 12.1, 12.2, 12.3

Standard	Primary Citations	Supporting Citations
7.7.1 Study the locations, landforms, and climates of Mexico, Central America, and South America and their effects on Mayan, Aztec, and Incan economies, trade, and development of urban societies.	**PUPIL & TEACHER & eEDITION** Common Pages: 366, **367–368, 369–371**, 372, 373, 382, 388, 390, 391, **394–395**, 396, **397–398**, 403, **404–407**, 408, 409, 416–417, 418–419 Add'l Teacher's Edition: 374 **PRINT COMPONENT(S)** CA Standards Enrichment Wrkbk: 101–102 **TRANSPARENCIES/TECHNOLOGY** CA Daily Standards Practice Transparencies: 37	**PRINT COMPONENT(S)** In-Depth Resources Unit 6: 3, 7 In-Depth Resources in Spanish Unit 6: 98, 103 CA Reading Toolkit: L37, L38, L39, L41 CA Modified Lesson Plans for English Learners: 77, 83, 85 CA Standards Planner & Lesson Plans: L73, L79, L81 **TRANSPARENCIES/TECHNOLOGY** Map Transparencies: 21 Critical Thinking Transparencies: 47, 52, 53 Benchmark Tests: 11.1, 12.1, 12.2 Power Presentations: 11.1, 12.1, 12.2
7.7.2 Study the roles of people in each society, including class structures, family life, warfare, religious beliefs and practices, and slavery.	**PUPIL & TEACHER & eEDITION** Common Pages: 361, 364–365, 372, **374–376**, 377, **382–384**, 390, 391, 396, **399–400**, 401–402, **411–413**, **414–415**, 416–417, 418–419 Add'l Teacher's Edition: 360 **PRINT COMPONENT(S)** CA Standards Enrichment Wrkbk: 103–104 **TRANSPARENCIES/TECHNOLOGY** CA Daily Standards Practice Transparencies: 39	**PRINT COMPONENT(S)** In-Depth Resources Unit 6: 5, 13, 23, 30 In-Depth Resources in Spanish Unit 6: 100 History Makers: 23–24 CA Reading Toolkit: L39, L40, L41 CA Modified Lesson Plans for English Learners: 81, 83, 85 CA Standards Planner & Lesson Plans: L77, L79, L81 **TRANSPARENCIES/TECHNOLOGY** Humanities Transparencies: 21, 23 Critical Thinking Transparencies: 49, 52, 53 Benchmark Tests: 11.3, 12.1, 12.2 Power Presentations: 11.3, 12.1, 12.2

Correlations to California History–Social Science Content Standards and Analysis Skills

Standard		Primary Citations	Supporting Citations
7.7.3	Explain how and where each empire arose and how the Aztec and Incan empires were defeated by the Spanish.	**PUPIL & TEACHER & eEDITION** Common Pages: 362–363, 366, **367–371**, 372, **373–377**, **378–379**, 380, **381–386**, 390, 392–393, 396, **397–402**, 404–407, 408, **409–415**, R49 **PRINT COMPONENT(S)** CA Standards Enrichment Wrkbk: 105–106 **TRANSPARENCIES/TECHNOLOGY** CA Daily Standards Practice Transparencies: 40	**PRINT COMPONENT(S)** In-Depth Resources Unit 6: 23, 27–28, 29, 30 In-Depth Resources in Spanish Unit 6: 113–114 History Makers: 23–24 CA Reading Toolkit: L38, L39, L40, L41 CA Modified Lesson Plans for English Learners: 81, 83, 85 CA Standards Planner & Lesson Plans: L77, L79, L81 **TRANSPARENCIES/TECHNOLOGY** Humanities Transparencies: 24 Map Transparencies: 23, 24 Critical Thinking Transparencies: 51 Benchmark Tests: 11.3, 12.1, 12.2 Power Presentations: 11.3, 12.1, 12.2
7.7.4	Describe the artistic and oral traditions and architecture in the three civilizations.	**PUPIL & TEACHER & eEDITION** Common Pages: **360–361**, 362–363, 372, 374, **375–376**, 377, 379, 380, 383, 384, 385, 392–393, 396, 399, **401–402**, 403, **404–407**, 412, **414–415**, R47 Add'l Teacher's Edition: 366 **PRINT COMPONENT(S)** CA Standards Enrichment Wrkbk: 107–108 **TRANSPARENCIES/TECHNOLOGY** CA Daily Standards Practice Transparencies: 38, 41	**PRINT COMPONENT(S)** History Makers: 21–22 CA Reading Toolkit: L38, L40 CA Modified Lesson Plans for English Learners: 81, 83, 85 CA Standards Planner & Lesson Plans: L77, L79, L81 **TRANSPARENCIES/TECHNOLOGY** Critical Thinking Transparencies: 52, 53 Benchmark Tests: 11.3, 12.1, 12.2 Power Presentations: 11.3, 12.1, 12.2

Standard		Primary Citations	Supporting Citations
7.7.5	Describe the Meso-American achievements in astronomy and mathematics, including the development of the calendar and the Meso-American knowledge of seasonal changes to the civilizations' agricultural systems.	**PUPIL & TEACHER & eEDITION** Common Pages: **360–361**, 370, 380, 382–383, 385–386, 387, 388–389, 391, 394–395, 396, 398, 402, 403, 408, 415 Add'l Teacher's Edition: 361 **PRINT COMPONENT(S)** CA Standards Enrichment Wrkbk: 109–110 **TRANSPARENCIES/TECHNOLOGY** CA Daily Standards Practice Transparencies: 41	**PRINT COMPONENT(S)** CA Reading Toolkit: L40, L41 CA Modified Lesson Plans for English Learners: 81, 83, 85 CA Standards Planner & Lesson Plans: L77, L79, L81 **TRANSPARENCIES/TECHNOLOGY** Humanities Transparencies: 22 Map Transparencies: 22 Critical Thinking Transparencies: 52, 53 Benchmark Tests: 11.3, 12.1 Power Presentations: 11.3, 12.1
7.8	**Students analyze the origins, accomplishments, and geographic diffusion of the Renaissance.**	**PUPIL & TEACHER & eEDITION** Common Pages: **422–423**, **424–425**, 426–427, 428, **429–433**, 434, **435–441**, 442–443, 444, **445–450**, 452–453, 454–455 Add'l Teacher's Edition: 422, 423 **PRINT COMPONENT(S)** CA Standards Enrichment Wrkbk: 111–112, 113–114, 115–116, 117–118, 119–120 **TRANSPARENCIES/TECHNOLOGY** CA Daily Standards Practice Transparencies: 42, 43, 44	**PRINT COMPONENT(S)** In-Depth Resources Unit 7: 1–2, 3, 4–5, 6, 11–12, 14 In-Depth Resources in Spanish Unit 7: 16, 117–118, 119, 123–124 History Makers: 26, 27 CA Standards Planner & Lesson Plans: L77, L83, L85, L87 **TRANSPARENCIES/TECHNOLOGY** Humanities Transparencies: 25–26 Map Transparencies: 25 Critical Thinking Transparencies: 54, 55–56 Benchmark Tests: 13.1, 13.2, 13.3 Power Presentations: 13.1, 13.2, 13.3
7.8.1	Describe the way in which the revival of classical learning and the arts fostered a new interest in humanism (i.e., a balance between intellect and religious faith).	**PUPIL & TEACHER & eEDITION** Common Pages: **431–433**, 434, **435–441**, 442–443, 444, **445–450**, 454–455 Add'l Teacher's Edition: 422, 423 **PRINT COMPONENT(S)** CA Standards Enrichment Wrkbk: 111–112 **TRANSPARENCIES/TECHNOLOGY** CA Daily Standards Practice Transparencies: 42	**PRINT COMPONENT(S)** In-Depth Resources Unit 7: 3, 6, 11–12, In-Depth Resources in Spanish Unit 7: 116, 119, 123–124 CA Reading Toolkit: L42 CA Modified Lesson Plans for English Learners: 87 CA Standards Planner & Lesson Plans: L77, L83 **TRANSPARENCIES/TECHNOLOGY** Critical Thinking Transparencies: 54 Benchmark Tests: 13.1 Power Presentations: 13.1

Correlations to California History–Social Science Content Standards and Analysis Skills

Standard	Primary Citations	Supporting Citations
7.8.2 Explain the importance of Florence in the early stages of the Renaissance and the growth of independent trading cities (e.g., Venice), with emphasis on the cities' importance in the spread of Renaissance ideas.	**PUPIL & TEACHER & eEDITION** Common Pages: **422–423, 436–437, 445–446,** 454 **PRINT COMPONENT(S)** CA Standards Enrichment Wrkbk: 113–114 **TRANSPARENCIES/TECHNOLOGY** CA Daily Standards Practice Transparencies: 43	**PRINT COMPONENT(S)** CA Reading Toolkit: L43 CA Modified Lesson Plans for English Learners: 89 CA Standards Planner & Lesson Plans: L85 **TRANSPARENCIES/TECHNOLOGY** Map Transparencies: 25 Benchmark Tests: 13.2 Power Presentations: 13.2
7.8.3 Understand the effects of the reopening of the ancient "Silk Road" between Europe and China, including Marco Polo's travels and the location of his routes.	**PUPIL & TEACHER & eEDITION** Common Pages: **430–431,** R43 **PRINT COMPONENT(S)** CA Standards Enrichment Wrkbk: 115–116	**PRINT COMPONENT(S)** CA Reading Toolkit: L42 CA Modified Lesson Plans for English Learners: 87 CA Standards Planner & Lesson Plans: L77, L83 **TRANSPARENCIES/TECHNOLOGY** Benchmark Tests: 13.1 Power Presentations: 13.1
7.8.4 Describe the growth and effects of new ways of disseminating information (e.g., the ability to manufacture paper, translation of the Bible into the vernacular, printing).	**PUPIL & TEACHER & eEDITION** Common Pages: **449–450, 454–455** **PRINT COMPONENT(S)** CA Standards Enrichment Wrkbk: 117–118 **TRANSPARENCIES/TECHNOLOGY** CA Daily Standards Practice Transparencies: 44	**PRINT COMPONENT(S)** In-Depth Resources Unit 7: 6 In-Depth Resources in Spanish Unit 7: 119 CA Reading Toolkit: L44 CA Modified Lesson Plans for English Learners: 91 CA Standards Planner & Lesson Plans: L87 **TRANSPARENCIES/TECHNOLOGY** Benchmark Tests: 13.3 Power Presentations: 13.3

Standard		Primary Citations	Supporting Citations
7.8.5	Detail advances made in literature, the arts, science, mathematics, cartography, engineering, and the understanding of human anatomy and astronomy (e.g., by Dante Alighieri, Leonardo da Vinci, Michelangelo di Buonarroti Simoni, Johann Gutenberg, William Shakespeare).	**PUPIL & TEACHER & eEDITION** Common Pages: **422–423, 439–440, 442–443,** 444, **448–450, 452–453,** 454–455, R50, R51 **PRINT COMPONENT(S)** CA Standards Enrichment Wrkbk: 119–120	**PRINT COMPONENT(S)** In-Depth Resources Unit 7: 1–2, 4–5, 14 In-Depth Resources in Spanish Unit 7: 117–118, History Makers: 25–27 CA Reading Toolkit: L43 CA Modified Lesson Plans for English Learners: 89, 91 CA Standards Planner & Lesson Plans: L85, L87 **TRANSPARENCIES/TECHNOLOGY** Critical Thinking Transparencies: 55–56 Humanities Transparencies: 25–26 Benchmark Tests: 13.2, 13.3 Power Presentations: 13.2, 13.3
7.9	**Students analyze the historical developments of the Reformation.**	**PUPIL & TEACHER & eEDITION** Common Pages: 136, 137, 456–457, **458–459,** 460, **461–465, 466–469,** 470, **471–475, 476–477,** 478, 479–480, 481, 482–484, 486–487 Add'l Teacher's Edition: 456, 491 **PRINT COMPONENT(S)** CA Standards Enrichment Wrkbk: 121–122, 123–124, 125–126, 127–128, 129–130, 131–132, 133–134 **TRANSPARENCIES/TECHNOLOGY** CA Daily Standards Practice Transparencies: 45, 46, 47	**PRINT COMPONENT(S)** In-Depth Resources Unit 7: 24, 29–30, 31 In-Depth Resources in Spanish Unit 7: 129, 131–132 History Makers: 27, 28 CA Standards Planner & Lesson Plans: L27, L89, L91, L93 **TRANSPARENCIES/TECHNOLOGY** Humanities Transparencies: 27, 28 Critical Thinking Transparencies: 58, 59, 60, 61 Benchmark Tests: 4.3, 14.1, 14.2, 14.3 Power Presentations: 4.3, 14.1, 14.2, 14.3
7.9.1	List the causes for the internal turmoil in and weakening of the Catholic church (e.g., tax policies, selling of indulgences).	**PUPIL & TEACHER & eEDITION** Common Pages: 456, 458–459, 460, **461–465,** 466–469, 470, **471–475,** 476–477, 478, 482–484, 486–487 **PRINT COMPONENT(S)** CA Standards Enrichment Wrkbk: 121–122	**PRINT COMPONENT(S)** CA Reading Toolkit: L45 CA Modified Lesson Plans for English Learners: 93 CA Standards Planner & Lesson Plans: L89 **TRANSPARENCIES/TECHNOLOGY** Critical Thinking Transparencies: 58, 61 Benchmark Tests: 14.1 Power Presentations: 14.1

Correlations to California History–Social Science Content Standards and Analysis Skills

Standard		Primary Citations	Supporting Citations
7.9.2	Describe the theological, political, and economic ideas of the major figures during the Reformation (e.g., Desiderius Erasmus, Martin Luther, John Calvin, William Tyndale).	**PUPIL & TEACHER & eEDITION** Common Pages: 458–459, 460, **463–465, 466–469, 472–475, 476–477,** 486–487, R55 Add'l Teacher's Edition: 456 **PRINT COMPONENT(S)** CA Standards Enrichment Wrkbk: 123–124 **TRANSPARENCIES/TECHNOLOGY** CA Daily Standards Practice Transparencies: 45	**PRINT COMPONENT(S)** In-Depth Resources Unit 7: 31 History Makers: 27–28 CA Reading Toolkit: L45, L46 CA Modified Lesson Plans for English Learners: 93, 95 CA Standards Planner & Lesson Plans: L89, L91 **TRANSPARENCIES/TECHNOLOGY** Humanities Transparencies: 27 Critical Thinking Transparencies: 58, 59, 61 Benchmark Tests: 14.1, 14.2 Power Presentations: 14.1, 14.2
7.9.3	Explain Protestants' new practices of church self-government and the influence of those practices on the development of democratic practices and ideas of federalism.	**PUPIL & TEACHER & eEDITION** Common Pages: **483–484,** 487 **PRINT COMPONENT(S)** CA Standards Enrichment Wrkbk: 125–126	**PRINT COMPONENT(S)** CA Modified Lesson Plans for English Learners: 97 CA Standards Planner & Lesson Plans: L93 **TRANSPARENCIES/TECHNOLOGY** Critical Thinking Transparencies: 60, 61 Benchmark Tests: 14.3 Power Presentations: 14.3
7.9.4	Identify and locate the European regions that remained Catholic and those that became Protestant and explain how the division affected the distribution of religions in the New World.	**PUPIL & TEACHER & eEDITION** Common Pages: **471,** 472, 473, **476–477,** 478, **479–482, 483–484,** 486–487 **PRINT COMPONENT(S)** CA Standards Enrichment Wrkbk: 127–128	**PRINT COMPONENT(S)** In-Depth Resources Unit 7: 24 In-Depth Resources in Spanish Unit 7: 129 CA Reading Toolkit: L47 CA Modified Lesson Plans for English Learners: 97 CA Standards Planner & Lesson Plans: L93 **TRANSPARENCIES/TECHNOLOGY** Critical Thinking Transparencies: 60, 61 Benchmark Tests: 14.3 Power Presentations: 14.3

Standard		Primary Citations	Supporting Citations
7.9.5	Analyze how the Counter-Reformation revitalized the Catholic church and the forces that fostered the movement (e.g., St. Ignatius of Loyola and the Jesuits, the Council of Trent).	**PUPIL & TEACHER & eEDITION** Common Pages: **473–475, 486** Add'l Teacher's Edition: 456 **PRINT COMPONENT(S)** CA Standards Enrichment Wrkbk: 129–130 **TRANSPARENCIES/TECHNOLOGY** CA Daily Standards Practice Transparencies: 46	**PRINT COMPONENT(S)** CA Reading Toolkit: L46 CA Modified Lesson Plans for English Learners: 95 CA Standards Planner & Lesson Plans: L91 **TRANSPARENCIES/TECHNOLOGY** Critical Thinking Transparencies: 59, 61 Benchmark Tests: 14.2 Power Presentations: 14.2
7.9.6	Understand the institution and impact of missionaries on Christianity and the diffusion of Christianity from Europe to other parts of the world in the medieval and early modern periods; locate missions on a world map.	**PUPIL & TEACHER & eEDITION** Common Pages: **479–480, 481, 482, 486, 487** Add'l Teacher's Edition: 491 **PRINT COMPONENT(S)** CA Standards Enrichment Wrkbk: 131–132 **TRANSPARENCIES/TECHNOLOGY** CA Daily Standards Practice Transparencies: 47	**PRINT COMPONENT(S)** In-Depth Resources Unit 7: 29–30 In-Depth Resources in Spanish Unit 7: 131–132 CA Reading Toolkit: L47 CA Modified Lesson Plans for English Learners: 97 CA Standards Planner & Lesson Plans: L93 **TRANSPARENCIES/TECHNOLOGY** Critical Thinking Transparencies: 60, 61 Benchmark Tests: 14.3 Power Presentations: 14.3
7.9.7	Describe the Golden Age of cooperation between Jews and Muslims in medieval Spain that promoted creativity in art, literature, and science, including how that cooperation was terminated by the religious persecution of individuals and groups (e.g., the Spanish Inquisition and the expulsion of Jews and Muslims from Spain in 1492).	**PUPIL & TEACHER & eEDITION** Common Pages: **136, 137**, 474 **PRINT COMPONENT(S)** CA Standards Enrichment Wrkbk: 133–134	**PRINT COMPONENT(S)** CA Modified Lesson Plans for English Learners: 31 CA Standards Planner & Lesson Plans: L27 **TRANSPARENCIES/TECHNOLOGY** Benchmark Tests: 4.3 Power Presentations: 4.3

Correlations to California History–Social Science Content Standards and Analysis Skills

Standard		Primary Citations	Supporting Citations
7.10	Students analyze the historical developments of the Scientific Revolution and its lasting effect on religious, political, and cultural institutions.	**PUPIL & TEACHER & eEDITION** Common Pages: 490–491, **492–493, 494–495, 496, 497–501,** 502, **503–507,** 528, 529 **PRINT COMPONENT(S)** CA Standards Enrichment Wrkbk: 135–136, 137–138, 139–140 **TRANSPARENCIES/TECHNOLOGY** CA Daily Standards Practice Transparencies: 48, 49	**PRINT COMPONENT(S)** In-Depth Resources Unit 8: 3, 4, 15 In-Depth Resources in Spanish Unit 8: 134, 135 History Makers: 29–30 CA Standards Planner & Lesson Plans: L95, L97 **TRANSPARENCIES/TECHNOLOGY** Humanities Transparencies: 29 Critical Thinking Transparencies: 62, 63 Benchmark Tests: 15.1, 15.2 Power Presentations: 15.1, 15.2
7.10.1	Discuss the roots of the Scientific Revolution (e.g., Greek rationalism; Jewish, Christian, and Muslim science; Renaissance humanism; new knowledge from global exploration).	**PUPIL & TEACHER & eEDITION** Common Pages: **496, 497–501,** 502, **503–507** **PRINT COMPONENT(S)** CA Standards Enrichment Wrkbk: 135–136 **TRANSPARENCIES/TECHNOLOGY** CA Daily Standards Practice Transparencies: 48	**PRINT COMPONENT(S)** In-Depth Resources Unit 8: 3 In-Depth Resources in Spanish Unit 8: 134 CA Reading Toolkit: L48, L50, L51 CA Modified Lesson Plans for English Learners: 99 CA Standards Planner & Lesson Plans: L95 **TRANSPARENCIES/TECHNOLOGY** Critical Thinking Transparencies: 62 Benchmark Tests: 15.1 Power Presentations: 15.1
7.10.2	Understand the significance of the new scientific theories (e.g., those of Copernicus, Galileo, Kepler, Newton) and the significance of new inventions (e.g., the telescope, microscope, thermometer, barometer).	**PUPIL & TEACHER & eEDITION** Common Pages: **492, 493,** 502, **503–507,** R56 **PRINT COMPONENT(S)** CA Standards Enrichment Wrkbk: 137–138 **TRANSPARENCIES/TECHNOLOGY** CA Daily Standards Practice Transparencies: 49	**PRINT COMPONENT(S)** In-Depth Resources Unit 8: 4, 15 In-Depth Resources in Spanish Unit 8: 135 History Makers: 29–30 CA Reading Toolkit: L49, L50 CA Modified Lesson Plans for English Learners: 101 CA Standards Planner & Lesson Plans: L97 **TRANSPARENCIES/TECHNOLOGY** Humanities Transparencies: 29 Critical Thinking Transparencies: 63 Benchmark Tests: 15.2 Power Presentations: 15.2

Standard	Primary Citations	Supporting Citations
7.10.3 Understand the scientific method advanced by Bacon and Descartes, the influence of new scientific rationalism on the growth of democratic ideas, and the coexistence of science with traditional religious beliefs.	**PUPIL & TEACHER & eEDITION** Common Pages: 493, **506, 507** **PRINT COMPONENT(S)** CA Standards Enrichment Wrkbk: 139–140	**PRINT COMPONENT(S)** CA Reading Toolkit: L49 CA Modified Lesson Plans for English Learners: 99, 101 CA Standards Planner & Lesson Plans: L95, L97 **TRANSPARENCIES/TECHNOLOGY** Benchmark Tests: 15.1, 15.2 Power Presentations: 15.1, 15.2
7.11 **Students analyze political and economic change in the sixteenth, seventeenth, and eighteenth centuries (the Age of Exploration, the Enlightenment, and the Age of Reason).**	**PUPIL & TEACHER & eEDITION** Common Pages: 341, 342, 510, **511–517**, 518–519, 520, **521–526**, 528–529, **530–531**, 532–533, 534, **535–539**, 540–541, 542, **543–548**, 550–553, 554, 555, R44 Add'l Teacher's Edition: 490, 491, 530 **PRINT COMPONENT(S)** CA Standards Enrichment Wrkbk: 141–142, 143–144, 145–146, 147–148, 149–150, 151–152 **TRANSPARENCIES/TECHNOLOGY** CA Daily Standards Practice Transparencies: 20, 50, 51, 52, 53	**PRINT COMPONENT(S)** In-Depth Resources Unit 3: 22–23, 31; Unit 8: 5, 6, 26, 33, 34 In-Depth Resources in Spanish Unit 3: 51; Unit 8: 136, 137, 147 History Makers: 31, 32 CA Standards Planner & Lesson Plans: L9, L99, L101, L103, L105 **TRANSPARENCIES/TECHNOLOGY** Humanities Transparencies: 30, 31, 32 Map Transparencies: 29, 30, 32 Critical Thinking Transparencies: 25, 64, 65, 67, 68, 69 Benchmark Tests: 6.3, 15.3, 15.4, 16.1, 16.2 Power Presentations: 6.3, 15.3, 15.4, 16.1, 16.2
7.11.1 Know the great voyages of discovery, the locations of the routes, and the influence of cartography in the development of a new European worldview.	**PUPIL & TEACHER & eEDITION** Common Pages: **510, 511–517**, 518–519, 520, **521–526**, 528–529, R57 Add'l Teacher's Edition: 490, 491 **PRINT COMPONENT(S)** CA Standards Enrichment Wrkbk: 141–142	**PRINT COMPONENT(S)** In-Depth Resources Unit 8: 5 In-Depth Resources in Spanish Unit 8: 136 CA Reading Toolkit: L50 CA Modified Lesson Plans for English Learners: 103 CA Standards Planner & Lesson Plans: L99 **TRANSPARENCIES/TECHNOLOGY** Map Transparencies: 29 Critical Thinking Transparencies: 64 Benchmark Tests: 15.3 Power Presentations: 15.3

Correlations to California History–Social Science Content Standards and Analysis Skills

Standard	Primary Citations	Supporting Citations
7.11.2 Discuss the exchanges of plants, animals, technology, culture, and ideas among Europe, Africa, Asia, and the Americas in the fifteenth and sixteenth centuries and the major economic and social effects on each continent.	**PUPIL & TEACHER & eEDITION** Common Pages: **520, 521–526, 528–529** **PRINT COMPONENT(S)** CA Standards Enrichment Wrkbk: 143–144 **TRANSPARENCIES/TECHNOLOGY** CA Daily Standards Practice Transparencies: 20, 51	**PRINT COMPONENT(S)** In-Depth Resources Unit 3: 22–23, 31; Unit 8: 6 In-Depth Resources in Spanish Unit 3: 51; Unit 8: 137 CA Reading Toolkit: L51 CA Modified Lesson Plans for English Learners: 43, 105 CA Standards Planner & Lesson Plans: L39, L101 **TRANSPARENCIES/TECHNOLOGY** Critical Thinking Transparencies: 25, 65 Benchmark Tests: 6.3, 15.4 Power Presentations: 6.3, 15.4
7.11.3 Examine the origins of modern capitalism; the influence of mercantilism and cottage industry; the elements and importance of a market economy in seventeenth-century Europe; the changing international trading and marketing patterns, including their locations on a world map; and the influence of explorers and map makers.	**PUPIL & TEACHER & eEDITION** Common Pages: 510, 511–517, 518–519, 520, 521–526, **524, 525**, 528–529 **PRINT COMPONENT(S)** CA Standards Enrichment Wrkbk: 145–146 **TRANSPARENCIES/TECHNOLOGY** CA Daily Standards Practice Transparencies: 50	**PRINT COMPONENT(S)** CA Modified Lesson Plans for English Learners: 105 CA Standards Planner & Lesson Plans: L101 **TRANSPARENCIES/TECHNOLOGY** Benchmark Tests: 15.4 Power Presentations: 15.4
7.11.4 Explain how the main ideas of the Enlightenment can be traced back to such movements as the Renaissance, the Reformation, and the Scientific Revolution and to the Greeks, Romans, and Christianity.	**PUPIL & TEACHER & eEDITION** Common Pages: **530–531, 534, 535–539** **PRINT COMPONENT(S)** CA Standards Enrichment Wrkbk: 147–148	**PRINT COMPONENT(S)** In-Depth Resources Unit 8: 34 CA Reading Toolkit: L53 CA Modified Lesson Plans for English Learners: 107 CA Standards Planner & Lesson Plans: L103 **TRANSPARENCIES/TECHNOLOGY** Critical Thinking Transparencies: 67, 69 Benchmark Tests: 16.1 Power Presentations: 16.1

Standard	Primary Citations	Supporting Citations
7.11.5 Describe how democratic thought and institutions were influenced by Enlightenment thinkers (e.g., John Locke, Charles-Louis Montesquieu, American founders).	**PUPIL & TEACHER & eEDITION** Common Pages: 534, **535–539**, 540–541, 542, **543–548**, 550–553, 554, 555 Add'l Teacher's Edition: 530 **PRINT COMPONENT(S)** CA Standards Enrichment Wrkbk: 149–150 **TRANSPARENCIES/TECHNOLOGY** CA Daily Standards Practice Transparencies: 52	**PRINT COMPONENT(S)** In-Depth Resources Unit 8: 33 History Makers: 31–32 CA Reading Toolkit: L52 CA Modified Lesson Plans for English Learners: 107, 109 CA Standards Planner & Lesson Plans: L103, L105 **TRANSPARENCIES/TECHNOLOGY** Critical Thinking Transparencies: 67, 69 Benchmark Tests: 16.1, 16.2 Power Presentations: 16.1, 16.2
7.11.6 Discuss how the principles in the Magna Carta were embodied in such documents as the English Bill of Rights and the American Declaration of Independence.	**PUPIL & TEACHER & eEDITION** Common Pages: **341, 342, 546, 547, R44, R58, R59** **PRINT COMPONENT(S)** CA Standards Enrichment Wrkbk: 151–152	**PRINT COMPONENT(S)** CA Reading Toolkit: L53 CA Modified Lesson Plans for English Learners: 109 CA Standards Planner & Lesson Plans: L105 **TRANSPARENCIES/TECHNOLOGY** Critical Thinking Transparencies: 68, 69 Humanities Transparencies: 32 Benchmark Tests: 16.2 Power Presentations: 16.2

Correlations to California Historical and Social Sciences Analysis Skills Grades 6–8

The intellectual skills noted below are to be learned through, and applied to, the content standards for grades six through eight. They are to be assessed only in conjunction with the content standards in grades six through eight.

In addition to the standards for grades six through eight, students demonstrate the following intellectual reasoning, reflection, and research skills:

Standard	Primary Citations	Supporting Citations
CHRONOLOGICAL AND SPATIAL THINKING		
CST(1) Students explain how major events are related to one another in time.	**PUPIL & TEACHER & eEDITION** Common Pages: **46**, 51, 98, 103, 116, 169, 203, 232, 237, **266, 271**, 279, 326, 331, **378–379**, 396, 402, 465, 496, 501, R15 Add'l Teacher's Edition: 4, **42**, 80, 101, 108, 176, 208, 246, 316, 362, 392, 456, 492 **PRINT COMPONENT(S)** CA Standards Enrichment Wrkbk: 1–16	**PRINT COMPONENT(S)** CA Reading Toolkit: L3, L4, L5, L6, L8, L10, L13, L14, L17, L19, L20, L23, L24, L25, L26, L29, L30, L31, L32, L34, L36, L42, L43, L44, L45, L46, L47, L49, L51, L52, L53 CA Modified Lesson Plans for English Learners: 15, 51, 73, 93 CA Standards Planner & Lesson Plans: L1, L3, L5, L7, L71 **TRANSPARENCIES/TECHNOLOGY** Critical Thinking Transparencies: 35, 58 Benchmark Tests: 1.1, 1.2, 1.3, 1.4, 10.5 Power Presentations: 1.1, 1.2, 1.3, 1.4, 10.5
CST(2) Students construct various time lines of key events, people, and periods of the historical era they are studying.	**PUPIL & TEACHER & eEDITION** Common Pages: 46, 51, 98, 103, **169**, **203**, 266, 271, 326, **331, 378–379**, 396, 402, 496, 501, **R15** Add'l Teacher's Edition: 16, 60, 135, 258, 328 **PRINT COMPONENT(S)** CA Standards Enrichment Wrkbk: 1–16	**PRINT COMPONENT(S)** In-Depth Resources Unit 4: 5 In-Depth Resources in Spanish Unit 4: 60 CA Reading Toolkit: L2, L19, L27, L33, L41, L48 CA Modified Lesson Plans for English Learners: 7, 13, 25, 45, 57, 101 CA Standards Planner & Lesson Plans: L1, L3, L5, L7, L71 **TRANSPARENCIES/TECHNOLOGY** Critical Thinking Transparencies: 29, 34, 42 Humanities Transparencies: 16 Benchmark Tests: 1.1, 1.2, 1.3, 1.4, 10.5 Power Presentations: 1.1, 1.2, 1.3, 1.4, 10.5

Standard	Primary Citations	Supporting Citations
CST(3) Students use a variety of maps and documents to identify physical and cultural features of neighborhoods, cities, states, and countries and to explain the historical migration of people, expansion and disintegration of empires, and the growth of economic systems.	**PUPIL & TEACHER & eEDITION** Common Pages: 15, 16, **17**, 18, 19, 22, **22–23**, 35, 40, 43, **97**, 114, 131, 134, 177, 182, 183, **192–193**, 196, 209, 215, 234, 240, 276, 281, 287, 317, 327, 328, 330, 334, 353, 363, 373, 376, 382, 393, 411, 425, 431, 457, 471, 481, 482, 493, **508–509**, 515, 522, 524, R9–R10 Add'l Teacher's Edition: 10, 66, 235, 513 **PRINT COMPONENT(S)** CA Standards Enrichment Wrkbk: 1–16 **TRANSPARENCIES/TECHNOLOGY** CA Daily Standards Practice Transparencies: 1, 2, 23	**PRINT COMPONENT(S)** In-Depth Resources Unit 2: 29–30; Unit 4: 8, 13–14; Unit 6: 11–12; Unit 7: 24; Unit 8: 14–15 In-Depth Resources in Spanish Unit 2: 37–38; Unit 4: 63, 66–67; Unit 6: 105–106; Unit 8: 141–142 CA Reading Toolkit: L1, L3, L7, L9, L12, L15, L18, L21, L22, L28, L37, L38, L39, L50 CA Modified Lesson Plans for English Learners: 3, 7, 9, 19, 21, 31, 37, 39, 61, 75, 81, 103, 105 CA Standards Planner & Lesson Plans: L1, L3, L5, L7, L71 **TRANSPARENCIES/TECHNOLOGY** Map Transparencies: 7, 8, 13, 14, 21, 22, 29, 30 Critical Thinking Transparencies: 2, 5 Benchmark Tests: 1.1, 1.2, 1.3, 1.4, 10.5 Power Presentations: 1.1, 1.2, 1.3, 1.4, 10.5

RESEARCH, EVIDENCE, AND POINT OF VIEW

Standard	Primary Citations	Supporting Citations
REP(1) Students frame questions that can be answered by historical study and research.	**PUPIL & TEACHER & eEDITION** Common Pages: **32, 35,** 40, **281, 380,** 386, **R18** **PRINT COMPONENT(S)** CA Standards Enrichment Wrkbk: 1–16 **TRANSPARENCIES/TECHNOLOGY** CA Daily Standards Practice Transparencies: 4	**PRINT COMPONENT(S)** In-Depth Resources Unit 6: 5 In-Depth Resources in Spanish Unit 6: 100 CA Reading Toolkit: L5, L9, L12, L14, L16, L20, L21, L22, L23, L25, L29, L30, L31, L32, L40, L49, L51, L52 CA Modified Lesson Plans for English Learners: 11, 17, 59, 73, 77, 81, 99, 107 CA Standards Planner & Lesson Plans: L1, L3, L5, L7, L71 **TRANSPARENCIES/TECHNOLOGY** Critical Thinking Transparencies: 4, 5 Benchmark Tests: 1.1, 1.2, 1.3, 1.4, 10.5 Power Presentations: 1.1, 1.2, 1.3, 1.4, 10.5

Correlations to California Historical and Social Sciences Analysis Skills

Standard	Primary Citations	Supporting Citations
REP(2) Students distinguish fact from opinion in historical narratives and stories.	**PUPIL & TEACHER & eEDITION** Common Pages: **508–509, R18** **PRINT COMPONENT(S)** CA Standards Enrichment Wrkbk: 1–16 **TRANSPARENCIES/TECHNOLOGY** CA Daily Standards Practice Transparencies: 48	**PRINT COMPONENT(S)** In-Depth Resources Unit 4: 36 CA Reading Toolkit: L3, L11, L18, L26, L32, L33, L38, L43, L46 CA Standards Planner & Lesson Plans: L1, L3, L5, L7, L71 **TRANSPARENCIES/TECHNOLOGY** Benchmark Tests: 1.1, 1.2, 1.3, 1.4, 10.5 Power Presentations: 1.1, 1.2, 1.3, 1.4, 10.5
REP(3) Students distinguish relevant from irrelevant information, essential from incidental information, and verifiable from unverifiable information in historical narratives and stories.	**PUPIL & TEACHER & eEDITION** Common Pages: 56, 63, 75, **104–105,** 106, 191, **192–193,** 203, **220–221,** 244, **312–313,** 371, 441, 444, 450, 455, 539, **R23,** R42 **PRINT COMPONENT(S)** CA Standards Enrichment Wrkbk: 1–16	**PRINT COMPONENT(S)** CA Reading Toolkit: L6, L19, L23, L30, L35, L44 CA Standards Planner & Lesson Plans: L1, L3, L5, L7, L71 **TRANSPARENCIES/TECHNOLOGY** Benchmark Tests: 1.1, 1.2, 1.3, 1.4, 10.5 Power Presentations: 1.1, 1.2, 1.3, 1.4, 10.5
REP(4) Students assess the credibility of primary and secondary sources and draw sound conclusions from them.	**PUPIL & TEACHER & eEDITION** Common Pages: **32–33,** 34, 35, 40, 104–105, **192–193,** 220–221, **312–313, 508–509, R24,** R25 Add'l Teacher's Edition: 87, 136, 159, 189, 225, 324 **PRINT COMPONENT(S)** CA Standards Enrichment Wrkbk: 1–16 **TRANSPARENCIES/TECHNOLOGY** CA Daily Standards Practice Transparencies: 4, 38, 50	**PRINT COMPONENT(S)** In-Depth Resources Unit 6: 7; Unit 8: 15 In-Depth Resources in Spanish Unit 7: 103 CA Reading Toolkit: L4, L8, L17, L34, L39, L45 CA Modified Lesson Plans for English Learners: 11 CA Standards Planner & Lesson Plans: L1, L3, L5, L7, L71 **TRANSPARENCIES/TECHNOLOGY** Critical Thinking Transparencies: 4, 5 Benchmark Tests: 1.1, 1.2, 1.3, 1.4, 10.5 Power Presentations: 1.1, 1.2, 1.3, 1.4, 10.5
REP(5) Students detect the different historical points of view on historical events and determine the context in which the historical statements were made (the questions asked, sources used, author's perspectives).	**PUPIL & TEACHER & eEDITION** Common Pages: **27–28,** 32–33, 34, **36–39, 192–193,** 220–221, 315, **508–509, R24,** R25 **PRINT COMPONENT(S)** CA Standards Enrichment Wrkbk: 1–16	**PRINT COMPONENT(S)** CA Reading Toolkit: L2, L40, L48 **TRANSPARENCIES/TECHNOLOGY** Benchmark Tests: 1.1, 1.2, 1.3, 1.4, 10.5 Power Presentations: 1.1, 1.2, 1.3, 1.4, 10.5

Standard	Primary Citations	Supporting Citations
HISTORICAL INTERPRETATION		
HI(1) Students explain the central issues and problems from the past, placing people and events in a matrix of time and place.	**PUPIL & TEACHER & eEDITION** Common Pages: 15, 16, 17, 18, 19, **22–23**, 35, 40, 43, 46, 51, **97**, 98, 103, 114, 116, 131, 134, 169, 177, 182, 183, 196, 203, 209, 215, 232, 234, 237, 240, 266, **271**, 276, 279, 281, 287, 317, 326, 327, 328, 330, 331, 334, 353, 363, 373, 376, 382, 393, 396, 402, 411, 425, 431, 457, 465, 471, 481, 482, 493, 496, 501, 515, 522, 524, **R9–R10**, R15 Add'l Teacher's Edition: 4, 42, 80, 101, 108, 176, 208, 246, 316, 362, 392, 456, 492 **PRINT COMPONENT(S)** CA Standards Enrichment Wrkbk: 1–16 **TRANSPARENCIES/TECHNOLOGY** CA Daily Standards Practice Transparencies: 3	**PRINT COMPONENT(S)** In-Depth Resources Unit 2: 22; Unit 4: 33–34 In-Depth Resources in Spanish Unit 22: 33; Unit 4: 75–76 CA Reading Toolkit: L5, L6, L9, L13, L16, L17, L19, L21, L23, L24, L27, L29, L30, L32, L34, L36, L39, L44, L45, L49 CA Modified Lesson Plans for English Learners: 17, 61, 75 CA Standards Planner & Lesson Plans: L1, L3, L5, L7, L71 **TRANSPARENCIES/TECHNOLOGY** Map Transparencies: 16 Critical Thinking Transparencies: 3, 5, 17, 45 Benchmark Tests: 1.1, 1.2, 1.3, 1.4, 10.5 Power Presentations: 1.1, 1.2, 1.3, 1.4, 10.5
HI(2) Students understand and distinguish cause, effect, sequence, and correlation in historical events, including the long- and short-term causal relations.	**PUPIL & TEACHER & eEDITION** Common Pages: 40, 46, 51, 58, 63, 96, 98, 103, 106, 116, 141, 161, 169, 184, 194, 199, 203, 212, 219, 229, 232, 237, 266, **271**, 279, 297, 302, 311, **318–319**, 326, 331, 357, **378–379**, 386, 395, 396, 402, 418, 455, 458–459, 465, **476–477**, 487, 496, 501, 520, 526, 548, R15, R26 Add'l Teacher's Edition: 4, 42, 80, 101, 108, 176, 208, 246, 316, 362, 392, 456, 492 **PRINT COMPONENT(S)** CA Standards Enrichment Wrkbk: 1–16 **TRANSPARENCIES/TECHNOLOGY** CA Daily Standards Practice Transparencies: 21, 28, 37	**PRINT COMPONENT(S)** In-Depth Resources Unit 2: 7; Unit 4: 3; Unit 8: 3, 6, 31–32 In-Depth Resources in Spanish Unit 2: 27; Unit 4: 58; Unit 8: 134, 137, 149–150 CA Reading Toolkit: L1, L7, L8, L11, L15, L20, L22, L25, L31, L35, L38, L42, L43, L46, L51 CA Modified Lesson Plans for English Learners: 9, 15, 17, 21, 49, 69, 71, 79, 91, 93, 95 CA Standards Planner & Lesson Plans: L1, L3, L5, L7, L71 **TRANSPARENCIES/TECHNOLOGY** Critical Thinking Transparencies: 3, 5, 27, 34, 35, 43, 59, 62, 65 Benchmark Tests: 1.1, 1.2, 1.3, 1.4, 10.5 Power Presentations: 1.1, 1.2, 1.3, 1.4, 10.5

Correlations to California Historical and Social Sciences Analysis Skills

Standard		Primary Citations	Supporting Citations
HI(3)	Students explain the sources of historical continuity and how the combination of ideas and events explains the emergence of new patterns.	**PUPIL & TEACHER & eEDITION** Common Pages: 40, 72–73, **138–139**, 200–201, 230–231, 338–339, **378–379**, 388–389, 442–443, **476–477**, 528, **540–541, R29** Add'l Teacher's Edition: 4, 42, 80, 101, 108, 176, 208, 246, 316, 362, 392, 456, 492 **PRINT COMPONENT(S)** CA Standards Enrichment Wrkbk: 1–16	**PRINT COMPONENT(S)** CA Reading Toolkit: L10, L18, L26, L28 CA Modified Lesson Plans for English Learners: 17, 21, 29, 47, 53, 65, 73, 89, 93, 101 CA Standards Planner & Lesson Plans: L1, L3, L5, L7, L71 **TRANSPARENCIES/TECHNOLOGY** Critical Thinking Transparencies: 5, 44 Benchmark Tests: 1.1, 1.2, 1.3, 1.4, 10.5 Power Presentations: 1.1, 1.2, 1.3, 1.4, 10.5
HI(4)	Students recognize the role of chance, oversight, and error in history.	**PUPIL & TEACHER & eEDITION** Common Pages: **27–28, 34–35, 36–39, 40, 41** **PRINT COMPONENT(S)** CA Standards Enrichment Wrkbk: 1–16	**PRINT COMPONENT(S)** CA Reading Toolkit: L40, L41, L47, L48, L50, L52, L53 **TRANSPARENCIES/TECHNOLOGY** Benchmark Tests: 1.1, 1.2, 1.3, 1.4, 10.5 Power Presentations: 1.1, 1.2, 1.3, 1.4, 10.5
HI(5)	Students recognize that interpretations of history are subject to change as new information is uncovered.	**PUPIL & TEACHER & eEDITION** Common Pages: 32–33, **34, 36–39, 192–193**, 220–221, **315, 508–509**, R24, R25, R35 **PRINT COMPONENT(S)** CA Standards Enrichment Wrkbk: 1–16 **TRANSPARENCIES/TECHNOLOGY** CA Daily Standards Practice Transparencies: 4	**PRINT COMPONENT(S)** History Makers: 1–2 CA Reading Toolkit: L2, L3, L4, L13, L33 CA Modified Lesson Plans for English learners: 11 CA Standards Planner & Lesson Plans: L1, L3, L5, L7, L71 **TRANSPARENCIES/TECHNOLOGY** Critical Thinking Transparencies: 3, 4, 5 Benchmark Tests: 1.1, 1.2, 1.3, 1.4, 10.5 Power Presentations: 1.1, 1.2, 1.3, 1.4, 10.5
HI(6)	Students interpret basic indicators of economic performance and conduct cost-benefit analyses of economic and political issues.	**PUPIL & TEACHER & eEDITION** Common Pages: **524–525, 526, 541, R30**; also see maps related to economics and trading systems: 61, 63, 87, 146, 183, 196, 376, 431, 512, 515, 522 **PRINT COMPONENT(S)** CA Standards Enrichment Wrkbk: 1–16	**PRINT COMPONENT(S)** CA Reading Toolkit: L12 CA Standards Planner & Lesson Plans: L1, L3, L5, L7, L71 **TRANSPARENCIES/TECHNOLOGY** Benchmark Tests: 1.1, 1.2, 1.3, 1.4, 10.5 Power Presentation: 1.1, 1.2, 1.3, 1.4, 10.5

California History–
Social Science Content Standards

Pacing Guide
Regular Scheduling

INSTRUCTIONAL SEGMENT WEEK 1

Reading 3.4

Writing 2.5

Day	Chapter Lesson	California Standards	Teach	Practice	Assess	Reteach
1	Ch. 1 Introduction & Starting with a Story	Reading 3.4 Writing 2.5	*PE/TE: 2-5* *PE/TE: 6-7*	*PE/TE: 7*		
2	1.1 Geography of the World		*PE/TE: 8-13* Reading Skill activity in *IDR: Unit 1, p. 3*	Critical Thinking: CT1		
3	1.1 Geography of the World		*PE/TE: 8-13* Humanities Transparency: HT1	*PE/TE: 13*		Reteaching activity in *IDR: Unit 1, p. 17*
4	1.2 Mapping the World		*PE/TE: 14-21* Reading Skill activity in *IDR: Unit 1, p. 4*	Critical Thinking: CT2	Formal Assessment: Lesson 1.1 Quiz, p. 5	
5	1.2 Mapping the World		*PE/TE: 14-21* Map Transparency: MT1 Literature activity in *IDR: Unit 1, p. 16*	*PE/TE: 21*		Reteaching activity in *IDR: Unit 1, p. 18*

Pacing Guide

INSTRUCTIONAL SEGMENT WEEK 2

Day	Chapter Lesson	California Standards	Teach	Practice	Assess	Reteach
1	Skillbuilder: Reading a Map		*PE/TE: 22-23*	*PE/TE: 23*	Formal Assessment: Lesson 1.2 Quiz, p. 6	
2	1.3 Discovering the Past		*PE/TE: 24-28* Reading Skill activity in *IDR: Unit 1, p. 5*	Critical Thinking: CT3 Skillbuilder Practice in *IDR: Unit 1, p. 8*		
3	1.3 Discovering the Past		*PE/TE: 24-28* Humanities Transparency: HT2	*PE/TE: 28* Geography Practice in *IDR: Unit 1, p. 13*		Reteaching activity in *IDR: Unit 1, p. 19*
4	1.3 Activity: Prepare a Time Capsule		*PE/TE: 29*	*PE/TE: 29*	Formal Assessment: Lesson 1.3 Quiz, p. 7	
5	1.3 Activity: Prepare a Time Capsule & 1.4 Interpreting the Past		*PE/TE: 29* *PE/TE: 30-35* Reading Skill activity in *IDR: Unit 1, p. 6*	Critical Thinking: CT4		

Pacing Guide

INSTRUCTIONAL SEGMENT WEEK 3

7.1.1   Study the early strengths and lasting contributions of Rome (e.g., significance of Roman citizenship; rights under Roman law; Roman art, architecture, engineering, and philosophy; preservation and transmission of Christianity) and its ultimate internal weaknesses (e.g., rise of autonomous military powers within the empire, undermining of citizenship by the growth of corruption and slavery, lack of education, and distribution of news).

7.1.2   Discuss the geographic borders of the empire at its height and the factors that threatened its territorial cohesion.

Reading 2.4, 3.4

Writing 2.2, 2.4

Day	Chapter Lesson	California Standards	Teach	Practice	Assess	Reteach
1	1.4 Interpreting the Past		PE/TE: 30-35 Map Transparency: MT2 History Makers: p. 1	PE/TE: 35 Critical Thinking: CT5		Reteaching activity in IDR: Unit 1, p. 20
2	Literature Connections	Reading 2.4 Writing 2.4	PE/TE: 36-39	PE/TE: 39	Formal Assessment: Lesson 1.4 Quiz, p. 8	
3	Ch. 2 Introduction & Starting with a Story	Reading 3.4 Writing 2.2	PE/TE: 42-43 PE/TE: 44-45	PE/TE: 45		
4	2.1 The Rise and Expansion of Rome	7.1.1 7.1.2	PE/TE: 46-51 Reading Skill activity in IDR: Unit 1, p. 23	Critical Thinking: CT6		
5	2.1 The Rise and Expansion of Rome	7.1.1 7.1.2	PE/TE: 46-51 Humanities Transparency: HT3 Map Transparency: MT3	PE/TE: 51		Reteaching activity in IDR: Unit 1, p. 37

INSTRUCTIONAL SEGMENT WEEK 4

7.1.1   Study the early strengths and lasting contributions of Rome (e.g., significance of Roman citizenship; rights under Roman law; Roman art, architecture, engineering, and philosophy; preservation and transmission of Christianity) and its ultimate internal weaknesses (e.g., rise of autonomous military powers within the empire, undermining of citizenship by the growth of corruption and slavery, lack of education, and distribution of news).

7.1.2   Discuss the geographic borders of the empire at its height and the factors that threatened its territorial cohesion.

7.1.3   Describe the establishment by Constantine of the new capital in Constantinople and the development of the Byzantine Empire, with an emphasis on the consequences of the development of two distinct European civilizations, Eastern Orthodox and Roman Catholic, and their two distinct views on church-state relations.

Writing 2.4

Day	Chapter Lesson	California Standards	Teach	Practice	Assess	Reteach
1	2.2 Decline and Fall of the Empire	7.1.1 7.1.2 7.1.3	*PE/TE: 52-56* Reading Skill activity in *IDR: Unit 1, p. 24*	Skillbuilder Practice in *IDR: Unit 1, p. 28* Critical Thinking: CT7	Formal Assessment: Lesson 2.1 Quiz, p. 21	
2	2.2 Decline and Fall of the Empire	7.1.1 7.1.2 7.1.3	*PE/TE: 52-56* Humanities Transparency: HT4	*PE/TE: 56*		Reteaching activity in *IDR: Unit 1, p. 38*
3	2.3 The Early Byzantine Empire	7.1.3	*PE/TE: 58-63* History Makers: p. 3 Reading Skill activity in *IDR: Unit 1, p. 25*	Critical Thinking: CT8	Formal Assessment: Lesson 2.2 Quiz, p. 22	
4	2.3 The Early Byzantine Empire	7.1.3	*PE/TE: 58-63* Primary Source activity in *IDR: Unit 1, p. 35*	*PE/TE: 63*		Reteaching activity in *IDR: Unit 1, p. 39*
5	Daily Life: Life in Constantinople	7.1.3 Writing 2.4	*PE/TE: 64-65*	*PE/TE: 65*	Formal Assessment: Lesson 2.3 Quiz, p. 23	

INSTRUCTIONAL SEGMENT WEEK 5

7.1.1　Study the early strengths and lasting contributions of Rome (e.g., significance of Roman citizenship; rights under Roman law; Roman art, architecture, engineering, and philosophy; preservation and transmission of Christianity) and its ultimate internal weaknesses (e.g., rise of autonomous military powers within the empire, undermining of citizenship by the growth of corruption and slavery, lack of education, and distribution of news).

Writing 2.3

Day	Chapter Lesson	California Standards	Teach	Practice	Assess	Reteach
1	2.4 The Legacy of Rome	7.1.1	*PE/TE: 66-71* Reading Skill activity in *IDR: Unit 1, p. 26*	Critical Thinking: CT9		
2	2.4 The Legacy of Rome	7.1.1	*PE/TE: 66-71* Literature activity in *IDR: Unit 1, p. 36* Map Transparency: MT4	*PE/TE: 71* Critical Thinking: CT10		Reteaching activity in *IDR: Unit 1, p. 40*
3	Connect to Today: Rome's Enduring Influence	7.1.1 Writing 2.3	*PE/TE: 72-73*	*PE/TE: 73*	Formal Assessment: Lesson 2.4 Quiz, p. 24	
4	Ch. 1 & Ch. 2 Review			*PE/TE: 40-41, 74-75*		
5	Ch. 1 & Ch. 2 Test				Formal Assessment: Ch. 1 & Ch. 2 Test	

Pacing Guide

INSTRUCTIONAL SEGMENT WEEK 6

7.2.1   Identify the physical features and describe the climate of the Arabian peninsula, its relationship to surrounding bodies of land and water, and nomadic and sedentary ways of life.

7.2.2   Trace the origins of Islam and the life and teachings of Muhammad, including Islamic teachings on the connection with Judaism and Christianity.

7.2.3   Explain the significance of the Qur'an and the Sunnah as the primary sources of Islamic beliefs, practice, and law, and their influence in Muslims' daily life.

7.2.4   Discuss the expansion of Muslim rule through military conquests and treaties, emphasizing the cultural blending within Muslim civilization and the spread and acceptance of Islam and the Arabic language.

7.2.5   Describe the growth of cities and the establishment of trade routes among Asia, Africa, and Europe, the products and inventions that traveled along these routes (e.g., spices, textiles, paper, steel, new crops), and the role of merchants in Arab society.

Reading 3.2

Writing 2.1, 2.2

Day	Chapter Lesson	California Standards	Teach	Practice	Assess	Reteach
1	Ch. 3 Introduction & Starting with a Story	Reading 3.2 Writing 2.2	*PE/TE: 80-81* *PE/TE: 82-83*	*PE/TE: 83*		
2	3.1 Life on the Arabian Peninsula	7.2.1 7.2.2 7.2.5	*PE/TE: 84-89* Reading Skill activity in *IDR: Unit 2, p. 3*	Critical Thinking: CT11 Geography Practice in *IDR: Unit 2, p. 11*		
3	3.1 Life on the Arabian Peninsula & Daily Life: Life Along a Trade Route	7.2.1 7.2.2 7.2.5 Writing 2.1	*PE/TE: 84-89* *PE/TE: 90-91* Map Transparency: MT5	*PE/TE: 89* *PE/TE: 91*		Reteaching activity in *IDR: Unit 2, p. 15*

continued on next page

Pacing Guide

4	3.2 Islam and Muhammad	7.2.2 7.2.3 7.2.4	*PE/TE: 92-96* Reading Skill activity in *IDR: Unit 2, p. 4*	Critical Thinking: CT12	Formal Assessment: Lesson 3.1 Quiz, p. 41	
5	3.2 Islam and Muhammad	7.2.2 7.2.3 7.2.4	*PE/TE: 92-96* Literature activity in *IDR: Unit 2, p. 14* Humanities Transparency: HT5	*PE/TE: 96*		Reteaching activity in *IDR: Unit 2, p. 16*

INSTRUCTIONAL SEGMENT WEEK 7

7.2.2   Trace the origins of Islam and the life and teachings of Muhammad, including Islamic teachings on the connection with Judaism and Christianity.

7.2.4   Discuss the expansion of Muslim rule through military conquests and treaties, emphasizing the cultural blending within Muslim civilization and the spread and acceptance of Islam and the Arabic language.

Reading 3.2

Writing 2.1

Day	Chapter Lesson	California Standards	Teach	Practice	Assess	Reteach
1	3.2 Activity		*PE/TE: 97*	*PE/TE: 97*	Formal Assessment: Lesson 3.2 Quiz, p. 42	
2	3.3 Islam After Muhammad's Death	7.2.2 7.2.4	*PE/TE: 98-103* Reading Skill activity in *IDR: Unit 2, p. 5* Map Transparency: MT6	Critical Thinking: CT13		
3	3.3 Islam After Muhammad's Death	7.2.2 7.2.4	*PE/TE: 98-103* Primary Source activity in *IDR: Unit 2, p. 13*	*PE/TE: 103* Skillbuilder Practice in *IDR: Unit 2, p. 7*		Reteaching activity in *IDR: Unit 2, p. 17*
4	Skillbuilder: Summarizing		*PE/TE: 104-105*	*PE/TE: 105*	Formal Assessment: Lesson 3.3 Quiz, p. 43	
5	Ch. 4 Introduction & Starting with a Story	Reading 3.2 Writing 2.1	*PE/TE: 108-109* *PE/TE: 110-111*	*PE/TE: 111*		

Pacing Guide

INSTRUCTIONAL SEGMENT WEEK 8

7.2.4   Discuss the expansion of Muslim rule through military conquests and treaties, emphasizing the cultural blending within Muslim civilization and the spread and acceptance of Islam and the Arabic language.

7.2.5   Describe the growth of cities and the establishment of trade routes among Asia, Africa, and Europe, the products and inventions that traveled along these routes (e.g., spices, textiles, paper, steel, new crops), and the role of merchants in Arab society.

7.2.6   Understand the intellectual exchanges among Muslim scholars of Eurasia and Africa and the contributions Muslim scholars made to later civilizations in the areas of science, geography, mathematics, philosophy, medicine, art, and literature.

Day	Chapter Lesson	California Standards	Teach	Practice	Assess	Reteach
1	4.1 The Expansion of Muslim Rule	7.2.4	*PE/TE: 112-116* Reading Skill activity in *IDR: Unit 2, p. 20*	Critical Thinking: CT15		
2	4.1 The Expansion of Muslim Rule	7.2.4	*PE/TE: 112-116* Humanities Transparency: HT7	*PE/TE: 116* Skillbuilder Practice in *IDR: Unit 2, p. 24*		Reteaching activity in *IDR: Unit 2, p. 33*
3	4.1 Activity	7.2.4	*PE/TE: 117*	*PE/TE: 117*	Formal Assessment: Lesson 4.1 Quiz, p. 59	
4	4.2 A Golden Age in the East	7.2.4 7.2.5 7.2.6	*PE/TE: 118-125* Map Transparency: MT7 Primary Source activity in *IDR: Unit 2, p. 31*	Geography Practice in *IDR: Unit 2, p. 29*		
5	4.2 A Golden Age in the East	7.2.4 7.2.5 7.2.6	*PE/TE: 118-125* Reading Skill activity in *IDR: Unit 2, p. 21*	*PE/TE: 125* Critical Thinking: CT16		Reteaching activity in *IDR: Unit 2, p. 34*

Pacing Guide

INSTRUCTIONAL SEGMENT WEEK 9

7.2.4   Discuss the expansion of Muslim rule through military conquests and treaties, emphasizing the cultural blending within Muslim civilization and the spread and acceptance of Islam and the Arabic language.

7.2.5   Describe the growth of cities and the establishment of trade routes among Asia, Africa, and Europe, the products and inventions that traveled along these routes (e.g., spices, textiles, paper, steel, new crops), and the role of merchants in Arab society.

7.2.6   Understand the intellectual exchanges among Muslim scholars of Eurasia and Africa and the contributions Muslim scholars made to later civilizations in the areas of science, geography, mathematics, philosophy, medicine, art, and literature.

7.9.7   Describe the Golden Age of cooperation between Jews and Muslims in medieval Spain that promoted creativity in art, literature, and science, including how that cooperation was terminated by the religious persecution of individuals and groups (e.g., the Spanish Inquisition and the expulsion of Jews and Muslims from Spain in 1492).

Reading 3.3

Writing 2.2, 2.4

Day	Chapter Lesson	California Standards	Teach	Practice	Assess	Reteach
1	Literature Connection	Reading 3.3 Writing 2.2	*PE/TE: 126-129*	*PE/TE: 129*	Formal Assessment: Lesson 4.2 Quiz, p. 60	
2	4.3 Muslim Rule in Spain	7.2.4 7.2.5 7.9.7	*PE/TE: 130-137* Humanities Transparency: HT8 Reading Skill activity in *IDR: Unit 2, p. 22*	Critical Thinking: CT16		
3	4.3 Muslim Rule in Spain	7.2.4 7.2.5 7.9.7	*PE/TE: 130-137* History Makers: p. 7 Map Transparency: MT8	*PE/TE: 137*		Reteaching activity in *IDR: Unit 2, p. 35*
4	Connect to Today: The Legacy of the Muslim Golden Age	7.2.6 Writing 2.4	*PE/TE: 138-139*	*PE/TE: 139*	Formal Assessment: Lesson 4.3 Quiz, p. 61	
5	Ch. 3 & Ch. 4 Review			*PE/TE: 106-107, 140-141*		

INSTRUCTIONAL SEGMENT WEEK 10

7.4.1   Study the Niger River and the relationship of vegetation zones of forest, savannah, and desert to trade in gold, salt, food, and slaves; and the growth of the Ghana and Mali empires.

7.4.2   Analyze the importance of family, labor specialization, and regional commerce in the development of states and cities in West Africa.

7.4.3   Describe the role of the trans-Saharan caravan trade in the changing religious and cultural characteristics of West Africa and the influence of Islamic beliefs, ethics, and law.

7.4.4   Trace the growth of the Arabic language in government, trade, and Islamic scholarship in West Africa.

7.4.5   Describe the importance of written and oral traditions in the transmission of African history and culture.

Reading 3.3

Writing 2.4

Day	Chapter Lesson	California Standards	Teach	Practice	Assess	Reteach
1	Ch. 3 & Ch. 4 Test				Formal Assessment: Ch. 3 & Ch. 4 Test	
2	Ch. 5 Introduction & Starting with a Story	Reading 3.3 Writing 2.4	*PE/TE: 146-147* *PE/TE: 148-149*	*PE/TE: 149*		
3	5.1 West African Culture and Daily Life	7.4.1 7.4.2 7.4.5	*PE/TE: 150-154* Humanities Transparency: HT9	*PE/TE: 154* Critical Thinking: CT19		Reteaching activity in *IDR: Unit 3, p. 15*
4	5.2 The Empire of Ghana	7.4.1 7.4.3 7.4.4	*PE/TE: 156-161* Humanities Transparency: HT10 Map Transparency: MT9	Geography Practice in *IDR: Unit 3, p. 11*	Formal Assessment: Lesson 5.1 Quiz, p. 78	
5	5.2 The Empire of Ghana	7.4.1 7.4.3 7.4.4	*PE/TE: 156-161* Reading Skill activity in *IDR: Unit 3, p. 4*	*PE/TE: 161* Critical Thinking: CT20		Reteaching activity in *IDR: Unit 3, p. 16*

Pacing Guide

INSTRUCTIONAL SEGMENT WEEK 11

7.4.1   Study the Niger River and the relationship of vegetation zones of forest, savannah, and desert to trade in gold, salt, food, and slaves; and the growth of the Ghana and Mali empires.

7.4.3   Describe the role of the trans-Saharan caravan trade in the changing religious and cultural characteristics of West Africa and the influence of Islamic beliefs, ethics, and law.

7.4.4   Trace the growth of the Arabic language in government, trade, and Islamic scholarship in West Africa.

7.4.5   Describe the importance of written and oral traditions in the transmission of African history and culture.

Reading 2.4, 3.3

Writing 2.2

Day	Chapter Lesson	California Standards	Teach	Practice	Assess	Reteach
1	Daily Life: Producing Salt & 5.3 The Empire of Mali	7.4.1 7.4.3 7.4.4 Writing 2.2	*PE/TE: 162-163* *PE/TE: 164-169* Map Transparency: MT10	*PE/TE: 163*	Formal Assessment: Lesson 5.2 Quiz, p. 79	
2	5.3 The Empire of Mali	7.4.1 7.4.3 7.4.4	*PE/TE: 164-169* Primary Source activity in *IDR: Unit 3, p. 13* History Makers: p. 9	Critical Thinking: CT21		
3	5.3 The Empire of Mali & Literature Connections	7.4.1 7.4.3 7.4.4 Reading 3.3 Writing 2.2	*PE/TE: 164-169* *PE/TE: 170-173*	*PE/TE: 169* *PE/TE: 173*		Reteaching activity in *IDR: Unit 3, p. 17*
4	Ch. 6 Introduction & Starting with a Story	Reading 2.4 Writing 2.2	*PE/TE: 176-177* *PE/TE: 178-179*	*PE/TE: 179*	Formal Assessment: Lesson 5.3 Quiz, p. 80	
5	6.1 The Growth of Coastal Trading Cities	7.2.4 7.2.5	*PE/TE: 180-184* Humanities Transparency: HT11 Map Transparency	*PE/TE: 184* Critical Thinking: CT23		Reteaching activity in *IDR: Unit 3, p. 33*

Pacing Guide

INSTRUCTIONAL SEGMENT WEEK 12

7.2.5   Describe the growth of cities and the establishment of trade routes among Asia, Africa, and Europe, the products and inventions that traveled along these routes (e.g., spices, textiles, paper, steel, new crops), and the role of merchants in Arab society.

7.4.5   Describe the importance of written and oral traditions in the transmission of African history and culture.

Day	Chapter Lesson	California Standards	Teach	Practice	Assess	Reteach
1	6.1 Activity		*PE/TE: 185*	*PE/TE: 185*	Formal Assessment: Lesson 6.1 Quiz, p. 96	
2	6.2 Empires Built on Gold and Trade	7.2.5 7.4.5	*PE/TE: 186-191* Literature activity in *IDR: Unit 3, p. 32* Map Transparency: MT12	Critical Thinking: CT24		
3	6.2 Empires Built on Gold and Trade	7.2.5 7.4.5	*PE/TE: 186-191* Humanities Transparency: HT12	*PE/TE: 191* Geography Practice in *IDR: Unit 3, p. 29*		Reteaching activity in *IDR: Unit 3, p. 34*
4	Skillbuilder: Drawing Conclusions from Sources		*PE/TE: 192-193*	*PE/TE: 193*	Formal Assessment: Lesson 6.2 Quiz, p. 97	
5	6.3 The Kongo Kingdom		*PE/TE: 194-199* History Makers: p. 11	*PE/TE: 199* Critical Thinking: CT25, CT26		Reteaching activity in *IDR: Unit 3, p. 35*

INSTRUCTIONAL SEGMENT WEEK 13

7.3.1 Describe the reunification of China under the Tang Dynasty and reasons for the spread of Buddhism in Tang China, Korea, and Japan.

7.3.2 Describe agricultural, technological, and commercial developments during the Tang and Sung periods.

7.3.3 Analyze the influences of Confucianism and changes in Confucian thought during the Sung and Mongol periods.

Reading 3.2

Writing 2.2

Day	Chapter Lesson	California Standards	Teach	Practice	Assess	Reteach
1	Ch. 5 & Ch. 6 Review			*PE/TE: 174-175, 202-203*	Formal Assessment: Lesson 6.3 Quiz, p. 98	
2	Ch. 5 & Ch. 6 Test				Formal Assessment: Ch. 5 & Ch. 6 Test	
3	Ch. 7 Introduction & Starting with a Story	Reading 3.2 Writing 2.2	*PE/TE: 208-209 PE/TE: 210-211*	*PE/TE: 211*		
4	7.1 Reunifying China	7.3.1 7.3.2 7.3.3	*PE/TE: 212-219* History Makers: p. 13	Critical Thinking: CT27		
5	7.1 Reunifying China	7.3.1 7.3.2 7.3.3	*PE/TE: 212-219* Map Transparency: MT13	*PE/TE: 219*		Reteaching activity in *IDR: Unit 4, p. 17*

Pacing Guide

INSTRUCTIONAL SEGMENT WEEK 14

7.3.2   Describe agricultural, technological, and commercial developments during the Tang and Sung periods.

7.3.3   Analyze the influences of Confucianism and changes in Confucian thought during the Sung and Mongol periods.

7.3.4   Understand the importance of both overland trade and maritime expeditions between China and other civilizations in the Mongol Ascendancy and Ming Dynasty.

7.3.5   Trace the historic influence of such discoveries as tea, the manufacture of paper, wood-block printing, the compass, and gunpowder.

7.3.6 Describe the development of the imperial state and the scholar-official class.

Writing 2.3

Day	Chapter Lesson	California Standards	Teach	Practice	Assess	Reteach
1	Skillbuilder: Identifying Issues and Problems		*PE/TE: 220-221*	*PE/TE: 221*	Formal Assessment: Lesson 7.1 Quiz, p. 115	
2	7.2 Advances Under the Tang and Song	7.3.2 7.3.5 7.3.6	*PE/TE: 222-229* Primary Source activity in *IDR: Unit 4, p. 15*	Geography Practice in *IDR: Unit 4, p. 13*		
3	7.2 Advances Under the Tang and Song	7.3.2 7.3.5 7.3.6	*PE/TE: 222-229* Map Transparency: MT14 Humanities Transparency: HT13	*PE/TE: 229* Critical Thinking: CT28		Reteaching activity in *IDR: Unit 4, p. 18*
4	Connect to Today: The Chinese Legacy	7.3.2 7.3.5 Writing 2.3	*PE/TE: 230-231*	*PE/TE: 231*	Formal Assessment: Lesson 7.2 Quiz, p. 116	
5	7.3 The Mongol Empire	7.3.3 7.3.4	*PE/TE: 232-237* Reading Skill activity in *IDR: Unit 4, p. 5*	Critical Thinking: CT29		

Pacing Guide

INSTRUCTIONAL SEGMENT WEEK 15

7.3.3   Analyze the influences of Confucianism and changes in Confucian thought during the Sung and Mongol periods.

7.3.4   Understand the importance of both overland trade and maritime expeditions between China and other civilizations in the Mongol Ascendancy and Ming Dynasty.

7.3.5   Trace the historic influence of such discoveries as tea, the manufacture of paper, wood-block printing, the compass, and gunpowder.

7.5.1   Describe the significance of Japan's proximity to China and Korea and the intellectual, linguistic, religious, and philosophical influence of those countries on Japan.

7.5.2   Discuss the reign of Prince Shotoku of Japan and the characteristics of Japanese society and family life during his reign.

Reading 3.4

Writing 2.2

Day	Chapter Lesson	California Standards	Teach	Practice	Assess	Reteach
1	7.3 The Mongol Empire	7.3.3 7.3.4	*PE/TE: 232-237* Humanities Transparency: HT14	*PE/TE: 237*		Reteaching activity in *IDR: Unit 4, p. 19*
2	7.4 A Return to Chinese Rule		*PE/TE: 238-242* Reading Skill activity in *IDR: Unit 4, p. 6*	Critical Thinking: CT30 Skillbuilder Practice in *IDR: Unit 4, p. 8*	Formal Assessment: Lesson 7.3 Quiz, p. 117	
3	7.4 A Return to Chinese Rule & 7.4 Activity	7.3.5	*PE/TE: 238-242* *PE/TE: 243*	*PE/TE: 242* *PE/TE: 243* Critical Thinking: CT31		Reteaching activity in *IDR: Unit 4, p. 20*
4	Ch. 8 Introduction & Starting with a Story	Reading 3.4 Writing 2.2	*PE/TE: 246-247* *PE/TE: 248-249*	*PE/TE: 249*	Formal Assessment: Lesson 7.4 Quiz, p. 118	
5	8.1 Land of the Rising Sun	7.5.1 7.5.2	*PE/TE: 250-254* Reading Skill activity in *IDR: Unit 4, p. 23*	Critical Thinking: CT32		

Pacing Guide

INSTRUCTIONAL SEGMENT WEEK 16

7.5.1   Describe the significance of Japan's proximity to China and Korea and the intellectual, linguistic, religious, and philosophical influence of those countries on Japan.

7.5.2   Discuss the reign of Prince Shotoku of Japan and the characteristics of Japanese society and family life during his reign.

7.5.4   Trace the development of distinctive forms of Japanese Buddhism.

7.5.5   Study the ninth and tenth centuries' golden age of literature, art, and drama and its lasting effects on culture today, including Murasaki Shikibu's *Tale of Genji*.

7.5.6   Analyze the rise of a military society in the late twelfth century and the role of the samurai in that society.

Writing 2.1

Day	Chapter Lesson	California Standards	Teach	Practice	Assess	Reteach
1	8.1 Land of the Rising Sun	7.5.1 7.5.2	*PE/TE:* 250-254 History Makers: p. 15	*PE/TE:* 254		Reteaching activity in *IDR: Unit 4, p. 37*
2	8.1 Activity	7.5.2	*PE/TE:* 255	*PE/TE:* 255	Formal Assessment: Lesson 8.1 Quiz, p. 134	
3	8.2 Growth of Japanese Culture	7.5.4 7.5.5	*PE/TE:* 256-261 Primary Source activity in *IDR: Unit 4, p. 35*	Critical Thinking: CT33		
4	8.2 Growth of Japanese Culture	7.5.4 7.5.5	*PE/TE:* 256-261 Humanities Transparency: HT15	*PE/TE:* 261		Reteaching activity in *IDR: Unit 4, p. 38*
5	Reader's Theater	7.5.6 Writing 2.1	*PE/TE:* 262-265	*PE/TE:* 265	Formal Assessment: Lesson 8.2 Quiz, p. 135	

INSTRUCTIONAL SEGMENT WEEK 17

7.3.1   Describe the reunification of China under the Tang Dynasty and reasons for the spread of Buddhism in Tang China, Korea, and Japan.

7.5.3   Describe the values, social customs, and traditions prescribed by the lord-vassal system consisting of *shogun, daimyo,* and *samurai* and the lasting influence of the warrior code in the twentieth century.

7.5.6   Analyze the rise of a military society in the late twelfth century and the role of the samurai in that society.

Writing 2.1

Day	Chapter Lesson	California Standards	Teach	Practice	Assess	Reteach
1	8.3 Samurai and Shoguns	7.5.3 7.5.6	*PE/TE: 266-271* Reading Skill activity in *IDR: Unit 4, p. 25*	Skillbuilder Practice in *IDR: Unit 4, p. 28*		
2	8.3 Samurai and Shoguns	7.5.3 7.5.6	*PE/TE: 266-271* Map Transparency: MT15	*PE/TE: 271* Critical Thinking: CT34		Reteaching activity in *IDR: Unit 4, p. 39*
3	Daily Life: An Inside Look at Himeji Castle	7.5.3 Writing 2.1	*PE/TE: 272-273*	*PE/TE: 273*	Formal Assessment: Lesson 8.3 Quiz, p. 136	
4	8.4 Korea and Southeast Asia	7.3.1	*PE/TE: 274-279* Literature activity in *IDR: Unit 4, p. 36*	Geography Practice in *IDR: Unit 4, p. 33*		
5	8.4 Korea and Southeast Asia	7.3.1	*PE/TE: 274-279* Humanities Transparency: HT16 Map Transparency: MT16	*PE/TE: 279* Critical Thinking: CT35, CT36		Reteaching activity in *IDR: Unit 4, p. 40*

Pacing Guide

INSTRUCTIONAL SEGMENT WEEK 18

Writing 2.3

Day	Chapter Lesson	California Standards	Teach	Practice	Assess	Reteach
1	Ch. 7 & Ch. 8 Review			*PE/TE: 244-245, 280-281*	Formal Assessment: Lesson 8.4 Quiz, p. 137	
2	Ch. 7 & Ch. 8 Test				Formal Assessment: Ch. 7 & Ch. 8 Test	
3	Writing about History: Expository Writing: Comparison and Contrast	Writing 2.3	*PE/TE: 316-317*			
4	Writing about History: Expository Writing: Comparison and Contrast	Writing 2.3	*PE/TE: 316-317*			
5	Writing about History: Expository Writing: Comparison and Contrast	Writing 2.3	*PE/TE: 316-317*			

INSTRUCTIONAL SEGMENT WEEK 19

7.6.1   Study the geography of the Europe and the Eurasian land mass, including its location, topography, waterways, vegetation, and climate and their relationship to ways of life in Medieval Europe.

7.6.2   Describe the spread of Christianity north of the Alps and the roles played by the early church and by monasteries in its diffusion after the fall of the western half of the Roman Empire.

7.6.3   Understand the development of feudalism, its role in the medieval European economy, the way in which it was influenced by physical geography (the role of the manor and the growth of towns), and how feudal relationships provided the foundation of political order.

Reading 3.4

Writing 2.5

Day	Chapter Lesson	California Standards	Teach	Practice	Assess	Reteach
1	Ch. 9 Introduction & Starting with a Story	Reading 3.4 Writing 2.5	PE/TE: 286-287 PE/TE: 288-289	PE/TE: 289		
2	9.1 The Development of Feudalism	7.6.1 7.6.2 7.6.3	PE/TE: 290-297 Map Transparency: MT17	Skillbuilder Practice in IDR: Unit 5, p. 7		
3	9.1 The Development of Feudalism	7.6.1 7.6.2 7.6.3	PE/TE: 290-297 History Makers: p. 17	PE/TE: 297 Critical Thinking: CT37		Reteaching activity in IDR: Unit 5, p. 15
4	9.2 Daily Life in Medieval Europe	7.6.3	PE/TE: 298-302 Literature activity in IDR: Unit 5, p. 14	Geography Practice in IDR: Unit 5, p. 11	Formal Assessment: Lesson 9.1 Quiz, p. 154	
5	9.2 Daily Life in Medieval Europe	7.6.3	PE/TE: 298-302 Humanities Transparency: HT17 Map Transparency: MT18	PE/TE: 302 Critical Thinking: CT38		Reteaching activity in IDR: Unit 5, p. 16

Pacing Guide

INSTRUCTIONAL SEGMENT WEEK 20

7.5.2   Discuss the reign of Prince Shotoku of Japan and the characteristics of Japanese society and family life during his reign.

7.6.3   Understand the development of feudalism, its role in the medieval European economy, the way in which it was influenced by physical geography (the role of the manor and the growth of towns), and how feudal relationships provided the foundation of political order.

Reading 2.3

Writing 2.1

Day	Chapter Lesson	California Standards	Teach	Practice	Assess	Reteach
1	9.2 Activity		PE/TE: 303	PE/TE: 303	Formal Assessment: Lesson 9.2 Quiz, p. 155	
2	9.3 Feudalism in Europe and Japan	7.5.2 7.6.3	PE/TE: 306-311 Reading Skill activity in IDR: Unit 5, p. 5	Critical Thinking: CT39		
3	9.3 Feudalism in Europe and Japan	7.5.2 7.6.3	PE/TE: 306-311 Humanities Transparency: HT18	PE/TE: 311		Reteaching activity in IDR: Unit 5, p. 17
4	Skillbuilder: Comparing and Contrasting		PE/TE: 312-313	PE/TE: 313	Formal Assessment: Lesson 9.3 Quiz, p. 156	
5	Ch. 10 Introduction & Starting with a Story	Reading 2.3 Writing 2.1	PE/TE: 316-317 PE/TE: 318-319	PE/TE: 319		

INSTRUCTIONAL SEGMENT WEEK 21

7.6.4 Demonstrate an understanding of the conflict and cooperation between the Papacy and European monarchs (e.g., Charlemagne, Gregory VII, Emperor Henry IV).

7.6.6 Discuss the causes and course of the religious Crusades and their effects on the Christian, Muslim, and Jewish populations in Europe, with emphasis on the increasing contact by Europeans with cultures of the Eastern Mediterranean world.

7.6.7 Map the spread of the bubonic plague from Central Asia to China, the Middle East, and Europe and describe its impact on global population.

7.6.8 Understand the importance of the Catholic church as a political, intellectual, and aesthetic institution (e.g., founding of universities, political and spiritual roles of the clergy, creation of monastic and mendicant religious orders, preservation of the Latin language and religious texts, St. Thomas Aquinas's synthesis of classical philosophy with Christian theology, and the concept of "natural law").

Day	Chapter Lesson	California Standards	Teach	Practice	Assess	Reteach
1	10.1 The Role of the Catholic Church	7.6.4 7.6.8	*PE/TE: 320-325* Humanities Transparency: HT19	Critical Thinking: CT41		
2	10.1 The Role of the Catholic Church	7.6.4 7.6.8	*PE/TE: 320-325* Primary Source activity in *IDR: Unit 5, p. 33*	*PE/TE: 325*		Reteaching activity in *IDR: Unit 5, p. 35*
3	10.2 The Crusades	7.6.6	*PE/TE: 326-331* Map Transparency: MT19	Skillbuilder Practice in *IDR: Unit 5, p. 26*	Formal Assessment: Lesson 10.1 Quiz, p. 172	
4	10.2 The Crusades	7.6.6	*PE/TE: 326-331* Reading Skill activity in *IDR: Unit 5, p. 21*	*PE/TE: 331* Critical Thinking: CT42		Reteaching activity in *IDR: Unit 5, p. 36*
5	10.3 Plague and the Hundred Years' War	7.6.7	*PE/TE: 332-337* History Makers: p. 19	Geography Practice in *IDR: Unit 5, p. 32*	Formal Assessment: Lesson 10.2 Quiz, p. 173	

Pacing Guide

Pacing Guide

INSTRUCTIONAL SEGMENT WEEK 22

7.6.5   Know the significance of developments in medieval English legal and constitutional practices and their importance in the rise of modern democratic thought and representative institutions (e.g., Magna Carta, parliament, development of habeas corpus, an independent judiciary in England).

7.6.7   Map the spread of the bubonic plague from Central Asia to China, the Middle East, and Europe and describe its impact on global population.

Writing 2.3

Day	Chapter Lesson	California Standards	Teach	Practice	Assess	Reteach
1	10.3 Plague and the Hundred Years' War	7.6.7	*PE/TE: 332-337* Primary Source activity in *IDR: Unit 5, p. 34*	*PE/TE: 337* Critical Thinking: CT43		Reteaching activity in *IDR: Unit 5, p. 37*
2	Connect to Today: Epidemics	7.6.7	*PE/TE: 338-339*	*PE/TE: 339*	Formal Assessment: Lesson 10.3 Quiz, p. 174	
3	10.4 Changes in Government and Economics	7.6.5	*PE/TE: 340-345* Reading Skill activity in *IDR: Unit 5, p. 23*	Geography Practice in *IDR: Unit 5, p. 31*		
4	10.4 Changes in Government and Economics	7.6.5	*PE/TE: 340-345*	*PE/TE: 345* Critical Thinking: CT44		Reteaching activity in *IDR: Unit 5, p. 38*
5	Reader's Theater	7.6.5 Writing 2.3	*PE/TE: 346-349*	*PE/TE: 349*	Formal Assessment: Lesson 10.4 Quiz, p. 175	

Copyright © by McDougal Littell, a division of Houghton Mifflin Company

INSTRUCTIONAL SEGMENT WEEK 23

7.6.6   Discuss the causes and course of the religious Crusades and their effects on the Christian, Muslim, and Jewish populations in Europe, with emphasis on the increasing contact by Europeans with cultures of the Eastern Mediterranean world.

Day	Chapter Lesson	California Standards	Teach	Practice	Assess	Reteach
1	10.5 The Ottoman Empire		*PE/TE: 350-354* Humanities Transparency: HT20 Map Transparency: MT20	Critical Thinking: CT45		
2	10.5 The Ottoman Empire		*PE/TE: 350-354* Reading Skill activity in *IDR: Unit 5, p. 24*	*PE/TE: 354* Critical Thinking: CT46		Reteaching activity in *IDR: Unit 5, p. 39*
3	10.5 Activity	7.6.6	*PE/TE: 355*	*PE/TE: 355*	Formal Assessment: Lesson 10.5 Quiz, p. 176	
4	Ch. 9 & Ch. 10 Review			*PE/TE: 314-315, 356-357*		
5	Ch. 9 & Ch. 10 Test				Formal Assessment: Ch. 9 & Ch. 10 Test	

INSTRUCTIONAL SEGMENT WEEK 24

7.7.1　Study the locations, landforms, and climates of Mexico, Central America, and South America and their effects on Mayan, Aztec, and Incan economies, trade, and development of urban societies.

Reading 3.2

Writing 2.1

Day	Chapter Lesson	California Standards	Teach	Practice	Assess	Reteach
1	Ch. 11 Introduction & Starting with a Story	Reading 3.2 Writing 2.1	*PE/TE: 362-363* *PE/TE: 364-365*	*PE/TE: 365*		
2	11.1 Geography and Agriculture in Meso-America	7.7.1	*PE/TE: 366-371* Map Transparency: MT21	Skillbuilder Practice in *IDR: Unit 6, p. 7*		
3	11.1 Geography and Agriculture in Meso-America	7.7.1	PE/TE: 366-371 Reading Skill activity in *IDR: Unit 6, p. 3*	*PE/TE: 371* Critical Thinking: CT47		Reteaching activity in *IDR: Unit 6, p. 15*
4	11.2 The Olmec Civilization		*PE/TE 372-377* Humanities Transparency: HT21	Geography Practice in *IDR: Unit 6, p. 11*	Formal Assessment: Lesson 11.1 Quiz, p. 193	
5	11.2 The Olmec Civilization		*PE/TE: 372-377* Reading Skill activity in *IDR: Unit 6, p. 4*	*PE/TE: 377* Critical Thinking: CT48		Reteaching activity in *IDR: Unit 6, p. 16*

INSTRUCTIONAL SEGMENT WEEK 25

7.7.2   Study the roles of people in each society, including class structures, family life, war-fare, religious beliefs and practices, and slavery.

7.7.3   Explain how and where each empire arose and how the Aztec and Incan empires were defeated by the Spanish.

7.7.4   Describe the artistic and oral traditions and architecture in the three civilizations.

7.7.5   Describe the Meso-American achievements in astronomy and mathematics, including the development of the calendar and the Meso-American knowledge of seasonal changes to the civilizations' agricultural systems.

Copyright © by McDougal Littell, a division of Houghton Mifflin Company

Day	Chapter Lesson	California Standards	Teach	Practice	Assess	Reteach
1	Skillbuilder: Explaining Chronological Order and Sequence		*PE/TE: 378-379*	*PE/TE: 379*	Formal Assessment: Lesson 11.2 Quiz, p. 194	
2	11.3 The Mayan Civilization	7.7.2 7.7.3 7.7.4 7.7.5	*PE/TE: 380-386* Humanities Transparency: HT22 Map Transparency: MT22	Critical Thinking: CT49		
3	11.3 The Mayan Civilization	7.7.2 7.7.3 7.7.4 7.7.5	*PE/TE: 380-386* Literature activity in *IDR: Unit 6, p. 14* History Makers: p.21	*PE/TE: 386*		Reteaching activity in *IDR: Unit 6, p. 17*
4	11.3 Activity	7.7.5	*PE/TE 387*	*PE/TE 387*	Formal Assessment: Lesson 11.3 Quiz, p. 195	
5	Ch. 12 Introduction & Starting with a Story		*PE/TE: 392-393* *PE/TE: 394-395*	*PE/TE: 395*		

INSTRUCTIONAL SEGMENT WEEK 26

7.7.1 Study the locations, landforms, and climates of Mexico, Central America, and South America and their effects on Mayan, Aztec, and Incan economies, trade, and development of urban societies.

7.7.2 Study the roles of people in each society, including class structures, family life, war-fare, religious beliefs and practices, and slavery.

7.7.3 Explain how and where each empire arose and how the Aztec and Incan empires were defeated by the Spanish.

7.7.4 Describe the artistic and oral traditions and architecture in the three civilizations.

7.7.5 Describe the Meso-American achievements in astronomy and mathematics, including the development of the calendar and the Meso-American knowledge of seasonal changes to the civilizations' agricultural systems.

Day	Chapter Lesson	California Standards	Teach	Practice	Assess	Reteach
1	12.1 The Aztecs	7.7.1 7.7.2 7.7.3 7.7.4 7.7.5	*PE/TE: 396-402* Humanities Transparency: HT23, HT24 Map Transparency: MT23	Geography Practice in *IDR: Unit 6, p. 27*		
2	12.1 The Aztecs	7.7.1 7.7.2 7.7.3 7.7.4 7.7.5	*PE/TE: 396-402* Primary Source activity in *IDR: Unit 6, p. 29*	Skillbuilder Practice in *IDR: Unit 6, p. 23*		
3	12.1 The Aztecs	7.7.1 7.7.2 7.7.3 7.7.4 7.7.5	*PE/TE: 396-402* Literature activity in *IDR: Unit 6, p. 30* Reading Skill activity in *IDR: Unit 6, p. 20*	*PE/TE: 402* Critical Thinking: CT51		Reteaching activity in *IDR: Unit 6, p. 31*
4	12.1 Activity	7.7.4	*PE/TE 403*	*PE/TE 403*	Formal Assessment: Lesson 12.1 Quiz, p. 211	
5	12.2 The Inca	7.7.1 7.7.2 7.7.3 7.7.4 7.7.5	*PE/TE: 408-415* Reading Skill activity in *IDR: Unit 6, p. 21*	Critical Thinking: CT52		

INSTRUCTIONAL SEGMENT WEEK 27

7.7.1   Study the locations, landforms, and climates of Mexico, Central America, and South America and their effects on Mayan, Aztec, and Incan economies, trade, and development of urban societies.

7.7.2   Study the roles of people in each society, including class structures, family life, war-fare, religious beliefs and practices, and slavery.

7.7.3   Explain how and where each empire arose and how the Aztec and Incan empires were defeated by the Spanish.

7.7.4   Describe the artistic and oral traditions and architecture in the three civilizations.

7.7.5   Describe the Meso-American achievements in astronomy and mathematics, including the development of the calendar and the Meso-American knowledge of seasonal changes to the civilizations' agricultural systems.

Writing 2.1, 2.2

Day	Chapter Lesson	California Standards	Teach	Practice	Assess	Reteach
1	12.2 The Inca	7.7.1 7.7.2 7.7.3 7.7.4 7.7.5	*PE/TE: 408-415* Map Transparency: MT24 History Makers: p. 23	*PE/TE: 415* Critical Thinking: CT53		Reteaching activity in *IDR: Unit 6, p. 32*
2	Daily Life: Runners on the Royal Road	7.7.2 Writing 2.1	*PE/TE: 416-417*	*PE/TE: 417*	Formal Assessment: Lesson 12.2 Quiz, p. 212	
3	Ch. 11 & Ch. 12 Review			*PE/TE: 390-391, 418-419*		
4	Ch. 11 & Ch. 12 Test				Formal Assessment: Ch. 11 & Ch. 12 Test	
5	Writing about History: Expository Writing: Problem and Solution	Writing 2.2	*PE/TE: 420-421*			

Pacing Guide

INSTRUCTIONAL SEGMENT WEEK 28

7.8.1 Describe the way in which the revival of classical learning and the arts fostered a new interest in humanism (i.e., a balance between intellect and religious faith).

7.8.2 Explain the importance of Florence in the early stages of the Renaissance and the growth of independent trading cities (e.g., Venice), with emphasis on the cities' importance in the spread of Renaissance ideas.

7.8.3 Understand the effects of the reopening of the ancient "Silk Road" between Europe and China, including Marco Polo's travels and the location of his routes.

7.8.5 Detail advances made in literature, the arts, science, mathematics, cartography, engineering, and the understanding of human anatomy and astronomy (e.g., by Dante Alighieri, Leonardo da Vinci, Michelangelo di Buonarroti Simoni, Johann Gutenberg, William Shakespeare).

Reading 3.3

Writing 2.2, 2.5

Day	Chapter Lesson	California Standards	Teach	Practice	Assess	Reteach
1	Writing about History: Expository Writing: Problem and Solution	Writing 2.2	*PE/TE: 420-421*			
2	Ch. 13 Introduction & Starting with a Story	Reading 3.3 Writing 2.5	*PE/TE: 424-425 PE/TE: 426-427*	*PE/TE: 427*		
3	13.1 Origins of the Renaissance	7.8.1 7.8.3	*PE/TE: 428-433* Primary Source activity in *IDR: Unit 7, p. 13*	Geography Practice in *IDR: Unit 7, p. 11*		
4	13.1 Origins of the Renaissance	7.8.1 7.8.3	*PE/TE: 428-433* Reading Skill activity in *IDR: Unit 7, p. 3*	*PE/TE: 433* Critical Thinking: CT54		Reteaching activity in *IDR: Unit 7, p. 15*
5	13.2 The Italian Renaissance	7.8.2 7.8.5	*PE/TE: 434-441* Humanities Transparency: HT25, HT26	Skillbuilder Practice in *IDR: Unit 7, p. 7*	Formal Assessment: Lesson 13.1 Quiz, p. 229	

INSTRUCTIONAL SEGMENT WEEK 29

7.8.2 Explain the importance of Florence in the early stages of the Renaissance and the growth of independent trading cities (e.g., Venice), with emphasis on the cities' importance in the spread of Renaissance ideas.

7.8.4 Describe the growth and effects of new ways of disseminating information (e.g., the ability to manufacture paper, translation of the Bible into the vernacular, printing).

7.8.5 Detail advances made in literature, the arts, science, mathematics, cartography, engineering, and the understanding of human anatomy and astronomy (e.g., by Dante Alighieri, Leonardo da Vinci, Michelangelo di Buonarroti Simoni, Johann Gutenberg, William Shakespeare).

Writing 2.4

Day	Chapter Lesson	California Standards	Teach	Practice	Assess	Reteach
1	13.2 The Italian Renaissance	7.8.2 7.8.5	*PE/TE: 434-441* Map Transparency: MT25 Reading Skill activity in *IDR: Unit 7, p. 4*	Critical Thinking: CT55		
2	13.2 The Italian Renaissance	7.8.2 7.8.5	*PE/TE: 434-441* Literature activity in *IDR: Unit 7, p. 14*	*PE/TE: 441*		Reteaching activity in *IDR: Unit 7, p. 16*
3	Connect to Today: Renaissance Advances	7.8.5 Writing 2.4	*PE/TE: 442-443*	*PE/TE: 443*	Formal Assessment: Lesson 13.2 Quiz, p. 230	
4	13.3 The Renaissance Spreads	7.8.4 7.8.5	*PE/TE: 444-450* Map Transparency: MT26	Critical Thinking: CT56		
5	13.3 The Renaissance Spreads	7.8.4 7.8.5	*PE/TE: 444-450* History Makers: p. 25	*PE/TE: 450* Critical Thinking: CT57		Reteaching activity in *IDR: Unit 7, p. 17*

Pacing Guide

INSTRUCTIONAL SEGMENT WEEK 30

7.8.5   Detail advances made in literature, the arts, science, mathematics, cartography, engineering, and the understanding of human anatomy and astronomy (e.g., by Dante Alighieri, Leonardo da Vinci, Michelangelo di Buonarroti Simoni, Johann Gutenberg, William Shakespeare).

7.9.1   List the causes for the internal turmoil in and weakening of the Catholic church (e.g., tax policies, selling of indulgences).

7.9.2   Describe the theological, political, and economic ideas of the major figures during the Reformation (e.g., Desiderius Erasmus, Martin Luther, John Calvin, William Tyndale).

Reading 2.3, 3.3

Writing 2.3, 2.4

Day	Chapter Lesson	California Standards	Teach	Practice	Assess	Reteach
1	Daily Life: Life at the Globe Theater	7.8.5 Writing 2.4	*PE/TE: 452-453*	*PE/TE: 453*	Formal Assessment: Lesson 13.3 Quiz, p. 231	
2	Ch. 14 Introduction & Starting with a Story	Reading 2.3 Writing 2.4	*PE/TE: 456-457* *PE/TE: 458-459*	*PE/TE: 459*		
3	14.1 Trouble for the Catholic Church	7.9.1 7.9.2	*PE/TE: 460-465* Humanities Transparency: HT27, HT28	Critical Thinking: CT58		
4	14.1 Trouble for the Catholic Church	7.9.1 7.9.2	*PE/TE: 460-465* Primary Source activity in *IDR: Unit 7, p. 31*	*PE/TE: 465*		Reteaching activity in *IDR: Unit 7, p. 33*
5	Literature Connection	Reading 3.3 Writing 2.3	*PE/TE: 466-469*	*PE/TE: 469*	Formal Assessment: Lesson 14.1 Quiz, p. 247	

INSTRUCTIONAL SEGMENT WEEK 31

7.9.2 Describe the theological, political, and economic ideas of the major figures during the Reformation (e.g., Desiderius Erasmus, Martin Luther, John Calvin, William Tyndale).

7.9.3 Explain Protestants' new practices of church self-government and the influence of those practices on the development of democratic practices and ideas of federalism.

7.9.4 Identify and locate the European regions that remained Catholic and those that became Protestant and explain how the division affected the distribution of religions in the New World.

7.9.5 Analyze how the Counter-Reformation revitalized the Catholic church and the forces that fostered the movement (e.g., St. Ignatius of Loyola and the Jesuits, the Council of Trent).

7.9.6 Understand the institution and impact of missionaries on Christianity and the diffusion of Christianity from Europe to other parts of the world in the medieval and early modern periods; locate missions on a world map.

Day	Chapter Lesson	California Standards	Teach	Practice	Assess	Reteach
1	14.2 Reform and Reaction	7.9.2 7.9.5	*PE/TE: 470-475* Map Transparency: MT27	Skillbuilder Practice in *IDR: Unit 7, p. 24*		
2	14.2 Reform and Reaction	7.9.2 7.9.5	*PE/TE: 470-475* Reading Skill activity in *IDR: Unit 7, p. 21*	*PE/TE: 475* Critical Thinking: CT59		Reteaching activity in *IDR: Unit 7, p. 34*
3	Skillbuilder: Understanding Cause and Effect		*PE/TE: 476-477*	*PE/TE: 477*	Formal Assessment: Lesson 14.2 Quiz, p. 248	
4	14.3 Expansion of Christianity	7.9.3 7.9.4 7.9.6	*PE/TE: 478-484* Map Transparency: MT28	Geography Practice in *IDR: Unit 7, p. 29* Critical Thinking: CT60		
5	14.3 Expansion of Christianity	7.9.3 7.9.4 7.9.6	*PE/TE: 478-484* Reading Skill activity in *IDR: Unit 7, p. 22*	*PE/TE: 484* Critical Thinking: CT61		Reteaching activity in *IDR: Unit 7, p. 35*

INSTRUCTIONAL SEGMENT WEEK 32

7.9.6   Understand the institution and impact of missionaries on Christianity and the diffusion of Christianity from Europe to other parts of the world in the medieval and early modern periods; locate missions on a world map.

Writing 2.4

Day	Chapter Lesson	California Standards	Teach	Practice	Assess	Reteach
1	14.3 Activity	7.9.6	*PE/TE: 485*	*PE/TE: 485*	Formal Assessment: Lesson 14.3 Quiz, p. 249	
2	Ch. 13 & Ch. 14 Review			*PE/TE: 454-455, 486-487*		
3	Ch. 13 & Ch. 14 Test				Formal Assessment: Ch. 13 & Ch. 14 Test	
4	Writing about History: Persuasive Writing	Writing 2.4	*PE/TE: 488-489*			
5	Writing about History: Persuasive Writing	Writing 2.4	*PE/TE: 488-489*			

INSTRUCTIONAL SEGMENT WEEK 33

7.10.1 Discuss the roots of the Scientific Revolution (e.g., Greek rationalism; Jewish, Christian, and Muslim science; Renaissance humanism; new knowledge from global exploration). \

7.10.2 Understand the significance of the new scientific theories (e.g., those of Copernicus, Galileo, Kepler, Newton) and the significance of new inventions (e.g., the telescope, microscope, thermometer, barometer).

7.10.3 Understand the scientific method advanced by Bacon and Descartes, the influence of new scientific rationalism on the growth of democratic ideas, and the coexistence of science with traditional religious beliefs.

Reading 3.2

Writing 2.1

Day	Chapter Lesson	California Standards	Teach	Practice	Assess	Reteach
1	Ch. 15 Introduction & Starting with a Story	Reading 3.2 Writing 2.1	PE/TE: 492-493 PE/TE: 494-495	PE/TE: 495		
2	15.1 History of Scientific Thought	7.10.1 7.10.3	PE/TE: 496-501 Reading Skill activity in IDR: Unit 8, p. 3	PE/TE: 501 Critical Thinking: CT62		Reteaching activity in IDR: Unit 8, p. 17
3	15.2 The Scientific Revolution	7.10.2 7.10.3	PE/TE: 502-507 Humanities Transparency: HT29 History Makers: p. 29	Critical Thinking: CT63	Formal Assessment: Lesson 15.1 Quiz, p. 266	
4	15.2 The Scientific Revolution	7.10.2 7.10.3	PE/TE: 502-507 Primary Source activity in IDR: Unit 8, p. 15	PE/TE: 507		Reteaching activity in IDR: Unit 8, p. 18
5	Skillbuilder: Distinguishing Fact from Opinion		PE/TE: 508-509	PE/TE: 509	Formal Assessment: Lesson 15.2 Quiz, p. 267	

INSTRUCTIONAL SEGMENT WEEK 34

7.11.1 Know the great voyages of discovery, the locations of the routes, and the influence of cartography in the development of a new European worldview.

7.11.2 Discuss the exchanges of plants, animals, technology, culture, and ideas among Europe, Africa, Asia, and the Americas in the fifteenth and sixteenth centuries and the major economic and social effects on each continent.

7.11.3 Examine the origins of modern capitalism; the influence of mercantilism and cottage industry; the elements and importance of a market economy in seventeenth-century Europe; the changing international trading and marketing patterns, including their locations on a world map; and the influence of explorers and map makers.

Writing 2.4

Day	Chapter Lesson	California Standards	Teach	Practice	Assess	Reteach
1	15.3 The Age of Exploration	7.11.1	*PE/TE: 510-517* Map Transparency: MT29	Skillbuilder Practice in *IDR: Unit 8, p. 8*		
2	15.3 The Age of Exploration	7.11.1	*PE/TE: 510-517* Reading Skill activity in *IDR: Unit 8, p. 5*	*PE/TE: 517* Critical Thinking: CT64		Reteaching activity in *IDR: Unit 8, p. 19*
3	Daily Life: Life on a Ship	7.11.1 Writing 2.4	*PE/TE: 518-519*	*PE/TE: 519*	Formal Assessment: Lesson 15.3 Quiz, p. 268	
4	15.4 Impact of Exploration	7.11.2 7.11.3	*PE/TE: 520-526* Literature activity in *IDR: Unit 8, p. 16*	Geography Practice in *IDR: Unit 8, p. 13* Critical Thinking: CT65		
5	15.4 Impact of Exploration	7.11.2 7.11.3	*PE/TE: 520-526* Humanities Transparency: HT30 Map Transparency: MT30	*PE/TE: 526* Critical Thinking: CT66		Reteaching activity in *IDR: Unit 8, p. 20*

INSTRUCTIONAL SEGMENT WEEK 35

7.11.4   Explain how the main ideas of the Enlightenment can be traced back to such movements as the Renaissance, the Reformation, and the Scientific Revolution and to the Greeks, Romans, and Christianity.

7.11.5   Describe how democratic thought and institutions were influenced by Enlightenment thinkers (e.g., John Locke, Charles-Louis Montesquieu, American founders).

7.11.6   Discuss how the principles in the Magna Carta were embodied in such documents as the English Bill of Rights and the American Declaration of Independence.

Reading 3.3

Writing 2.4

Day	Chapter Lesson	California Standards	Teach	Practice	Assess	Reteach
1	15.4 Activity		*PE/TE: 527*	*PE/TE: 527*	Formal Assessment: Lesson 15.4 Quiz, p. 269	
2	Ch. 16 Introduction & Starting with a Story	Reading 3.3 Writing 2.4	*PE/TE: 530-531 PE/TE: 532-533*	*PE/TE: 533*		
3	16.1 The Enlightenment	7.11.4 7.11.5	*PE/TE: 534-539* Humanities Transparency: HT31 Map Transparency: MT31	Critical Thinking: CT67		
4	16.1 The Enlightenment	7.11.4 7.11.5	*PE/TE: 534-539* History Makers: p. 31 Literature activity in *IDR: Unit 8, p. 34*	*PE/TE: 539*		Reteaching activity in *IDR: Unit 8, p. 35*
5	16.2 Democratic Ideas Develop	7.11.5 7.11.6	*PE/TE: 542-548* Humanities Transparency: HT32	Critical Thinking: CT68 Geography Practice in *IDR: Unit 8, p. 31*	Formal Assessment: Lesson 16.1 Quiz, p. 285	

Pacing Guide

INSTRUCTIONAL SEGMENT WEEK 36

7.11.5   Describe how democratic thought and institutions were influenced by Enlightenment thinkers (e.g., John Locke, Charles-Louis Montesquieu, American founders).

7.11.6   Discuss how the principles in the Magna Carta were embodied in such documents as the English Bill of Rights and the American Declaration of Independence.

Writing 2.1

Day	Chapter Lesson	California Standards	Teach	Practice	Assess	Reteach
1	16.2 Democratic Ideas Develop	7.11.5 7.11.6	*PE/TE: 542-548* Map Transparency: MT32	*PE/TE: 548* Critical Thinking: CT69		Reteaching activity in *IDR: Unit 8, p. 36*
2	16.2 Activity	7.11.5	*PE/TE: 549*	*PE/TE: 549*	Formal Assessment: Lesson 16.2 Quiz, p. 286	
3	Reader's Theater	7.11.6 Writing 2.1	*PE/TE: 550-553*	*PE/TE: 553*		
4	Ch. 15 & Ch. 16 Review			*PE/TE: 528-529, 554-555*		
5	Ch. 15 & Ch. 16 Test				Formal Assessment: Ch. 15 & Ch. 16 Test	

California History–
Social Science Content Standards

Pacing Guide
Block Scheduling

Pacing Guide–Block Schedule

INSTRUCTIONAL SEGMENT WEEK 1

Reading 3.4

Writing 2.5

Day	Chapter Lesson	California Standards	Teach	Practice	Assess	Reteach
1	Ch. 1 Introduction & 1.1 Geography of the World	Reading 3.4 Writing 2.5	*PE/TE: 2-7* *PE/TE: 8-13* Reading Skill activity in *IDR: Unit 1, p. 3*	*PE/TE: 7* Critical Thinking: CT1		
2	1.1 Geography of the World & 1.2 Mapping the World		*PE/TE: 8-13* *PE/TE: 14-21* Humanities Transparency: HT1 Reading Skill activity in *IDR: Unit 1, p. 4*	*PE/TE: 13* Critical Thinking: CT2	Formal Assessment: Lesson 1.1 Quiz, p. 5	Reteaching activity in *IDR: Unit 1, p. 17*
3	1.2 Mapping the World & Skillbuilder: Reading a Map		*PE/TE: 14-21* *PE/TE: 22-23* Map Transparency: MT1 Literature activity in *IDR: Unit 1, p. 16*	*PE/TE: 21* *PE/TE: 23*	Formal Assessment: Lesson 1.2 Quiz, p. 6	Reteaching activity in *IDR: Unit 1, p. 18*

continued on next page

| 4 | 1.3 Discovering the Past | | *PE/TE: 24-28*

Reading Skill activity in *IDR: Unit 1, p. 5*

Humanities Transparency: HT2 | *PE/TE: 28*

Critical Thinking: CT3

Skillbuilder Practice in *IDR: Unit 1, p. 8* | | Reteaching activity in *IDR: Unit 1, p. 19* |
| 5 | 1.3 Activity: Prepare a Time Capsule & 1.4 Interpreting the Past | | *PE/TE: 29*
PE/TE: 30-35

Reading Skill activity in *IDR: Unit 1, p. 6* | *PE/TE: 29*

Critical Thinking: CT4 | Formal Assessment: Lesson 1.3 Quiz, p. 7 | |

Pacing Guide–Block Schedule

INSTRUCTIONAL SEGMENT WEEK 2

7.1.1 Study the early strengths and lasting contributions of Rome (e.g., significance of Roman citizenship; rights under Roman law; Roman art, architecture, engineering, and philosophy; preservation and transmission of Christianity) and its ultimate internal weaknesses (e.g., rise of autonomous military powers within the empire, undermining of citizenship by the growth of corruption and slavery, lack of education, and distribution of news).

7.1.2 Discuss the geographic borders of the empire at its height and the factors that threatened its territorial cohesion.

7.1.3 Describe the establishment by Constantine of the new capital in Constantinople and the development of the Byzantine Empire, with an emphasis on the consequences of the development of two distinct European civilizations, Eastern Orthodox and Roman Catholic, and their two distinct views on church-state relations.

Reading 2.4, 3.4

Writing 2.2, 2.4

Day	Chapter Lesson	California Standards	Teach	Practice	Assess	Reteach
1	1.4 Interpreting the Past & Literature Connections	Reading 2.4 Writing 2.4	*PE/TE: 30-35* *PE/TE: 36-39* Map Transparency: MT2 History Makers: p. 1	*PE/TE: 35* *PE/TE: 39* Critical Thinking: CT5	Formal Assessment: Lesson 1.4 Quiz, p. 8	Reteaching activity in *IDR: Unit 1, p. 20*
2	Ch. 2 Introduction & 2.1 The Rise and Expansion of Rome	7.1.1 7.1.2 Reading 3.4 Writing 2.2	*PE/TE: 42-45* *PE/TE: 46-51* Reading Skill activity in *IDR: Unit 1, p. 23*	*PE/TE: 45* Critical Thinking: CT6		
3	2.1 The Rise and Expansion of Rome & 2.2 Decline and Fall of the Empire	7.1.1 7.1.2 7.1.3	*PE/TE: 46-51* *PE/TE: 52-56* Humanities Transparency: HT3 Reading Skill activity in *IDR: Unit 1, p. 24*	*PE/TE: 51* Skillbuilder Practice in *IDR: Unit 1, p. 28* Critical Thinking: CT7	Formal Assessment: Lesson 2.1 Quiz, p. 21	Reteaching activity in *IDR: Unit 1, p. 37*

continued on next page

| 4 | 2.2 Decline and Fall of the Empire & 2.3 The Early Byzantine Empire | 7.1.1 7.1.2 7.1.3 | *PE/TE: 52-56* *PE/TE: 58-63* History Makers: p. 3 Humanities Transparency: HT4 | *PE/TE: 56* Critical Thinking: CT8 | Formal Assessment: Lesson 2.2 Quiz, p. 22 | Reteaching activity in *IDR: Unit 1, p. 38* |
| 5 | 2.3 The Early Byzantine Empire & Daily Life: Life in Constantinople | 7.1.3 Writing 2.4 | *PE/TE: 58-63* *PE/TE: 64-65* Primary Source activity in *IDR: Unit 1, p. 35* | *PE/TE: 63* *PE/TE: 65* | Formal Assessment: Lesson 2.3 Quiz, p. 23 | Reteaching activity in *IDR: Unit 1, p. 39* |

Pacing Guide–Block Schedule

Pacing Guide–Block Schedule

INSTRUCTIONAL SEGMENT WEEK 3

7.1.1   Study the early strengths and lasting contributions of Rome (e.g., significance of Roman citizenship; rights under Roman law; Roman art, architecture, engineering, and philosophy; preservation and transmission of Christianity) and its ultimate internal weaknesses (e.g., rise of autonomous military powers within the empire, undermining of citizenship by the growth of corruption and slavery, lack of education, and distribution of news).

7.2.1   Identify the physical features and describe the climate of the Arabian peninsula, its relationship to surrounding bodies of land and water, and nomadic and sedentary ways of life.

7.2.2   Trace the origins of Islam and the life and teachings of Muhammad, including Islamic teachings on the connection with Judaism and Christianity.

7.2.3   Explain the significance of the Qur'an and the Sunnah as the primary sources of Islamic beliefs, practice, and law, and their influence in Muslims' daily life.

7.2.4   Discuss the expansion of Muslim rule through military conquests and treaties, emphasizing the cultural blending within Muslim civilization and the spread and acceptance of Islam and the Arabic language.

7.2.5   Describe the growth of cities and the establishment of trade routes among Asia, Africa, and Europe, the products and inventions that traveled along these routes (e.g., spices, textiles, paper, steel, new crops), and the role of merchants in Arab society.

Reading 3.2

Writing 2.1, 2.2, 2.3

Day	Chapter Lesson	California Standards	Teach	Practice	Assess	Reteach
1	2.4 The Legacy of Rome	7.1.1	*PE/TE: 66-71* Literature activity in *IDR: Unit 1, p. 36* Map Transparency: MT4	*PE/TE: 71* Critical Thinking: CT9, CT10		Reteaching activity in *IDR: Unit 1, p. 40*
2	Connect to Today: Rome's Enduring Influence & Ch. 1 & Ch. 2 Review	7.1.1 Writing 2.3	*PE/TE: 72-73*	*PE/TE: 73* *PE/TE: 40-41, 74-75*	Formal Assessment: Lesson 2.4 Quiz, p. 24	

continued on next page

3	Ch. 1 & Ch. 2 Test & Ch. 3 Introduction	Reading 3.2 Writing 2.2	*PE/TE: 80-81* *PE/TE: 82-83*	*PE/TE: 83*	Formal Assessment: Ch. 1 & Ch. 2 Test	
4	3.1 Life on the Arabian Peninsula & Daily Life: Life Along a Trade Route	7.2.1 7.2.2 7.2.5 Writing 2.1	*PE/TE: 84-89* *PE/TE: 90-91* Map Transparency: MT5 Reading Skill activity in *IDR: Unit 2, p. 3*	*PE/TE: 89* *PE/TE: 91* Critical Thinking: CT11 Geography Practice in *IDR: Unit 2, p. 11*		Reteaching activity in *IDR: Unit 2, p. 15*
5	3.2 Islam and Muhammad	7.2.2 7.2.3 7.2.4	*PE/TE: 92-96* Literature activity in *IDR: Unit 2, p. 14* Humanities Transparency: HT5	*PE/TE: 96* Critical Thinking: CT12	Formal Assessment: Lesson 3.1 Quiz, p. 41	Reteaching activity in *IDR: Unit 2, p. 16*

Copyright © by McDougal Littell, a division of Houghton Mifflin Company

INSTRUCTIONAL SEGMENT WEEK 4

7.2.2 Trace the origins of Islam and the life and teachings of Muhammad, including Islamic teachings on the connection with Judaism and Christianity.

7.2.4 Discuss the expansion of Muslim rule through military conquests and treaties, emphasizing the cultural blending within Muslim civilization and the spread and acceptance of Islam and the Arabic language.

7.2.5 Describe the growth of cities and the establishment of trade routes among Asia, Africa, and Europe, the products and inventions that traveled along these routes (e.g., spices, textiles, paper, steel, new crops), and the role of merchants in Arab society.

7.2.6 Understand the intellectual exchanges among Muslim scholars of Eurasia and Africa and the contributions Muslim scholars made to later civilizations in the areas of science, geography, mathematics, philosophy, medicine, art, and literature.

Reading 3.2

Writing 2.1

Day	Chapter Lesson	California Standards	Teach	Practice	Assess	Reteach
1	3.2 Activity & 3.3 Islam After Muhammad's Death	7.2.2 7.2.4	*PE/TE: 97* *PE/TE: 98-103* Reading Skill activity in *IDR: Unit 2, p. 5* Map Transparency: MT6	*PE/TE: 97* Critical Thinking: CT13	Formal Assessment: Lesson 3.2 Quiz, p. 42	
2	3.3 Islam After Muhammad's Death & Skillbuilder: Summarizing	7.2.2 7.2.4	*PE/TE: 98-103* *PE/TE: 104-105* Primary Source activity in *IDR: Unit 2, p. 13*	*PE/TE: 103* *PE/TE: 105* Skillbuilder Practice in *IDR: Unit 2, p. 7*	Formal Assessment: Lesson 3.3 Quiz, p. 43	Reteaching activity in *IDR: Unit 2, p. 17*
3	Ch. 4 Introduction & 4.1 The Expansion of Muslim Rule	7.2.4 Reading 3.2 Writing 2.1	*PE/TE: 108-111* *PE/TE: 112-116* Reading Skill activity in *IDR: Unit 2, p. 20*	*PE/TE: 111* Critical Thinking: CT15		

continued on next page

| 4 | 4.1 The Expansion of Muslim Rule & 4.1 Activity | 7.2.4 | *PE/TE: 112-116* *PE/TE: 117* Humanities Transparency: HT7 | *PE/TE: 116* *PE/TE: 117* Skillbuilder Practice in *IDR: Unit 2, p. 24* | Formal Assessment: Lesson 4.1 Quiz, p. 59 | Reteaching activity in *IDR: Unit 2, p. 33* |
| 5 | 4.2 A Golden Age in the East | 7.2.4 7.2.5 7.2.6 | *PE/TE: 118-125* Map Transparency: MT7 Primary Source activity in *IDR: Unit 2, p. 31* | *PE/TE: 125* Critical Thinking: CT16 Geography Practice in *IDR: Unit 2, p. 29* | | Reteaching activity in *IDR: Unit 2, p. 34* |

Pacing Guide–Block Schedule

INSTRUCTIONAL SEGMENT WEEK 5

7.2.4   Discuss the expansion of Muslim rule through military conquests and treaties, emphasizing the cultural blending within Muslim civilization and the spread and acceptance of Islam and the Arabic language.

7.2.5   Describe the growth of cities and the establishment of trade routes among Asia, Africa, and Europe, the products and inventions that traveled along these routes (e.g., spices, textiles, paper, steel, new crops), and the role of merchants in Arab society.

7.2.6   Understand the intellectual exchanges among Muslim scholars of Eurasia and Africa and the contributions Muslim scholars made to later civilizations in the areas of science, geography, mathematics, philosophy, medicine, art, and literature.

7.4.1   Study the Niger River and the relationship of vegetation zones of forest, savannah, and desert to trade in gold, salt, food, and slaves; and the growth of the Ghana and Mali empires.

7.4.2   Analyze the importance of family, labor specialization, and regional commerce in the development of states and cities in West Africa.

7.4.3   Describe the role of the trans-Saharan caravan trade in the changing religious and cultural characteristics of West Africa and the influence of Islamic beliefs, ethics, and law.

7.4.4   Trace the growth of the Arabic language in government, trade, and Islamic scholarship in West Africa.

7.4.5   Describe the importance of written and oral traditions in the transmission of African history and culture.

7.9.7   Describe the Golden Age of cooperation between Jews and Muslims in medieval Spain that promoted creativity in art, literature, and science, including how that cooperation was terminated by the religious persecution of individuals and groups (e.g., the Spanish Inquisition and the expulsion of Jews and Muslims from Spain in 1492).

Reading 3.3

Writing 2.2, 2.4

Day	Chapter Lesson	California Standards	Teach	Practice	Assess	Reteach
1	Literature Connection & 4.3 Muslim Rule in Spain	7.2.4 7.2.5 7.9.7 Reading 3.3 Writing 2.2	PE/TE: 126-129 PE/TE: 130-137 Humanities Transparency: HT8 Reading Skill activity in IDR: Unit 2, p. 22	PE/TE: 129 Critical Thinking: CT16	Formal Assessment: Lesson 4.2 Quiz, p. 60	

continued on next page

2	4.3 Muslim Rule in Spain & Connect to Today: The Legacy of the Muslim Golden Age	7.2.4 7.2.5 7.2.6 7.9.7 Writing 2.4	*PE/TE: 130-137* *PE/TE: 138-139* History Makers: p. 7 Map Transparency: MT8	*PE/TE: 137* *PE/TE: 139*	Formal Assessment: Lesson 4.3 Quiz, p. 61	Reteaching activity in *IDR: Unit 2, p. 35*
3	Ch. 3 & Ch. 4 Review & Ch. 3 & Ch. 4 Test			*PE/TE: 106-107, 140-141*	Formal Assessment: Ch. 3 & Ch. 4 Test	
4	Ch. 5 Introduction & 5.1 West African Culture and Daily Life	7.4.1 7.4.2 7.4.5 Reading 3.3 Writing 2.4	*PE/TE: 146-149* *PE/TE: 150-154* Humanities Transparency: HT9	*PE/TE: 149* *PE/TE: 154* Critical Thinking: CT19		Reteaching activity in *IDR: Unit 3, p. 15*
5	5.2 The Empire of Ghana	7.4.1 7.4.3 7.4.4	*PE/TE: 156-161* Reading Skill activity in *IDR: Unit 3, p. 4* Map Transparency: MT9	*PE/TE: 161* Critical Thinking: CT20 Geography Practice in *IDR: Unit 3, p. 11*	Formal Assessment: Lesson 5.1 Quiz, p. 78	Reteaching activity in *IDR: Unit 3, p. 16*

Pacing Guide–Block Schedule

Copyright © by McDougal Littell, a division of Houghton Mifflin Company

PACING GUIDE BLOCK SCHEDULE **SP49**

INSTRUCTIONAL SEGMENT WEEK 6

7.2.5   Describe the growth of cities and the establishment of trade routes among Asia, Africa, and Europe, the products and inventions that traveled along these routes (e.g., spices, textiles, paper, steel, new crops), and the role of merchants in Arab society.

7.4.1   Study the Niger River and the relationship of vegetation zones of forest, savannah, and desert to trade in gold, salt, food, and slaves; and the growth of the Ghana and Mali empires.

7.4.3   Describe the role of the trans-Saharan caravan trade in the changing religious and cultural characteristics of West Africa and the influence of Islamic beliefs, ethics, and law.

7.4.4   Trace the growth of the Arabic language in government, trade, and Islamic scholarship in West Africa.

7.4.5   Describe the importance of written and oral traditions in the transmission of African history and culture.

Reading 2.4, 3.3

Writing 2.2

Day	Chapter Lesson	California Standards	Teach	Practice	Assess	Reteach
1	Daily Life: Producing Salt & 5.3 The Empire of Mali	7.4.1 7.4.3 7.4.4 Writing 2.2	PE/TE: 162-163 PE/TE: 164-169 Map Transparency: MT10 Primary Source activity in IDR: Unit 3, p. 13	PE/TE: 163 Critical Thinking: CT21	Formal Assessment: Lesson 5.2 Quiz, p. 79	
2	5.3 The Empire of Mali & Ch. 6 Introduction	7.4.1 7.4.3 7.4.4 Reading 2.4, 3.3 Writing 2.2	PE/TE: 164-173 PE/TE: 176-179	PE/TE: 169, 173 PE/TE: 179	Formal Assessment: Lesson 5.3 Quiz, p. 80	Reteaching activity in IDR: Unit 3, p. 17
3	6.1 The Growth of Coastal Trading Cities & 6.1 Activity	7.2.4 7.2.5	PE/TE: 180-184 PE/TE: 185 Humanities Transparency: HT11 Map Transparency	PE/TE: 184 PE/TE: 185 Critical Thinking: CT23	Formal Assessment: Lesson 6.1 Quiz, p. 96	Reteaching activity in IDR: Unit 3, p. 33

continued on next page

| 4 | 6.2 Empires Built on Gold and Trade & Skillbuilder: Drawing Conclusions from Sources | 7.2.5 7.4.5 | *PE/TE: 186-191* *PE/TE: 192-193* Humanities Transparency: HT12 | *PE/TE: 191* *PE/TE: 193* Geography Practice in *IDR: Unit 3, p. 29* | Formal Assessment: Lesson 6.2 Quiz, p. 97 | Reteaching activity in *IDR: Unit 3, p. 34* |
| 5 | Skillbuilder: Drawing Conclusions from Sources & 6.3 The Kongo Kingdom | | *PE/TE: 192-193* *PE/TE: 194-199* History Makers: p. 11 | *PE/TE: 193* *PE/TE: 199* Critical Thinking: CT25, CT26 | Formal Assessment: Lesson 6.2 Quiz, p. 97 | Reteaching activity in *IDR: Unit 3, p. 35* |

Pacing Guide–Block Schedule

INSTRUCTIONAL SEGMENT WEEK 7

7.3.1   Describe the reunification of China under the Tang Dynasty and reasons for the spread of Buddhism in Tang China, Korea, and Japan.

7.3.2   Describe agricultural, technological, and commercial developments during the Tang and Sung periods.

7.3.3   Analyze the influences of Confucianism and changes in Confucian thought during the Sung and Mongol periods.

7.3.4   Understand the importance of both overland trade and maritime expeditions between China and other civilizations in the Mongol Ascendancy and Ming Dynasty.

7.3.5   Trace the historic influence of such discoveries as tea, the manufacture of paper, wood-block printing, the compass, and gunpowder.

7.3.6   Describe the development of the imperial state and the scholar-official class.

Reading 3.2

Writing 2.2, 2.3

Day	Chapter Lesson	California Standards	Teach	Practice	Assess	Reteach
1	Ch. 5 & Ch. 6 Review & Ch. 5 & Ch. 6 Test			PE/TE: 174-175, 202-203	Formal Assessment: Lesson 6.3 Quiz, p. 98 Formal Assessment: Ch. 5 & Ch. 6 Test	
2	Ch. 7 Introduction & 7.1 Reunifying China	7.3.1 7.3.2 7.3.3 Reading 3.2 Writing 2.2	PE/TE: 208-211 PE/TE: 212-219 History Makers: p. 13	PE/TE: 211 Critical Thinking: CT27		
3	7.1 Reunifying China & Skillbuilder: Identifying Issues and Problems	7.3.1 7.3.2 7.3.3	PE/TE: 212-219 PE/TE: 220-221 Map Transparency: MT13	PE/TE: 219 PE/TE: 221	Formal Assessment: Lesson 7.1 Quiz, p. 115	Reteaching activity in IDR: Unit 4, p. 17

continued on next page

4	7.2 Advances Under the Tang and Song	7.3.2 7.3.5 7.3.6	*PE/TE: 222-229* Primary Source activity in *IDR: Unit 4, p. 15* Humanities Transparency: HT13	*PE/TE: 229* Critical Thinking: CT28 Geography Practice in *IDR: Unit 4, p. 13*		Reteaching activity in *IDR: Unit 4, p. 18*
5	Connect to Today: The Chinese Legacy & 7.3 The Mongol Empire	7.3.2 7.3.3 7.3.4 7.3.5 Writing 2.3	*PE/TE: 230-231* *PE/TE: 232-237* Reading Skill activity in *IDR: Unit 4, p. 5*	*PE/TE: 231* Critical Thinking: CT29	Formal Assessment: Lesson 7.2 Quiz, p. 116	

INSTRUCTIONAL SEGMENT WEEK 8

7.3.3   Analyze the influences of Confucianism and changes in Confucian thought during the Sung and Mongol periods.

7.3.4   Understand the importance of both overland trade and maritime expeditions between China and other civilizations in the Mongol Ascendancy and Ming Dynasty.

7.3.5   Trace the historic influence of such discoveries as tea, the manufacture of paper, wood-block printing, the compass, and gunpowder.

7.5.1   Describe the significance of Japan's proximity to China and Korea and the intellectual, linguistic, religious, and philosophical influence of those countries on Japan.

7.5.2   Discuss the reign of Prince Shotoku of Japan and the characteristics of Japanese society and family life during his reign.

7.5.4   Trace the development of distinctive forms of Japanese Buddhism.

7.5.5   Study the ninth and tenth centuries' golden age of literature, art, and drama and its lasting effects on culture today, including Murasaki Shikibu's *Tale of Genji*.

7.5.6   Analyze the rise of a military society in the late twelfth century and the role of the samurai in that society.

Reading 3.4

Writing 2.1, 2.2

Day	Chapter Lesson	California Standards	Teach	Practice	Assess	Reteach
1	7.3 The Mongol Empire & 7.4 A Return to Chinese Rule	7.3.3 7.3.4	*PE/TE: 232-237* *PE/TE: 238-242* Reading Skill activity in *IDR: Unit 4, p. 6* Humanities Transparency: HT14	*PE/TE: 237* Critical Thinking: CT30 Skillbuilder Practice in *IDR: Unit 4, p. 8*	Formal Assessment: Lesson 7.3 Quiz, p. 117	Reteaching activity in *IDR: Unit 4, p. 19*
2	7.4 A Return to Chinese Rule & Ch. 8 Introduction	7.3.5 Reading 3.4 Writing 2.2	*PE/TE: 238-243* *PE/TE: 246-249*	*PE/TE: 242, 243* *PE/TE: 249* Critical Thinking: CT31	Formal Assessment: Lesson 7.4 Quiz, p. 118	Reteaching activity in *IDR: Unit 4, p. 20*
3	8.1 Land of the Rising Sun	7.5.1 7.5.2	*PE/TE: 250-254* Reading Skill activity in *IDR: Unit 4, p. 23* History Makers: p. 15	*PE/TE: 254* Critical Thinking: CT32		Reteaching activity in *IDR: Unit 4, p. 37*

continued on next page

4	8.1 Activity & 8.2 Growth of Japanese Culture	7.5.2 7.5.4 7.5.5	*PE/TE: 255* *PE/TE: 256-261* Primary Source activity in *IDR: Unit 4, p. 35*	*PE/TE: 255* Critical Thinking: CT33	Formal Assessment: Lesson 8.1 Quiz, p. 134	
5	8.2 Growth of Japanese Culture & Reader's Theater	7.5.4 7.5.5 7.5.6 Writing 2.1	*PE/TE: 256-261* *PE/TE: 262-265* Humanities Transparency: HT15	*PE/TE: 261* *PE/TE: 265*	Formal Assessment: Lesson 8.2 Quiz, p. 135	Reteaching activity in *IDR: Unit 4, p. 38*

Pacing Guide–Block Schedule

INSTRUCTIONAL SEGMENT WEEK 9

7.3.1 Describe the reunification of China under the Tang Dynasty and reasons for the spread of Buddhism in Tang China, Korea, and Japan.

7.5.3 Describe the values, social customs, and traditions prescribed by the lord-vassal system consisting of *shogun, daimyo,* and *samurai* and the lasting influence of the warrior code in the twentieth century.

7.5.6 Analyze the rise of a military society in the late twelfth century and the role of the samurai in that society.

Writing 2.1, 2.3

Day	Chapter Lesson	California Standards	Teach	Practice	Assess	Reteach
1	8.3 Samurai and Shoguns	7.5.3 7.5.6	*PE/TE: 266-271* Reading Skill activity in *IDR: Unit 4, p. 25* Map Transparency: MT15	*PE/TE: 271* Critical Thinking: CT34 Skillbuilder Practice in *IDR: Unit 4, p. 28*		Reteaching activity in *IDR: Unit 4, p. 39*
2	Daily Life: An Inside Look at Himeji Castle & 8.4 Korea and Southeast Asia	7.3.1 7.5.3 Writing 2.1	*PE/TE: 272-273 PE/TE: 274-279* Literature activity in *IDR: Unit 4, p. 36*	*PE/TE: 273* Geography Practice in *IDR: Unit 4, p. 33*	Formal Assessment: Lesson 8.3 Quiz, p. 136	
3	8.4 Korea and Southeast Asia & Ch. 7 & Ch. 8 Review	7.3.1	*PE/TE: 274-279* Humanities Transparency: HT16 Map Transparency: MT16	*PE/TE: 279 PE/TE: 244-245, 280-281* Critical Thinking: CT35, CT36	Formal Assessment: Lesson 8.4 Quiz, p. 137	Reteaching activity in *IDR: Unit 4, p. 40*

continued on next page

| 4 | Ch. 7 & Ch. 8 Test & Writing about History: Expository Writing: Comparison and Contrast | Writing 2.3 | *PE/TE: 316-317* | | Formal Assessment: Ch. 7 & Ch. 8 Test | |
| 5 | Writing about History: Expository Writing: Comparison and Contrast | Writing 2.3 | *PE/TE: 316-317* | | | |

Pacing Guide–Block Schedule

INSTRUCTIONAL SEGMENT WEEK 10

7.5.2 Discuss the reign of Prince Shotoku of Japan and the characteristics of Japanese society and family life during his reign.

7.6.1 Study the geography of the Europe and the Eurasian land mass, including its location, topography, waterways, vegetation, and climate and their relationship to ways of life in Medieval Europe.

7.6.2 Describe the spread of Christianity north of the Alps and the roles played by the early church and by monasteries in its diffusion after the fall of the western half of the Roman Empire.

7.6.3 Understand the development of feudalism, its role in the medieval European economy, the way in which it was influenced by physical geography (the role of the manor and the growth of towns), and how feudal relationships provided the foundation of political order.

Reading 2.3, 3.4

Writing 2.1, 2.5

Day	Chapter Lesson	California Standards	Teach	Practice	Assess	Reteach
1	Ch. 9 Introduction & 9.1 The Development of Feudalism	7.6.1 7.6.2 7.6.3 Reading 3.4 Writing 2.5	PE/TE: 286-289 PE/TE: 290-297 Map Transparency: MT17	PE/TE: 289 Skillbuilder Practice in IDR: Unit 5, p. 7		
2	9.1 The Development of Feudalism & 9.2 Daily Life in Medieval Europe	7.6.1 7.6.2 7.6.3	PE/TE: 290-297 PE/TE: 298-302 Literature activity in IDR: Unit 5, p. 14 History Makers: p. 17	PE/TE: 297 Critical Thinking: CT37 Geography Practice in IDR: Unit 5, p. 11	Formal Assessment: Lesson 9.1 Quiz, p. 154	Reteaching activity in IDR: Unit 5, p. 15
3	9.2 Daily Life in Medieval Europe & 9.2 Activity	7.6.3	PE/TE: 298-302 PE/TE: 303 Humanities Transparency: HT17 Map Transparency: MT18	PE/TE: 302 PE/TE: 303 Critical Thinking: CT38	Formal Assessment: Lesson 9.2 Quiz, p. 155	Reteaching activity in IDR: Unit 5, p. 16

continued on next page

4	9.3 Feudalism in Europe and Japan	7.5.2 7.6.3	*PE/TE: 306-311* Reading Skill activity in *IDR: Unit 5, p. 5* Humanities Transparency: HT18	*PE/TE: 311* Critical Thinking: CT39		Reteaching activity in *IDR: Unit 5, p. 17*
5	Skillbuilder: Comparing and Contrasting & Ch. 10 Introduction	Reading 2.3 Writing 2.1	*PE/TE: 312-313* *PE/TE: 316-319*	*PE/TE: 313* *PE/TE: 319*	Formal Assessment: Lesson 9.3 Quiz, p. 156	

Pacing Guide–Block Schedule

INSTRUCTIONAL SEGMENT WEEK 11

7.6.4   Demonstrate an understanding of the conflict and cooperation between the Papacy and European monarchs (e.g., Charlemagne, Gregory VII, Emperor Henry IV).

7.6.5   Know the significance of developments in medieval English legal and constitutional practices and their importance in the rise of modern democratic thought and representative institutions (e.g., Magna Carta, parliament, development of habeas corpus, an independent judiciary in England).

7.6.6   Discuss the causes and course of the religious Crusades and their effects on the Christian, Muslim, and Jewish populations in Europe, with emphasis on the increasing contact by Europeans with cultures of the Eastern Mediterranean world.

7.6.7   Map the spread of the bubonic plague from Central Asia to China, the Middle East, and Europe and describe its impact on global population.

7.6.8   Understand the importance of the Catholic church as a political, intellectual, and aesthetic institution (e.g., founding of universities, political and spiritual roles of the clergy, creation of monastic and mendicant religious orders, preservation of the Latin language and religious texts, St. Thomas Aquinas's synthesis of classical philosophy with Christian theology, and the concept of "natural law").

Writing 2.3

Day	Chapter Lesson	California Standards	Teach	Practice	Assess	Reteach
1	10.1 The Role of the Catholic Church	7.6.4 7.6.8	*PE/TE: 320-325* Humanities Transparency: HT19 Primary Source activity in *IDR: Unit 5, p. 33*	*PE/TE: 325* Critical Thinking: CT41		Reteaching activity in *IDR: Unit 5, p. 35*
2	10.2 The Crusades	7.6.6	*PE/TE: 326-331* Map Transparency: MT19 Reading Skill activity in *IDR: Unit 5, p. 21*	*PE/TE: 331* Critical Thinking: CT42 Skillbuilder Practice in *IDR: Unit 5, p. 26*	Formal Assessment: Lesson 10.1 Quiz, p. 172	Reteaching activity in *IDR: Unit 5, p. 36*

continued on next page

3	10.3 Plague and the Hundred Years' War	7.6.7	PE/TE: 332-337 History Makers: p. 19 Primary Source activity in *IDR: Unit 5, p. 34*	PE/TE: 337 Critical Thinking: CT43 Geography Practice in *IDR: Unit 5, p. 32*	Formal Assessment: Lesson 10.2 Quiz, p. 173	Reteaching activity in *IDR: Unit 5, p. 37*
4	Connect to Today: Epidemics & 10.4 Changes in Government and Economics	7.6.5 7.6.7	PE/TE: 338-339 PE/TE: 340-345 Reading Skill activity in *IDR: Unit 5, p. 23*	PE/TE: 339 Geography Practice in *IDR: Unit 5, p. 31*	Formal Assessment: Lesson 10.3 Quiz, p. 174	
5	10.4 Changes in Government and Economics & Reader's Theater	7.6.5 Writing 2.3	PE/TE: 340-345 PE/TE: 346-349	PE/TE: 345 PE/TE: 349 Critical Thinking: CT44	Formal Assessment: Lesson 10.4 Quiz, p. 175	Reteaching activity in *IDR: Unit 5, p. 38*

Pacing Guide–Block Schedule

Copyright © by McDougal Littell, a division of Houghton Mifflin Company

PACING GUIDE BLOCK SCHEDULE **SP61**

INSTRUCTIONAL SEGMENT WEEK 12

7.6.6   Discuss the causes and course of the religious Crusades and their effects on the Christian, Muslim, and Jewish populations in Europe, with emphasis on the increasing contact by Europeans with cultures of the Eastern Mediterranean world.

7.7.1   Study the locations, landforms, and climates of Mexico, Central America, and South America and their effects on Mayan, Aztec, and Incan economies, trade, and development of urban societies.

Reading 3.2

Writing 2.1

Day	Chapter Lesson	California Standards	Teach	Practice	Assess	Reteach
1	10.5 The Ottoman Empire		*PE/TE: 350-354* Humanities Transparency: HT20 Reading Skill activity in *IDR: Unit 5, p. 24*	*PE/TE: 354* Critical Thinking: CT45, CT46		Reteaching activity in *IDR: Unit 5, p. 39*
2	10.5 Activity & Ch. 9 & Ch. 10 Review	7.6.6	*PE/TE: 355*	*PE/TE: 355* *PE/TE: 314-315, 356-357*	Formal Assessment: Lesson 10.5 Quiz, p. 176	
3	Ch. 9 & Ch. 10 Test & Ch. 11 Introduction	Reading 3.2 Writing 2.1	*PE/TE: 362-363* *PE/TE: 364-365*	*PE/TE: 365*	Formal Assessment: Ch. 9 & Ch. 10 Test	
4	11.1 Geography and Agriculture in Meso-America	7.7.1	*PE/TE: 366-371* Map Transparency: MT21 Reading Skill activity in *IDR: Unit 6, p. 3*	*PE/TE: 371* Critical Thinking: CT47 Skillbuilder Practice in *IDR: Unit 6, p. 7*		Reteaching activity in *IDR: Unit 6, p. 15*
5	11.2 The Olmec Civilization		*PE/TE 372-377* Humanities Transparency: HT21 Reading Skill activity in *IDR: Unit 6, p. 4*	*PE/TE: 377* Critical Thinking: CT48 Geography Practice in *IDR: Unit 6, p. 11*	Formal Assessment: Lesson 11.1 Quiz, p. 193	Reteaching activity in *IDR: Unit 6, p. 16*

Pacing Guide–Block Schedule

Pacing Guide–Block Schedule

INSTRUCTIONAL SEGMENT WEEK 13

7.7.1   Study the locations, landforms, and climates of Mexico, Central America, and South America and their effects on Mayan, Aztec, and Incan economies, trade, and development of urban societies.

7.7.2   Study the roles of people in each society, including class structures, family life, war-fare, religious beliefs and practices, and slavery.

7.7.3   Explain how and where each empire arose and how the Aztec and Incan empires were defeated by the Spanish.

7.7.4   Describe the artistic and oral traditions and architecture in the three civilizations.

7.7.5   Describe the Meso-American achievements in astronomy and mathematics, including the development of the calendar and the Meso-American knowledge of seasonal changes to the civilizations' agricultural systems.

Day	Chapter Lesson	California Standards	Teach	Practice	Assess	Reteach
1	Skillbuilder: Explaining Chronological Order and Sequence & 11.3 The Mayan Civilization	7.7.2 7.7.3 7.7.4 7.7.5	*PE/TE: 378-379* *PE/TE: 380-386* Humanities Transparency: HT22 Map Transparency: MT22	*PE/TE: 379* Critical Thinking: CT49	Formal Assessment: Lesson 11.2 Quiz, p. 194	
2	11.3 The Mayan Civilization & 11.3 Activity	7.7.2 7.7.3 7.7.4 7.7.5	*PE/TE: 380-386* *PE/TE 387* Literature activity in *IDR: Unit 6, p. 14* History Makers: p.21	*PE/TE: 386* *PE/TE: 387*	Formal Assessment: Lesson 11.3 Quiz, p. 195	Reteaching activity in *IDR: Unit 6, p. 17*
3	Ch. 12 Introduction & 12.1 The Aztecs	7.7.1 7.7.2 7.7.3 7.7.4 7.7.5	*PE/TE: 392-395* *PE/TE: 396-402* Humanities Transparency: HT23, HT24 Map Transparency: MT23	*PE/TE: 395* Geography Practice in *IDR: Unit 6, p. 27*		

continued on next page

4	12.1 The Aztecs	7.7.1 7.7.2 7.7.3 7.7.4 7.7.5	*PE/TE: 396-402* Literature activity in *IDR: Unit 6, p. 30* Reading Skill activity in *IDR: Unit 6, p. 20*	*PE/TE: 402* Critical Thinking: CT51 Skillbuilder Practice in IDR: Unit 6, p. 23		Reteaching activity in *IDR: Unit 6, p. 31*
5	12.1 Activity & 12.2 The Inca	7.7.1 7.7.2 7.7.3 7.7.4 7.7.5	*PE/TE 403* *PE/TE: 408-415* Reading Skill activity in *IDR: Unit 6, p. 21*	*PE/TE: 403* Critical Thinking: CT52	Formal Assessment: Lesson 12.1 Quiz, p. 211	

INSTRUCTIONAL SEGMENT WEEK 14

7.7.1   Study the locations, landforms, and climates of Mexico, Central America, and South America and their effects on Mayan, Aztec, and Incan economies, trade, and development of urban societies.

7.7.2   Study the roles of people in each society, including class structures, family life, war-fare, religious beliefs and practices, and slavery.

7.7.3   Explain how and where each empire arose and how the Aztec and Incan empires were defeated by the Spanish.

7.7.4   Describe the artistic and oral traditions and architecture in the three civilizations.

7.7.5   Describe the Meso-American achievements in astronomy and mathematics, including the development of the calendar and the Meso-American knowledge of seasonal changes to the civilizations' agricultural systems.

7.8.1   Describe the way in which the revival of classical learning and the arts fostered a new interest in humanism (i.e., a balance between intellect and religious faith).

7.8.2   Explain the importance of Florence in the early stages of the Renaissance and the growth of independent trading cities (e.g., Venice), with emphasis on the cities' importance in the spread of Renaissance ideas.

7.8.3   Understand the effects of the reopening of the ancient "Silk Road" between Europe and China, including Marco Polo's travels and the location of his routes.

7.8.5   Detail advances made in literature, the arts, science, mathematics, cartography, engineering, and the understanding of human anatomy and astronomy (e.g., by Dante Alighieri, Leonardo da Vinci, Michelangelo di Buonarroti Simoni, Johann Gutenberg, William Shakespeare).

Reading 3.3

Writing 2.1, 2.2, 2.5

Day	Chapter Lesson	California Standards	Teach	Practice	Assess	Reteach
1	12.2 The Inca & Daily Life: Runners on the Royal Road	7.7.1 7.7.2 7.7.3 7.7.4 7.7.5 Writing 2.1	*PE/TE: 408-415* *PE/TE: 416-417* Map Transparency: MT24 History Makers: p. 23	*PE/TE: 415* *PE/TE: 417* Critical Thinking: CT53	Formal Assessment: Lesson 12.2 Quiz, p. 212	Reteaching activity in *IDR: Unit 6, p. 32*
2	Ch. 11 & Ch. 12 Review & Ch. 11 & Ch. 12 Test			*PE/TE: 390-391, 418-419*	Formal Assessment: Ch. 11 & Ch. 12 Test	

continued on next page

3	Writing about History: Expository Writing: Problem and Solution	Writing 2.2	PE/TE: 420-421			
4	Ch. 13 Introduction & 13.1 Origins of the Renaissance	7.8.1 7.8.3 Reading 3.3 Writing 2.5	PE/TE: 424-427 PE/TE: 428-433 Primary Source activity in *IDR: Unit 7, p. 13*	PE/TE: 427 Geography Practice in *IDR: Unit 7, p. 11*		
5	13.1 Origins of the Renaissance & 13.2 The Italian Renaissance	7.8.1 7.8.2 7.8.3 7.8.5	PE/TE: 428-433 PE/TE: 434-441 Humanities Transparency: HT25, HT26 Reading Skill activity in *IDR: Unit 7, p. 3*	PE/TE: 433 Critical Thinking: CT54 Skillbuilder Practice in *IDR: Unit 7, p. 7*	Formal Assessment: Lesson 13.1 Quiz, p. 229	Reteaching activity in *IDR: Unit 7, p. 15*

INSTRUCTIONAL SEGMENT WEEK 15

7.8.2   Explain the importance of Florence in the early stages of the Renaissance and the growth of independent trading cities (e.g., Venice), with emphasis on the cities' importance in the spread of Renaissance ideas.

7.8.4   Describe the growth and effects of new ways of disseminating information (e.g., the ability to manufacture paper, translation of the Bible into the vernacular, printing).

7.8.5   Detail advances made in literature, the arts, science, mathematics, cartography, engineering, and the understanding of human anatomy and astronomy (e.g., by Dante Alighieri, Leonardo da Vinci, Michelangelo di Buonarroti Simoni, Johann Gutenberg, William Shakespeare).

7.9.1   List the causes for the internal turmoil in and weakening of the Catholic church (e.g., tax policies, selling of indulgences).

7.9.2   Describe the theological, political, and economic ideas of the major figures during the Reformation (e.g., Desiderius Erasmus, Martin Luther, John Calvin, William Tyndale).

Reading 2.3, 3.3

Writing 2.3, 2.4

Day	Chapter Lesson	California Standards	Teach	Practice	Assess	Reteach
1	13.2 The Italian Renaissance	7.8.2 7.8.5	*PE/TE: 434-441* Map Transparency: MT25 Literature activity in *IDR: Unit 7, p. 14*	*PE/TE: 441* Critical Thinking: CT55		Reteaching activity in *IDR: Unit 7, p. 16*
2	Connect to Today: Renaissance Advances & 13.3 The Renaissance Spreads	7.8.4 7.8.5 Writing 2.4	*PE/TE: 442-443* *PE/TE: 444-450* Map Transparency: MT26	*PE/TE: 443* Critical Thinking: CT56	Formal Assessment: Lesson 13.2 Quiz, p. 230	
3	13.3 The Renaissance Spreads & Daily Life: Life at the Globe Theater	7.8.4 7.8.5 Writing 2.4	*PE/TE: 444-450* *PE/TE: 452-453* History Makers: p. 25	*PE/TE: 450* *PE/TE: 453* Critical Thinking: CT57	Formal Assessment: Lesson 13.3 Quiz, p. 231	Reteaching activity in *IDR: Unit 7, p. 17*

continued on next page

4	Ch. 14 Introduction & 14.1 Trouble for the Catholic Church	7.9.1 7.9.2 Reading 2.3 Writing 2.4	*PE/TE: 456-459* *PE/TE: 460-465* Humanities Transparency: HT27, HT28	*PE/TE: 459* Critical Thinking: CT58		
5	14.1 Trouble for the Catholic Church & Literature Connection	7.9.1 7.9.2 Reading 3.3 Writing 2.3	*PE/TE: 460-465* *PE/TE: 466-469* Primary Source activity in *IDR: Unit 7, p. 31*	*PE/TE: 465* *PE/TE: 469*	Formal Assessment: Lesson 14.1 Quiz, p. 247	Reteaching activity in *IDR: Unit 7, p. 33*

INSTRUCTIONAL SEGMENT WEEK 16

7.9.2   Describe the theological, political, and economic ideas of the major figures during the Reformation (e.g., Desiderius Erasmus, Martin Luther, John Calvin, William Tyndale).

7.9.3   Explain Protestants' new practices of church self-government and the influence of those practices on the development of democratic practices and ideas of federalism.

7.9.4   Identify and locate the European regions that remained Catholic and those that became Protestant and explain how the division affected the distribution of religions in the New World.

7.9.5   Analyze how the Counter-Reformation revitalized the Catholic church and the forces that fostered the movement (e.g., St. Ignatius of Loyola and the Jesuits, the Council of Trent).

7.9.6   Understand the institution and impact of missionaries on Christianity and the diffusion of Christianity from Europe to other parts of the world in the medieval and early modern periods; locate missions on a world map.

Writing 2.4

Day	Chapter Lesson	California Standards	Teach	Practice	Assess	Reteach
1	14.2 Reform and Reaction	7.9.2 7.9.5	*PE/TE: 470-475* Map Transparency: MT27 Reading Skill activity in *IDR: Unit 7, p. 21*	*PE/TE: 475* Critical Thinking: CT59 Skillbuilder Practice in *IDR: Unit 7, p. 24*		Reteaching activity in *IDR: Unit 7, p. 34*
2	Skillbuilder: Understanding Cause and Effect & 14.3 Expansion of Christianity	7.9.3 7.9.4 7.9.6	*PE/TE: 476-477* *PE/TE: 478-484* Map Transparency: MT28	*PE/TE: 477* Geography Practice in *IDR: Unit 7, p. 29*	Formal Assessment: Lesson 14.2 Quiz, p. 248	
3	14.3 Expansion of Christianity & 14.3 Activity	7.9.3 7.9.4 7.9.6	*PE/TE: 478-484* *PE/TE: 485* Reading Skill activity in *IDR: Unit 7, p. 22*	*PE/TE: 484* *PE/TE: 485* Critical Thinking: CT61	Formal Assessment: Lesson 14.3 Quiz, p. 249	Reteaching activity in *IDR: Unit 7, p. 35*
4	Ch. 13 & Ch. 14 Review & Ch. 13 & Ch. 14 Test			*PE/TE: 454-455, 486-487*	Formal Assessment: Ch. 13 & Ch. 14 Test	
5	Writing about History: Persuasive Writing	Writing 2.4	*PE/TE: 488-489*			

INSTRUCTIONAL SEGMENT WEEK 17

7.10.1 Discuss the roots of the Scientific Revolution (e.g., Greek rationalism; Jewish, Christian, and Muslim science; Renaissance humanism; new knowledge from global exploration). \

7.10.2 Understand the significance of the new scientific theories (e.g., those of Copernicus, Galileo, Kepler, Newton) and the significance of new inventions (e.g., the telescope, microscope, thermometer, barometer).

7.10.3 Understand the scientific method advanced by Bacon and Descartes, the influence of new scientific rationalism on the growth of democratic ideas, and the coexistence of science with traditional religious beliefs.

7.11.1 Know the great voyages of discovery, the locations of the routes, and the influence of cartography in the development of a new European worldview.

7.11.2 Discuss the exchanges of plants, animals, technology, culture, and ideas among Europe, Africa, Asia, and the Americas in the fifteenth and sixteenth centuries and the major economic and social effects on each continent.

7.11.3 Examine the origins of modern capitalism; the influence of mercantilism and cottage industry; the elements and importance of a market economy in seventeenth-century Europe; the changing international trading and marketing patterns, including their locations on a world map; and the influence of explorers and map makers.

Reading 3.2

Writing 2.1, 2.4

Day	Chapter Lesson	California Standards	Teach	Practice	Assess	Reteach
1	Ch. 15 Introduction & 15.1 History of Scientific Thought	7.10.1 7.10.3 Reading 3.2 Writing 2.1	PE/TE: 492-495 PE/TE: 496-501 Reading Skill activity in IDR: Unit 8, p. 3	PE/TE: 495 PE/TE: 501 Critical Thinking: CT62		Reteaching activity in IDR: Unit 8, p. 17
2	15.2 The Scientific Revolution	7.10.2 7.10.3	PE/TE: 502-507 Humanities Transparency: HT29 History Makers: p. 29	PE/TE: 507 Critical Thinking: CT63	Formal Assessment: Lesson 15.1 Quiz, p. 266	Reteaching activity in IDR: Unit 8, p. 18
3	Skillbuilder: Distinguishing Fact from Opinion & 15.3 The Age of Exploration	7.11.1	PE/TE: 508-509 PE/TE: 510-517 Map Transparency: MT29	PE/TE: 509 Skillbuilder Practice in IDR: Unit 8, p. 8	Formal Assessment: Lesson 15.2 Quiz, p. 267	

continued on next page

| 4 | 15.3 The Age of Exploration & Daily Life: Life on a Ship | 7.11.1

 Writing 2.4 | *PE/TE: 510-517*
 PE/TE: 518-519

 Reading Skill activity in *IDR: Unit 8, p. 5* | *PE/TE: 517*
 PE/TE: 519

 Critical Thinking: CT64 | Formal Assessment: Lesson 15.3 Quiz, p. 268 | Reteaching activity in *IDR: Unit 8, p. 19* |
| 5 | 15.4 Impact of Exploration | 7.11.2
 7.11.3 | *PE/TE: 520-526*

 Literature activity in *IDR: Unit 8, p. 16*

 Humanities Transparency: HT30 | *PE/TE: 526*

 Geography Practice in *IDR: Unit 8, p. 13*

 Critical Thinking: CT65, CT66 | | Reteaching activity in *IDR: Unit 8, p. 20* |

Pacing Guide–Block Schedule

INSTRUCTIONAL SEGMENT WEEK 18

7.11.4 Explain how the main ideas of the Enlightenment can be traced back to such movements as the Renaissance, the Reformation, and the Scientific Revolution and to the Greeks, Romans, and Christianity.

7.11.5 Describe how democratic thought and institutions were influenced by Enlightenment thinkers (e.g., John Locke, Charles-Louis Montesquieu, American founders).

7.11.6 Discuss how the principles in the Magna Carta were embodied in such documents as the English Bill of Rights and the American Declaration of Independence.

Reading 3.3

Writing 2.1, 2.4

Day	Chapter Lesson	California Standards	Teach	Practice	Assess	Reteach
1	15.4 Activity & Ch. 16 Introduction	Reading 3.3 Writing 2.4	PE/TE: 527 PE/TE: 530-533	PE/TE: 527 PE/TE: 533	Formal Assessment: Lesson 15.4 Quiz, p. 269	
2	16.1 The Enlightenment	7.11.4 7.11.5	PE/TE: 534-539 Humanities Transparency: HT31 History Makers: p. 31	PE/TE: 539 Critical Thinking: CT67		Reteaching activity in IDR: Unit 8, p. 35
3	16.2 Democratic Ideas Develop	7.11.5 7.11.6	PE/TE: 542-548 Humanities Transparency: HT32 Map Transparency: MT32	PE/TE: 548 Critical Thinking: CT68, CT69 Geography Practice in IDR: Unit 8, p. 31	Formal Assessment: Lesson 16.1 Quiz, p. 285	Reteaching activity in IDR: Unit 8, p. 36
4	16.2 Activity & Reader's Theater	7.11.5 7.11.6 Writing 2.1	PE/TE: 549 PE/TE: 550-553	PE/TE: 549 PE/TE: 553	Formal Assessment: Lesson 16.2 Quiz, p. 286	
5	Ch. 15 & Ch. 16 Review & Ch. 15 & Ch. 16 Test			PE/TE: 528-529, 554-555	Formal Assessment: Ch. 15 & Ch. 16 Test	

McDougal Littell
World History: Medieval and Early Modern Times

Lesson Plans

CHAPTER 1 *Lesson 1*   Lesson Plan

Geography of the World

INTRODUCE THE UNIT AND CHAPTER

UNIT 1: INTERACT WITH HISTORY: Roman City of Pompeii, about A.D. 60, *PE/TE pp. 2–3*

CHAPTER OBJECTIVE: Identify the ways that historians gain knowledge about the past.

❑   Before You Read: Knowledge Rating, *PE/TE p. 4*

❑   Big Ideas: Science and Technology, *PE p. 4, TE p. 5*

❑   Time Line Discussion, *TE p. 4*

❑   Map: Archaeological Sites of the World, *PE/TE p. 5*

> *PE = Pupil's Edition*
> *TE = Teacher's Edition*
> *IDR = In-Depth Resources*
> *IDRS = IDR in Spanish*
> *RSG = Reading Study Guide*

STARTING WITH A STORY: The Buried City of Pompeii, *PE/TE pp. 6–7;* California eEdition CD-ROM

PLAN AND PREPARE

Lesson Objectives

❑   Define and use terms that describe geographical features.

❑   Analyze the interaction between people and their environments.

❑   Identify the five themes that organize the study of geography.

❑   **Language Objective:** Use personal experience to gain a deeper understanding of the five themes of geography.

California Standards

Reading 3.5

Writing 2.2

CST 1

CST 3

HI 2

How to Teach the California Standards, *TE p. 8*

FOCUS AND MOTIVATE

❑   MAIN IDEAS, *PE/TE p. 8*

❑   TERMS & NAMES, *PE/TE p. 9*

❑   READING SKILL: Finding Main Ideas, *PE/TE p. 8*

TEACH

Struggling Readers	**On-level**	**Gifted and Talented**	**English Learners**
TE	**PE**	**TE**	**TE**
❑ Chart Causes and Effects, p. 11	❑ History Makers: the Iceman, p. 11	❑ Create Clay Maps, p. 10	❑ Describe Geograpy Themes, p. 10
IDR Unit 1	**IDR Unit 1**	**Interdisciplinary Projects**	**IDRS**
❑ Reading Skill: Finding Main Ideas, p. 3	❑ Family Newsletter (English and Spanish), pp. 1–2	❑ Science, p. 2	❑ Reading Skill: Finding Main Ideas, p. 2
❑ Vocabulary Cards p. 11			**RSG (Spanish)**
❑ Reteaching Activity, p. 17	❑ Reading Skill: Finding Main Ideas, p. 3		❑ Lesson 1, p. 5
Reading Study Guide	❑ Vocabulary Study Guide, p. 9		❑ **California Modified Lesson Plans for English Learners, p. 3**
❑ Lesson 1, p. 5	❑ Vocabulary Cards, p. 11		
❑ RSG Audio CD			❑ **Multi-Language Glossary of Social Studies Terms**
California Reading Toolkit, p. L1			

Lesson Plans

Inclusion

- ❏ **TE:** Define Graphically, p. 11
- ❏ **California EasyPlanner CD-ROM:** Reading Skill, Vocabulary Study Guide, Vocabulary Cards

All Students

- ❏ California Reading Toolkit, p. L1

PE

- ❏ Taking Notes: Finding Main Ideas, p. 8

TE

- ❏ More About Climate Classifications, p. 10; Vegetation, p. 11

IDR Unit 1

- ❏ Family Newsletter (English and Spanish), pp. 1–2

REVIEW AND ENRICH

Integrate Technology

Transparencies

- ❏ Critical Thinking: CT1 Finding Main Ideas
- ❏ Humanities: HT1 Statue of Apollo in Pompeii

Power Presentations

- ❏ Lesson 1 Lecture Notes

CD-ROMS

- ❏ California EasyPlanner CD-ROM
- ❏ California eEdition CD-ROM
- ❏ California Test Generator CD-ROM

Interdisciplinary Activities

TE

- ❏ Science: Chart Climate Factors, p. 10
- ❏ Art: Illustrate the Five Themes of Geography, p. 12

Interdisciplinary Projects

- ❏ Science, p. 2

Transparencies

- ❏ Humanities: HT1 Statue of Apollo in Pompeii

ASSESS

Content Assessment

- ❏ Lesson Review, *PE p. 13*
- ❏ Lesson Quiz, *FA p. 5*
- ❏ California Test Generator CD-ROM: Lesson 1 Quiz
- ❏ Integrated Assessment

Standards Practice

- ❏ California Standards Enrichment Workbook, pp. 1–16
- ❏ California Daily Standards Practice Transparencies TT1
- ❏ California Standards Planner and Lesson Plans, p. L1
- ❏ California Online Test Practice: **ClassZone.com**

RETEACH

- ❏ Reteaching Activity, *IDR Unit 1, p. 17*

Mapping the World

PE = Pupil's Edition	IDRS = IDR in Spanish
TE = Teacher's Edition	RSG = Reading Study Guide
IDR = In-Depth Resources	

PLAN AND PREPARE

Lesson Objectives

❑ Describe advances in mapmaking over the centuries.

❑ Identify features and kinds of maps.

❑ Explain the effect of technology on the accuracy of maps.

❑ **Language Objective:** Explore cognates to acquire information and make the text more comprehensible.

California Standards

How to Teach the California Standards, *TE p. 8*

FOCUS AND MOTIVATE

❑ MAIN IDEAS, *PE/TE p. 14*

❑ READING SKILL: Summarizing, *PE/TE p. 14*

❑ TERMS & NAMES, *PE/TE p. 15*

TEACH

Struggling Readers	On-level	Gifted and Talented	English Learners
TE	**PE**	**TE**	**TE**
❑ Compare and Contrast Map Types, p. 18	❑ Geography: Map Projections, p. 16	❑ Research Longitude, p. 17	❑ Find Similar Words, p. 17
IDR Unit 1	❑ Skillbuilder: Reading a Map, pp. 22–23	❑ Plan Map Data, p. 20	**IDRS**
❑ Reading Skill, p. 4	**IDR Unit 1**	**IDR Unit 1**	❑ Reading Skill, p. 3
❑ Reteaching Activity, p. 18	❑ Reading Skill: Summarizing, p. 4	❑ Literature: "Mapping the Sahara," p. 16	**RSG (Spanish)**
Reading Study Guide	❑ Vocabulary Study Guide, p. 9	**Interdisciplinary Projects**	❑ Lesson 2, p. 7
❑ Lesson 2, p. 7	❑ Vocabulary Cards, p. 11	❑ Math, p. 1	❑ **California Modified Lesson Plans for English Learners, p. 7**
❑ RSG Audio CD			❑ **Multi-Language Glossary of Social Studies Terms**
California Reading Toolkit, p. L2			

Lesson Plans

Inclusion

- ☐ **TE:** Read Aloud, p. 18; View GPS Demonstration, p. 20
- ☐ **California EasyPlanner CD-ROM:** Reading Skill, Vocabulary Study Guide, Vocabulary Cards

All Students

- ☐ California Reading Toolkit, p. L2

PE

- ☐ Taking Notes: Summarizing, p. 14
- ☐ **Extend Lesson 2** Skillbuilder: Reading a Map, pp. 22–23

TE

- ☐ More About Map Projections, p. 16; The Compass Rose, p. 18; Geographic Information Systems, p. 20; Scale, p 23; Inset Maps, p. 23

REVIEW AND ENRICH

Integrate Technology

Transparencies

- ☐ Critical Thinking: CT2 Summarizing
- ☐ Map: MT1 Latitude and Longitude

Power Presentations

- ☐ Lesson 2 Lecture Notes

CD-ROMS

- ☐ California EasyPlanner CD-ROM
- ☐ California eEdition CD-ROM
- ☐ California Test Generator CD-ROM

Interdisciplinary Activities

TE

- ☐ Science: Create a Time Line, p. 16
- ☐ Art: Show Distortion, p. 16
- ☐ Math: Present Statistics, p. 19
- ☐ Art: Map Sports Teams, p. 19

Interdisciplinary Projects

- ☐ Math, p. 1

Transparencies

- ☐ Geography: MT1 Latitude and Longitude

ASSESS

Content Assessment

- ☐ Lesson Review, *PE p. 21*
- ☐ Lesson Quiz, *FA p. 6*
- ☐ California Test Generator CD-ROM: Lesson 2 Quiz
- ☐ Integrated Assessment

Standards Practice

- ☐ California Standards Enrichment Workbook, pp. 1–16
- ☐ California Daily Standards Practice Transparencies TT2
- ☐ California Standards Planner and Lesson Plans, p. L3
- ☐ California Online Test Practice: **ClassZone.com**

RETEACH

- ☐ Reteaching Activity, *IDR Unit 1, p. 18*

Discovering the Past

> PE = Pupil's Edition
> TE = Teacher's Edition
> IDR = In-Depth Resources
>
> IDRS = IDR in Spanish
> RSG = Reading Study Guide

PLAN AND PREPARE

Lesson Objectives

- ❑ Examine the steps taken by archaeologists to uncover evidence from the past.

- ❑ Compare the functions of archaeologists and anthropologists.

- ❑ Analyze how additional knowledge affects perception of the past.

- ❑ **Language Objective:** Use a K-W-L chart to connect to prior knowledge, formulate questions to guide reading, make notes, and organize a summary.

California Standards

HI 1
HI 2
HI 5
Reading 3.2
Writing 2.1
How to Teach the California Standards, *TE p. 24*

FOCUS AND MOTIVATE

- ❑ MAIN IDEAS, *PE/TE p. 24*

- ❑ READING SKILL: Making Generalizations, *PE/TE p. 24*

- ❑ TERMS & NAMES, *PE/TE p. 25*

TEACH

Struggling Readers

TE

- ❑ Outline Text, p. 26

IDR Unit 1

- ❑ Reading Skill: Making Generalizations, p. 5

- ❑ Vocabulary Cards, p. 11

- ❑ Reteaching Activity, p. 19

Reading Study Guide

- ❑ Lesson 3, p. 9

- ❑ RSG Audio CD

California Reading Toolkit, p. L3

On-level

PE

- ❑ Activity: Prepare a Time Capsule, p. 29

IDR Unit 1

- ❑ Reading Skill: Making Generalizations, p. 5

- ❑ Skillbuilder Practice: Finding Main Ideas, p. 8

- ❑ Vocabulary Study Guide, p. 9

- ❑ Geography Practice, p. 13

Gifted and Talented

TE

- ❑ Research Archaeologists and Anthropologists, p. 27

IDR Unit 1

- ❑ Primary Source: Understanding Anthropology, p. 15

Interdisciplinary Projects

- ❑ Art, p. 4

English Learners

TE

- ❑ Read Maps, p. 22

- ❑ Use K-W-L Chart, p. 27

IDRS

- ❑ Reading Skill, p. 4

RSG (Spanish)

- ❑ Lesson 3, p. 9

- ❑ **California Modified Lesson Plans for English Learners, p. 9**

- ❑ **Multi-Language Glossary of Social Studies Terms**

Lesson Plans

Inclusion

- ☐ **TE:** Summarize Orally, p. 26
- ☐ **California EasyPlanner CD-ROM:** Reading Skill, Vocabulary Study Guide, Vocabulary Cards

All Students

- ☐ California Reading Toolkit, p. L3

PE

- ☐ Taking Notes: Making Generalizations, p. 24
- ☐ **Extend Lesson 3** Activity: Prepare a Time Capsule, p. 29

TE

- ☐ More About Margaret Mead, p. 27

REVIEW AND ENRICH

Integrate Technology

Transparencies

- ☐ Critical Thinking: CT3 Making Generalizations
- ☐ Humanities: HT2 Archaeological Dig at Cancuén

Power Presentations

- ☐ Lesson 3 Lecture Notes

CD-ROMS

- ☐ California EasyPlanner CD-ROM
- ☐ California eEdition CD-ROM
- ☐ California Test Generator CD-ROM

Interdisciplinary Activities

Interdisciplinary Projects

- ☐ Art, p. 4

Transparencies

- ☐ Humanities: HT2 Archaeological Dig at Cancuén

ASSESS

Content Assessment

- ☐ Lesson Review, *PE p. 28*
- ☐ Lesson Quiz, *FA p. 7*
- ☐ California Test Generator CD-ROM: Lesson 3 Quiz
- ☐ Integrated Assessment

Standards Practice

- ☐ California Standards Enrichment Workbook, pp. 1–16
- ☐ California Daily Standards Practice Transparencies TT3
- ☐ California Standards Planner and Lesson Plans, p. L5
- ☐ California Online Test Practice: **ClassZone.com**

RETEACH

Interpreting the Past

PE = Pupil's Edition   IDRS = IDR in Spanish
TE = Teacher's Edition   RSG = Reading Study Guide
IDR = In-Depth Resources

PLAN AND PREPARE

Lesson Objectives

❏ Analyze the importance of history.

❏ Identify questions used by historians to acquire information.

❏ Examine the kinds of evidence used by historians to explore the past, and analyze what they do with their knowledge.

❏ **Language Objective:** Listen as scenarios are presented and document evidence to discuss whether the scenarios depict a primary source, secondary source, or oral history.

California Standards

REP 1
REP 4
HI 5
Reading 2.4
Writing 2.4
How to Teach the California Standards, *TE p. 30*

FOCUS AND MOTIVATE

❏ MAIN IDEAS, *PE/TE p. 30*

❏ READING SKILL: Finding Main Ideas, *PE/TE p. 30*

❏ TERMS & NAMES, *PE/TE p. 31*

TEACH

Struggling Readers	**On-level**	**Gifted and Talented**	**English Learners**
TE	**PE**	**TE**	**TE**
❏ Create Bulletin Board Display, p. 32	❏ Primary Source: from *Concerning the Islands Recently Discovered in the Indian Sea,* p. 33	❏ Compare Primary and Secondary Sources, p. 33	❏ Find Sources, p. 33
❏ Sequence the Action, p. 37		❏ Read Further, p. 38	❏ Sequence Events, p. 37
IDR Unit 1	❏ Literature: from *Discovering the Inca ice Maiden,* pp. 36–39	**History Makers**	**IDRS**
❏ Reading Skill: Finding Main Ideas, p. 6		❏ William McNiell, p. 1	❏ Reading Skill, p. 5
❏ Reteaching Activity, p. 20	**IDR Unit 1**	**Interdisciplinary Projects**	**RSG (Spanish)**
Reading Study Guide	❏ Reading Skill: Finding Main Ideas, p. 6	❏ Language Arts, p. 3	❏ Lesson 4, p. 11
❏ Lesson 4, p. 11	❏ Vocabulary Study Guide, p. 9		❏ **California Modified Lesson Plans for English Learners, p. 11**
❏ RSG Audio CD	❏ Vocabulary Cards, p. 11		❏ **Multi-Language Glossary of Social Studies Terms**
California Reading Toolkit, p. L4			

Lesson Plans

Inclusion

- ❏ **TE:** Share Oral Histories, p. 32; Make a Graphic Organizer, p. 38
- ❏ **California EasyPlanner CD-ROM:** Reading Skill, Vocabulary Study Guide, Vocabulary Cards

All Students

- ❏ California Reading Toolkit, p. L4

PE

- ❏ Taking Notes: Finding Main Ideas, p. 30

TE

- ❏ More About Using Primary Sources, p. 33; Sacrifices of the Inda, p. 36; Ampato, p. 37; Preserving the Mummy, p. 38; Other Frozen Mummies, p. 39

REVIEW AND ENRICH

Integrate Technology

Transparencies

- ❏ Critical Thinking: CT4 Finding Main Ideas
- ❏ Map: MT2 Columbus's First Voyage, 1492

Power Presentations

- ❏ Lesson 4 Lecture Notes

CD-ROMS

- ❏ California EasyPlanner CD-ROM
- ❏ California eEdition CD-ROM
- ❏ California Test Generator CD-ROM

Interdisciplinary Activities

TE

- ❏ Language Arts: Write Primary and Secondary Sources, p. 34
- ❏ Art: Museum Display, p. 34

Interdisciplinary Projects

- ❏ Language Arts, p. 3

Transparencies

- ❏ Geography: MT2 Columbus's First Voyage, 1492

ASSESS

Content Assessment

- ❏ Lesson Review, *PE p. 35*
- ❏ Chapter Review, *PE pp. 40–41*
- ❏ Lesson Quiz, *FA p. 8*
- ❏ California Test Generator CD-ROM: Lesson 4 Quiz
- ❏ Integrated Assessment

Standards Practice

- ❏ California Standards Enrichment Workbook, pp. 1–16
- ❏ California Daily Standards Practice Transparencies TT4
- ❏ California Standards Planner and Lesson Plans, p. L7
- ❏ California Online Test Practice: **ClassZone.com**

Struggling Readers	On-Level	Gifted and Talented	English Learners
❏ Test Form A, *FA pp. 9–12*	❏ Test Form B, *FA pp. 13–16*	❏ Test Form C, *FA pp. 17–20*	❏ Test Generator: Forms A, B, and C in Spanish

RETEACH

- ❏ Reteaching Activity, *IDR Unit 1, p. 20*

CHAPTER 2 Lesson 1   **Lesson Plan**

The Rise and Expansion of Rome

INTRODUCE THE CHAPTER

CHAPTER OBJECTIVE: Analyze the rise and fall of the Roman Empire and the Romans' lasting contributions to civilization.

❏ Before You Read: People Search, *PE/TE p. 42*
❏ Big Ideas: Government, *PE p. 42, TE p. 43*
❏ Time Line Discussion, *TE p. 42*
❏ Map: Roman Empire, A.D. 120, *PE/TE p. 43*

> *PE = Pupil's Edition*
> *TE = Teacher's Edition*
> *IDR = In-Depth Resources*
> *IDRS = IDR in Spanish*
> *RSG = Reading Study Guide*

STARTING WITH A STORY: A Dangerous Race, *PE/TE pp. 44–45;* California eEdition CD-ROM

PLAN AND PREPARE

Lesson Objectives	California Standards
❏ Describe the factors influencing the settlement of Rome. ❏ Identify the characteristics of the Roman Republic. ❏ Explain reasons for the growth of the Roman Empire and the emergence of Christianity. ❏ **Language Objective:** Use note-taking skills to organize the key information in the lesson.	Reading 3.4 Writing 2.2 7.1.1 7.1.2 CST 3 How to Teach the California Standards, *TE p. 46*

FOCUS AND MOTIVATE

❏ MAIN IDEAS, *PE/TE p. 46*
❏ TERMS & NAMES, *PE/TE p. 47*

❏ READING SKILL: Explaining Sequence, *PE/TE p. 46*

TEACH

Struggling Readers	On-level	Gifted and Talented	English Learners
TE ❏ Characterize Governments, p. 49 **IDR Unit 1** ❏ Reading Skill: Explaining Sequence, p. 23 ❏ Reteaching Activity, p. 37 **Reading Study Guide** ❏ Lesson 1, p. 15 ❏ RSG Audio CD **California Reading Toolkit, p. L5**	**IDR Unit 1** ❏ Family Newsletter (English and Spanish), pp. 21–22 ❏ Reading Skill: Explaining Sequence, p. 23 ❏ Vocabulary Cards, p. 31	**TE** ❏ Develop Handouts, p. 49 **Interdisciplinary Projects** ❏ Art, p. 10	**TE** ❏ Taking Notes, p. 48 **IDRS** ❏ Reading Skill, p. 11 **RSG (Spanish)** ❏ Lesson 1, p. 15 ❏ **California Modified Lesson Plans for English Learners, p. 13** ❏ **Multi-Language Glossary of Social Studies Terms**

Lesson Plans

Inclusion

- ❑ **TE:** Order Events, p. 48

- ❑ **California EasyPlanner CD-ROM:** Reading Skill, Vocabulary Study Guide, Reteaching Activity

All Students

- ❑ California Reading Toolkit, p. L5

PE

- ❑ Taking Notes: Explaining Sequence, p. 46

TE

- ❑ More About Tarquin the Proud, p. 48; Julius Caesar, p. 49; Augustus, p. 49; Persecution of Christians, p. 50

REVIEW AND ENRICH

Integrate Technology

Transparencies

- ❑ Critical Thinking: CT6 Explaining Sequence
- ❑ Map: MT3 City of Rome
- ❑ Humanities: HT3 Peter's Basilica

Power Presentations

- ❑ Lesson 1 Lecture Notes

CD-ROMS

- ❑ California EasyPlanner CD-ROM
- ❑ California eEdition CD-ROM
- ❑ California Test Generator CD-ROM

Interdisciplinary Activities

TE

- ❑ Journalism: Report on Christianity, p. 50
- ❑ Art: Illustrate the Roman Pantheon, p. 50

Interdisciplinary Projects

- ❑ Art, p. 10

Transparencies

- ❑ Geography: MT3 City of Rome
- ❑ Art: HT3 Peter's Basilica

ASSESS

Content Assessment

- ❑ Lesson Review, *PE p. 51*
- ❑ Lesson Quiz, *FA p. 21*
- ❑ California Test Generator CD-ROM: Lesson 1 Quiz
- ❑ Integrated Assessment

Standards Practice

- ❑ California Standards Enrichment Workbook, pp. 31–34
- ❑ California Daily Standards Practice Transparencies TT5
- ❑ California Standards Planner and Lesson Plans, p. L9
- ❑ California Online Test Practice: **ClassZone.com**

RETEACH

- ❑ Reteaching Activity, *IDR Unit 1, p. 37*

Decline and Fall of the Empire

PE = Pupil's Edition   IDRS = IDR in Spanish
TE = Teacher's Edition   RSG = Reading Study Guide
IDR = In-Depth Resources

PLAN AND PREPARE

Lesson Objectives

❑ Trace the development of the Shona Empire.

❑ Explain the relationship between the gold trade and the growth of Great Zimbabwe.

❑ Describe the rise of the Mutapa Empire.

❑ **Language Objective:** Formulate statements that compare and contrast details from expository text to identify ways people, characters, events, and ideas are alike and different.

California Standards

7.1.1

7.1.2

7.1.3

How to Teach the California Standards, *TE p. 52*

FOCUS AND MOTIVATE

❑ MAIN IDEAS, *PE/TE p. 52*

❑ READING SKILL: Categorizing, *PE/TE p. 52*

❑ TERMS & NAMES, *PE/TE p. 53*

TEACH

Struggling Readers	**On-level**	**Gifted and Talented**	**English Learners**
TE	**IDR Unit 1**	**TE**	**TE**
❑ Take Notes, p. 55	❑ Reading Skill: Categorizing, p. 25	❑ Interview Emperors, p. 54	❑ Understanding Cause and Effect, p. 54
IDR Unit 1	❑ Skillbuilder Practice: Categorizing, p. 28	**Interdisciplinary Projects**	**IDRS**
❑ Reading Skill: Categorizing, p. 25	❑ Vocabulary Cards, p. 31	❑ Science, p. 8	❑ Reading Skill, p. 12
❑ Reteaching Activity, p. 38		❑ Language Arts, p. 9	**RSG (Spanish)**
Reading Study Guide			❑ Lesson 2, p. 17
❑ Lesson 2, p. 17			❑ **California Modified Lesson Plans for English Learners, p. 15**
❑ RSG Audio CD			❑ **Multi-Language Glossary**
California Reading Toolkit, p. L6			

Lesson Plans

Inclusion

- ☐ **TE:** Use the Map, p. 55
- ☐ **California EasyPlanner CD-ROM:** Reading Skill, Vocabulary Study Guide, Reteaching Activity

All Students

- ☐ California Reading Toolkit, p. L6

PE

- ☐ Taking Notes: Categorizing, p. 52
- ☐ **Extend Lesson 2** Activity: Play a Board Game, p. 57

TE

- ☐ More About Diocletian, p. 54; Constantine and Christianity, p. 54

REVIEW AND ENRICH

Integrate Technology

Transparencies

- ☐ Critical Thinking: CT7 Categorizing
- ☐ Humanities: HT4 Constantine the Great

Power Presentations

- ☐ Lesson 2 Lecture Notes

CD-ROMS

- ☐ California EasyPlanner CD-ROM
- ☐ California eEdition CD-ROM
- ☐ California Test Generator CD-ROM

Interdisciplinary Activities

Interdisciplinary Projects

- ☐ Science, p. 8
- ☐ Language Arts, p. 9

Transparencies

- ☐ Art: HT4 Constantine the Great

ASSESS

Content Assessment

- ☐ Lesson Review, *PE p. 56*
- ☐ Lesson Quiz, *FA p. 22*
- ☐ California Test Generator CD-ROM: Lesson 2 Quiz
- ☐ Integrated Assessment

Standards Practice

- ☐ California Standards Enrichment Workbook, pp. 31–34
- ☐ California Daily Standards Practice Transparencies TT6
- ☐ California Standards Planner and Lesson Plans, p. L11
- ☐ California Online Test Practice: **ClassZone.com**

RETEACH

- ☐ Reteaching Activity, *IDR Unit 1, p. 38*

Lesson Plans

Name _____ Date _____

The Early Byzantine Empire

PE = Pupil's Edition   IDRS = IDR in Spanish
TE = Teacher's Edition   RSG = Reading Study Guide
IDR = In-Depth Resources

PLAN AND PREPARE

Lesson Objectives	California Standards
❏ Identify Justinian's accomplishments.	7.1.3
❏ Describe life in Constantinople.	HI 1
❏ Analyze the causes and effects of the split in Christianity.	CST 3
❏ **Language Objective:** Analyze the similarities and differences between two things in order to make comparisons between them.	How to Teach the California Standards, *TE p. 58*

FOCUS AND MOTIVATE

❏ MAIN IDEAS, *PE/TE p. 58*

❏ READING SKILL: Understanding Cause and Effect, *PE/TE p. 58*

❏ TERMS & NAMES, *PE/TE p. 59*

TEACH

Struggling Readers	On-level	Gifted and Talented	English Learners
TE	**PE**	**TE**	**TE**
❏ Annotate a Time Line, p. 60	❏ History Makers: Theodora and Justinian, p. 60	❏ Prepare a Flow Chart, p. 62	❏ Comparing and Contrasting, p. 62
❏ Write a Letter, p. 64	❏ Comparisons Across Cultures, p. 62	**IDR Unit 1**	❏ Illustrate Ideas, p. 62
IDR Unit 1	**IDR Unit 1**	❏ Primary Source: Justinian Code, p. 35	**IDRS**
❏ Reading Skill, p. 25	❏ Reading Skill: Understanding Cause and Effect, p. 25	**Interdisciplinary Projects**	❏ Reading Skill, p. 13
❏ Reteaching Activity, p. 39	❏ Vocabulary Cards, p. 32	❏ Math, p. 7	**RSG (Spanish)**
Reading Study Guide			❏ Lesson 3, p. 19
❏ Lesson 3, p. 19			❏ **California Modified Lesson Plans for English Learners, p. 17**
❏ RSG Audio CD			❏ **Multi-Language Glossary**
California Reading Toolkit, p. L7			

Lesson Plans

Inclusion

- ❏ **TE:** Read in Pairs, p. 60
- ❏ **California EasyPlanner CD-ROM:** Reading Skill, Vocabulary Study Guide, Reteaching Activity

All Students

- ❏ California Reading Toolkit, p. L7

PE

- ❏ Taking Notes: Understanding Cause and Effect, p. 58
- ❏ **Extend Lesson 3** Daily Life: Life in Constantinople, pp. 64–65

TE

- ❏ More About Icons, p. 62; The Hippodrome, p. 65; Hagia Sophia, p. 65

REVIEW AND ENRICH

Integrate Technology

Transparencies

- ❏ Critical Thinking: CT8 Understanding Cause and Effect

Power Presentations

- ❏ Lesson 3 Lecture Notes

CD-ROMS

- ❏ California EasyPlanner CD-ROM
- ❏ California eEdition CD-ROM
- ❏ California Test Generator CD-ROM

Interdisciplinary Activities

TE

- ❏ Art: Prepare an Art Lecture, p. 61
- ❏ Language Arts: Write a Television Script, p. 61

Interdisciplinary Projects

- ❏ Math, p. 7

ASSESS

Content Assessment

- ❏ Lesson Review, *PE p. 63*
- ❏ Lesson Quiz, *FA p. 23*
- ❏ California Test Generator CD-ROM: Lesson 3 Quiz
- ❏ Integrated Assessment

Standards Practice

- ❏ California Standards Enrichment Workbook, pp. 35–36
- ❏ California Daily Standards Practice Transparencies TT7
- ❏ California Standards Planner and Lesson Plans, p. L13
- ❏ California Online Test Practice: **ClassZone.com**

RETEACH

- ❏ Reteaching Activity, *IDR Unit 1, p. 39*

Name _____ Date _____

The Legacy of Rome

PE = Pupil's Edition	IDRS = IDR in Spanish
TE = Teacher's Edition	RSG = Reading Study Guide
IDR = In-Depth Resources	

PLAN AND PREPARE

Lesson Objectives

❑ Describe the rise and fall of the Mali empire.

❑ Analyze the importance of strong leadership and government organization to the rise of the Songhai empire.

❑ Outline the reasons for the fall of Songhai.

❑ **Language Objective:** Use antonyms to present different sides of a situation or event.

California Standards

7.1.1

HI 3

REP 4

How to Teach the California Standards, *TE p. 66*

FOCUS AND MOTIVATE

❑ MAIN IDEAS, *PE/TE p. 66*

❑ READING SKILL: Finding Main Ideas, *PE/TE p. 66*

❑ TERMS & NAMES, *PE/TE p. 67*

TEACH

Struggling Readers	On-level	Gifted and Talented	English Learners
TE	**PE**	**TE**	**TE**
❑ Design a Building, p. 69	❑ Primary Source: from "On Duty", p. 68	❑ Use Latin Prefixes and Roots, p. 68	❑ Use Context Clues, p. 69
IDR Unit 1	**IDR Unit 1**	**IDR Unit 1**	**IDRS**
❑ Reading Skill, p. 26	❑ Reading Skill: Finding Main Ideas, p. 26	❑ Geography Practice: Roman Roads, p. 33 Literature: The Aeneid, p. 36	❑ Reading Skill, p. 14
❑ Reteaching Activity, p. 40	❑ Vocabulary Cards, p. 32		**RSG (Spanish)**
Reading Study Guide			❑ Lesson 4, p. 21
❑ Lesson 4, p. 21			❑ **California Modified Lesson Plans for English Learners, p. 19**
❑ RSG Audio CD			❑ **Multi-Language Glossary of Social Studies Terms**
California Reading Toolkit, p. L8			

Lesson Plans

Inclusion

- ☐ **TE:** Use Flash Cards, p. 68
- ☐ **California EasyPlanner CD-ROM:** Reading Skill, Vocabulary Study Guide, Reteaching Activity

All Students

- ☐ California Reading Toolkit, p. L8

PE

- ☐ Taking Notes: Finding Main Ideas, p. 66
- ☐ **Extend Lesson 4** Connect to Today: Rome's Enduring Influence, pp. 72–73

TE

- ☐ More About Cicero, p. 68; Aqueducts, p. 69; Roman Roads, p. 69; Roman Law, p. 70

REVIEW AND ENRICH

Integrate Technology

Transparencies

- ☐ Critical Thinking: CT9 Finding Main Ideas
- ☐ Map: MT4 Spread of Christianity

Power Presentations

- ☐ Lesson 4 Lecture Notes

CD-ROMS

- ☐ California EasyPlanner CD-ROM
- ☐ California eEdition CD-ROM
- ☐ California Test Generator CD-ROM

Interdisciplinary Activities

TE

- ☐ Language Arts: Present Political Speeches, p. 70
- ☐ Language Arts: Write a Reflection, p. 70

Transparencies

- ☐ Geography: MT4 Spread of Christianity

ASSESS

Content Assessment

- ☐ Lesson Review, *PE p. 71*
- ☐ Chapter Review, *PE pp. 74–75*
- ☐ Lesson Quiz, *FA p. 24*
- ☐ California Test Generator CD-ROM: Lesson 4 Quiz
- ☐ Integrated Assessment

Standards Practice

- ☐ California Standards Enrichment Workbook, pp. 31–32
- ☐ California Daily Standards Practice Transparencies TT8
- ☐ California Standards Planner and Lesson Plans, p. L15
- ☐ California Online Test Practice: **ClassZone.com**

Struggling Readers	On-Level	Gifted and Talented	English Learners
☐ Test Form A, *FA pp. 25–28*	☐ Test Form B, *FA pp. 29–32*	☐ Test Form C, *FA pp. 33–36*	☐ Test Generator: Forms A, B, and C in Spanish

RETEACH

- ☐ Reteaching Activity, *IDR Unit 1, p. 40*

CHAPTER 3 Lesson 1

Life on the Arabian Peninsula

INTRODUCE THE UNIT AND CHAPTER

UNIT 2: INTERACT WITH HISTORY: The Holy City of Mecca, about A.D. 660, *PE/TE pp. 78–79*

CHAPTER OBJECTIVE: Trace the origins of Islam and the life and teachings of Muhammad.

❏ Before You Read: K-W-L, *PE/TE p. 80*

❏ Big Ideas: Belief Systems, *PE p. 80, TE p. 81*

❏ Time Line Discussion, *TE p. 80*

❏ Map: Spread of Islam, A.D. 661, *PE/TE p. 81*

> *PE = Pupil's Edition*
> *TE = Teacher's Edition*
> *IDR = In-Depth Resources*
> *IDRS = IDR in Spanish*
> *RSG = Reading Study Guide*

STARTING WITH A STORY: A Journey to Mecca, *PE/TE pp. 82–83;* California eEdition CD-ROM

PLAN AND PREPARE

Lesson Objectives

❏ Explain how the desert climate of the Arabian peninsula affected the lives of different people.

❏ Summarize the origins and teachings of Islam.

❏ Describe the trade routes on the Arabian Peninsula and the goods that moved along these routes.

❏ **Language Objective:** Use a KWL chart to connect to prior knowledge, formulate questions to guide reading, make notes, and organize a summary.

California Standards

Reading 3.2
Writing 2.2
7.2.1
7.2.2
7.2.5
How to Teach the California Standards, *TE p. 84*

FOCUS AND MOTIVATE

❏ MAIN IDEAS, *PE/TE p. 84*   ❏ READING SKILL: Categorizing, *PE/TE p. 84*   ❏ TERMS & NAMES, *PE/TE p. 85*

TEACH

Struggling Readers	On-level	Gifted and Talented	English Learners
TE	**PE**	**TE**	**TE**
❏ Make a Cause-and-Effect Chart, p. 87	❏ Geography: Oasis, p. 86	❏ Research Travel in the 600s, p. 87	❏ Create a KWL Chart, p. 86
❏ Role-Play: Be a Trader, p. 90	**IDR Unit 2**	**Interdisciplinary Projects**	❏ Study the Illustration, p. 90
IDR Unit 2	❏ Family Newsletter (English and Spanish), pp. 1–2	❏ Science, p. 14	**IDRS**
❏ Reading Skill: Categorizing, p. 3	❏ Reading Skill: Categorizing, p. 3		❏ Reading Skill, p. 22
❏ Reteaching Activity, p. 15	❏ Vocabulary Study Guide, p. 8		**RSG (Spanish)**
Reading Study Guide	❏ Vocabulary Cards, p. 9		❏ Lesson 1, p. 25
❏ Lesson 1, p. 25	❏ Geography Practice: Water Resources of the Arabian Peninsula, p. 11		❏ **California Modified Lesson Plans for English Learners, p. 21**
❏ RSG Audio CD			❏ **Multi-Language Glossary of Social Studies Terms**
California Reading Toolkit, p. L9			

Lesson Plans

Inclusion

- ❑ **TE:** Use the Visual, p. 86
- ❑ **California EasyPlanner CD-ROM:** Reading Skill, Vocabulary Study Guide, Reteaching Activity

All Students

- ❑ California Reading Toolkit, p. L9

PE

- ❑ Taking Notes: Categorizing, p. 84
- ❑ **Extend Lesson 1** Daily Life: Life Along a Trade Route, pp. 90–91

TE

- ❑ More About The Ka'aba, p. 79; Bedouins, p. 86; Silk, p. 91

IDR Unit 2

- ❑ Family Newsletter (English and Spanish), pp. 1–2

REVIEW AND ENRICH

Integrate Technology

Transparencies
- ❑ Critical Thinking: CT11 Categorizing
- ❑ Map: MT5 The Hajj

Power Presentations
- ❑ Lesson 1 Lecture Notes

CD-ROMS
- ❑ California EasyPlanner CD-ROM
- ❑ California eEdition CD-ROM
- ❑ California Test Generator CD-ROM

Interdisciplinary Activities

PE
- ❑ Geography: Oasis, p. 86

TE
- ❑ Language Arts: Report on Worship at the Ka'aba, p. 88
- ❑ Science: Create a Poster on Inventions of the 600s, p. 88

Interdisciplinary Projects
- ❑ Science, p. 14

Transparencies
- ❑ Geography: MT5 The Hajj

ASSESS

Content Assessment

- ❑ Lesson Review, *PE p. 89*
- ❑ Lesson Quiz, *FA p. 41*
- ❑ California Test Generator CD-ROM: Lesson 1 Quiz
- ❑ Integrated Assessment

Standards Practice

- ❑ California Standards Enrichment Workbook, pp. 37–40, 45–46
- ❑ California Daily Standards Practice Transparencies TT9
- ❑ California Standards Planner and Lesson Plans, p. L17
- ❑ California Online Test Practice: **ClassZone.com**

RETEACH

- ❑ Reteaching Activity, *IDR Unit 2, p. 15*

Lesson Plans

Copyright © by McDougal Littell, a division of Houghton Mifflin Company

Islam and Muhammad

PE = Pupil's Edition	IDRS = IDR in Spanish
TE = Teacher's Edition	RSG = Reading Study Guide
IDR = In-Depth Resources	

PLAN AND PREPARE

Lesson Objectives	California Standards
❏ Summarize the life and teachings of Muhammad.	7.2.2
❏ Explain how the teachings of Islam provide laws and guidelines for the religious practice and everyday life of Muslims.	7.2.3 7.2.4 How to Teach the California Standards, *TE p. 92*
❏ Describe the connections between Islam and Judaism and Christianity.	
❏ **Language Objective:** Construct time lines using summaries that tell the order in which important, related events take place.	

FOCUS AND MOTIVATE

❏ MAIN IDEAS, *PE/TE p. 92*

❏ READING SKILL: Summarizing, *PE/TE p. 92*

❏ TERMS & NAMES, *PE/TE p. 93*

TEACH

Struggling Readers	On-level	Gifted and Talented	English Learners
TE	**IDR Unit 2**	**TE**	**TE**
❏ Adjust Reading Rate, p. 94	❏ Reading Skill: Summarizing, p. 4	❏ Make a Model of a Mosque, p. 95	❏ Interpret a Time Line, p. 94
IDR Unit 2	❏ Vocabulary Cards, p. 9	**IDR Unit 2**	**IDRS**
❏ Reading Skill: Summarizing, p. 4		❏ Literature, p. 14	❏ Reading Skill, p. 23
❏ Reteaching Activity, p. 16		**Interdisciplinary Projects**	**RSG (Spanish)**
Reading Study Guide		❏ Math, p. 13	❏ Lesson 2, p. 27
❏ Lesson 2, p. 27		❏ Language Arts, p. 15	❏ **California Modified Lesson Plans for English Learners, p. 23**
❏ RSG Audio CD			❏ **Multi-Language Glossary of Social Studies Terms**
California Reading Toolkit, p. L10			

Inclusion

❑ **TE:** Use the Graphic Organizer, p. 95

❑ **California EasyPlanner CD-ROM:** Reading Skill, Vocabulary Study Guide, Reteaching Activity

All Students

❑ California Reading Toolkit, p. L10

PE

❑ Taking Notes: Summarizing, p. 92

❑ **Extend Lesson 2** Activity: Create a Distribution Map, p. 97

TE

❑ More About The Qur'an in Muslim Daily Life, p. 95

REVIEW AND ENRICH

Integrate Technology

Transparencies

❑ Critical Thinking: CT12 Summarizing

❑ Humanities: HT5 Detail from the Koran

Power Presentations

❑ Lesson 2 Lecture Notes

CD-ROMS

❑ California EasyPlanner CD-ROM

❑ California eEdition CD-ROM

❑ California Test Generator CD-ROM

Interdisciplinary Activities

Interdisciplinary Projects

❑ Math, p. 13

❑ Language Arts, p. 15

Transparencies

❑ Art: HT5 Detail from the Koran

ASSESS

Content Assessment

❑ Lesson Review, *PE p. 96*

❑ Lesson Quiz, *FA p. 42*

❑ California Test Generator CD-ROM: Lesson 2 Quiz

❑ Integrated Assessment

Standards Practice

❑ California Standards Enrichment Workbook, pp. 39–44

❑ California Daily Standards Practice Transparencies TT10

❑ California Standards Planner and Lesson Plans, p. L19

❑ California Online Test Practice: **ClassZone.com**

RETEACH

❑ Reteaching Activity, *IDR Unit 2, p. 16*

Lesson Plans

Islam After Muhammad's Death

> *PE = Pupil's Edition*   *IDRS = IDR in Spanish*
> *TE = Teacher's Edition*   *RSG = Reading Study Guide*
> *IDR = In-Depth Resources*

PLAN AND PREPARE

Lesson Objectives	California Standards
❑ Describe the role of Islamic leaders in the spread of Islam after Muhammad's death.	7.2.2
	7.2.4
❑ Explain how tolerance affected the expansion of the Muslim Empire.	HI 2
	How to Teach the California Standards, *TE p. 98*
❑ Analyze the issues behind the split in the Islamic community.	
❑ **Language Objective:** Complete cause and effect chains to derive the meaning of the text in the lesson.	

FOCUS AND MOTIVATE

❑ MAIN IDEAS, *PE/TE p. 98*

❑ READING SKILL: Explaining Chronological Order and Sequence, *PE/TE p. 98*

❑ TERMS & NAMES, *PE/TE p. 99*

TEACH

Struggling Readers	On-level	Gifted and Talented	English Learners
TE	**PE**	**TE**	**TE**
❑ Compare and Contrast Islamic Groups, p. 102	❑ History Makers: Abu Bakr, p. 100	❑ Debate Leadership Issues, p. 102	❑ Locate Cause and Effect Chains, p. 101
IDR Unit 2	❑ Primary Source: from the Qur'an, p. 102	**IDR Unit 2**	**IDRS**
❑ Reading Skill, p. 5	**IDR Unit 2**	❑ Primary Source: from the Sunnah, p. 13	❑ Reading Skill, p. 24
❑ Reteaching Activity, p. 17	❑ Reading Skill: Explaining Chronological Order and Sequence, p. 5	**Interdisciplinary Projects**	**RSG (Spanish)**
Reading Study Guide		❑ Art, p. 16	❑ Lesson 3, p. 29
❑ Lesson 3, p. 29	❑ Skillbuilder Practice: Making Decisions, p. 7	**History Makers**	❑ **California Modified Lesson Plans for English Learners, p. 25**
❑ RSG Audio CD		❑ Umar, p. 5	
California Reading Toolkit, p. L11	❑ Vocabulary Cards, p. 9		❑ **Multi-Language Glossary**

Lesson Plans

Inclusion

- ❏ **TE:** Structure Class Discussion, p. 101; Find Synonyms, p. 104
- ❏ **California EasyPlanner CD-ROM:** Reading Skill, Vocabulary Study Guide, Reteaching Activity

All Students

- ❏ California Reading Toolkit, p. L11

PE
- ❏ Taking Notes: Explaining Chronological Order and Sequence, p. 98
- ❏ **Extend Lesson 3** Skillbuilder: Summarizing, pp. 104–105

TE
- ❏ More About Blending of Cultures, p. 101

REVIEW AND ENRICH

Integrate Technology

Transparencies
- ❏ Critical Thinking: CT13 Explaining Chronological Order and Sequence
- ❏ Map: MT6 The Islamic World
- ❏ Humanities: HT6 Dome of the Rock Ceramic Wall Tiles

Power Presentations
- ❏ Lesson 3 Lecture Notes

CD-ROMS
- ❏ California EasyPlanner CD-ROM
- ❏ California eEdition CD-ROM
- ❏ California Test Generator CD-ROM

Interdisciplinary Activities

TE
- ❏ Language Arts: Create an Arabic Glossary, p. 100
- ❏ Language Arts: Role-Play the Election of Abu Bakr, p. 100

Transparencies
- ❏ Geography: MT6 The Islamic World
- ❏ Art: HT6 Dome of the Rock Ceramic Wall Tiles

ASSESS

Content Assessment

- ❏ Lesson Review, *PE p. 103*
- ❏ Chapter Review, *PE pp. 106–107*
- ❏ Lesson Quiz, *FA p. 43*
- ❏ California Test Generator CD-ROM: Lesson 3 Quiz
- ❏ Integrated Assessment

Standards Practice

- ❏ California Standards Enrichment Workbook, pp. 39–40, 43–44
- ❏ California Daily Standards Practice Transparencies TT11
- ❏ California Standards Planner and Lesson Plans, p. L21
- ❏ California Online Test Practice: **ClassZone.com**

Struggling Readers	On-Level	Gifted and Talented	English Learners
❏ Test Form A, *FA pp. 44–48*	❏ Test Form B, *FA pp. 49–53*	❏ Test Form C, *FA pp. 54–58*	❏ Test Generator: Forms A, B, and C in Spanish

RETEACH

- ❏ Reteaching Activity, *IDR Unit 2, p. 17*

Lesson Plans

The Expansion of Muslim Rule

INTRODUCE THE CHAPTER

CHAPTER OBJECTIVE: Describe the origins and features of the Umayyad and Abbasid empires.

- ❑ Before You Read: Knowledge Rating, *PE/TE p. 108*
- ❑ Big Ideas: Geography, *PE p. 108, TE p. 109*
- ❑ Time Line Discussion, *TE p. 108*
- ❑ Map: Muslim World, A.D. 1200, *PE/TE p. 109*

> *PE = Pupil's Edition*
> *TE = Teacher's Edition*
> *IDR = In-Depth Resources*
> *IDRS = IDR in Spanish*
> *RSG = Reading Study Guide*

STARTING WITH A STORY: The Magic of Baghdad, *PE/TE pp. 110–111;* California eEdition CD-ROM

PLAN AND PREPARE

Lesson Objectives

- ❑ Identify the areas under Umayyad rule.
- ❑ Describe the features of the Umayyad Empire.
- ❑ Explain the causes of the Umayyad downfall.

California Standards

Reading 3.2

Writing 2.1

7.2.4

CST 1

CST 3

How to Teach the Standards, *TE p. 112*

FOCUS AND MOTIVATE

- ❑ MAIN IDEAS, *PE/TE p. 112*
- ❑ TERMS & NAMES, *PE/TE p. 113*
- ❑ READING SKILL: Finding Main Ideas, *PE/TE p. 112*

TEACH

Struggling Readers	On-level	Gifted and Talented	English Learners
TE	**IDR Unit 2**	**TE**	**TE**
❑ Write Newspaper Headlines, p. 115	❑ Family Newsletter (English and Spanish), pp. 18–19	❑ Present Comparisons, p. 114	❑ Formulating Questions, p. 114
IDR Unit 2	❑ Reading Skill: Finding Main Ideas, p. 20	**Interdisciplinary Projects**	**IDRS**
❑ Reading Skill: Finding Main Ideas, p. 20	❑ Skillbuilder Practice, p. 24	❑ Language Arts, p. 21	❑ Reading Skill, p. 23
❑ Reteaching Activity, p. 33	❑ Vocabulary Cards, p. 27	❑ Art, p. 22	❑ Skillbuilder Practice, p. 24
Reading Study Guide			**RSG (Spanish)**
❑ Lesson 1, p. 33			❑ Lesson 1, p. 33
❑ RSG Audio CD			❑ **California Modified Lesson Plans for English Learners, p. 27**
California Reading Toolkit, p. L12			❑ **Multi-Language Glossary**

Lesson Plans

Inclusion

- ❑ **TE:** Identify Problems and Solutions, p. 115
- ❑ **California EasyPlanner CD-ROM:** Reading Skill, Vocabulary Study Guide, Reteaching Activity

All Students

- ❑ California Reading Toolkit, p. L12

PE

- ❑ Taking Notes: Finding Main Ideas, p. 112
- ❑ **Extend Lesson 1** Activity: Make a Travel Brochure, p. 117

TE

- ❑ More About Early Islamic Coins, p. 115; The Hajj, p. 115

IDR Unit 2

- ❑ Family Newsletter (English and Spanish), pp. 18–19

REVIEW AND ENRICH

Integrate Technology

Transparencies

- ❑ Critical Thinking: CT15 Finding Main Ideas
- ❑ Humanities: HT7 Mosque and Minaret, Mahur, Iran

Power Presentations

- ❑ Lesson 1 Lecture Notes

CD-ROMS

- ❑ California EasyPlanner CD-ROM
- ❑ California eEdition CD-ROM
- ❑ California Test Generator CD-ROM

Interdisciplinary Projects

- ❑ Language Arts, p. 21
- ❑ Art, p. 22

Transparencies

- ❑ Art: HT7 Mosque and Minaret, Mahur, Iran

ASSESS

Content Assessment

- ❑ Lesson Review, *PE p. 116*
- ❑ Lesson Quiz, *FA p. 59*
- ❑ California Test Generator CD-ROM: Lesson 1 Quiz
- ❑ Integrated Assessment

Standards Practice

- ❑ California Standards Enrichment Workbook, pp. 43–44
- ❑ California Daily Standards Practice Transparencies TT12
- ❑ California Standards Planner and Lesson Plans, p. L23
- ❑ California Online Test Practice: **ClassZone.com**

RETEACH

- ❑ Reteaching Activity, *IDR Unit 2, p. 33*

Lesson Plans

CHAPTER 4 Lesson 2   **Lesson Plan**

A Golden Age in the East

PE = Pupil's Edition   IDRS = IDR in Spanish
TE = Teacher's Edition   RSG = Reading Study Guide
IDR = In-Depth Resources

PLAN AND PREPARE

Lesson Objectives

❑ Examine the effects of self-rule on Roman society.

❑ Describe how Rome's republican government was organized.

❑ Analyze the causes and effects of Roman expansion.

❑ **Language Objective:** Interpret information in a chart to compare the government of the Roman Republic with the government of the present-day United States.

California Standards

7.2.4

7.2.5

7.2.6

How to Teach the Standards, *TE p. 118*

FOCUS AND MOTIVATE

❑ MAIN IDEAS, *PE/TE p. 436*

❑ READING SKILL: Understanding Cause and Effect, *PE/TE p. 436*

❑ TERMS & NAMES, *PE/TE p. 437*

TEACH

Struggling Readers	On-level	Gifted and Talented	English Learners
TE	**PE**	**TE**	**TE**
❑ Make a Collage, p. 122	❑ Comparisons Across Cultures, p. 121	❑ Interpret Poetry, p. 122	❑ Build a Cluster Map, p. 121
❑ Summarize Graphically, p. 128	❑ Primary Source: from the *Rubaiyat,* p. 122	❑ Write an Analysis, p. 128	❑ Identify character, Plot, and Setting, p. 127
IDR Unit 2	**IDR Unit 2**	**IDR Unit 2**	**IDRS**
❑ Reading Skill, p. 21	❑ Reading Skill: Forming and Supporting Opinions, p. 21	❑ Primary Source, p. 31	❑ Reading Skill, p. 32
❑ Vocabulary Cards, p. 27		Literature, p. 32	**RSG (Spanish)**
❑ Reteaching Activity, p. 34	❑ Vocabulary Cards, p. 27	**Interdisciplinary Projects**	❑ Lesson 2, p. 35
Reading Study Guide	❑ Geography Practice: Baghdad, p. 29	❑ Science, p. 20	❑ **California Modified Lesson Plans for English Learners, p. 29**
❑ Lesson 2, p. 35			
❑ RSG Audio CD			❑ **Multi-Language Glossary**
California Reading Toolkit, p. L13			

Lesson Plans

Inclusion

- ❏ **TE:** Enlarge Images, p. 121; Map the Plot, p. 127
- ❏ **California EasyPlanner CD-ROM:** Reading Skill, Vocabulary Study Guide, Reteaching Activity

All Students

- ❏ California Reading Toolkit, p. L13

PE

- ❏ Taking Notes: Forming and Supporting Opinions, p. 118
- ❏ **Extend Lesson 2** Literature Connections: The Second Voyage of Sindbad the Sailor, pp. 126–129

TE

- ❏ More About The Abbasids, p. 120; Samarra, p. 120; Papermaking, p. 122; Omar Khayyam's Calendar, p. 123; Muslim Hospitals, p. 123; The Frame Story of *The Thousand and One Nights,* p. 126; The Origin of *The Thousand and One Nights,* p. 127; Sindbad's Adventures, p. 128; Literary Parallels Between Sindbad and Other Tales, p. 129

REVIEW AND ENRICH

Integrate Technology

Transparencies

- ❏ Critical Thinking: CT16 Forming and Supporting Opinions
- ❏ Map: MT7 The Abbasid Empire, c. 850

Power Presentations

- ❏ Lesson 2 Lecture Notes

CD-ROMS

- ❏ California EasyPlanner CD-ROM
- ❏ California eEdition CD-ROM
- ❏ California Test Generator CD-ROM

Interdisciplinary Activities

TE

- ❏ Art: Present Info-Poster, p. 120
- ❏ Language Arts: Catalog Archaeological Finds, p. 120; Role Play: Be a Merchant, p. 124
- ❏ Math: Calculate with Arabic and Roman Numerals, p. 123
- ❏ Science: Write a Biographical Pamphlet, p. 123
- ❏ Art: Create Collages, p. 124

Interdisciplinary Projects

- ❏ Science, p. 20

Transparencies

- ❏ Geography: MT7 The Abbasid Empire, c. 850

ASSESS

Content Assessment

- ❏ Lesson Review, *PE p. 125*
- ❏ Lesson Quiz, *FA p. 60*
- ❏ California Test Generator CD-ROM: Lesson 2 Quiz
- ❏ Integrated Assessment

Standards Practice

- ❏ California Standards Enrichment Workbook, pp. 43–48
- ❏ California Daily Standards Practice Transparencies TT13
- ❏ California Standards Planner and Lesson Plans, p. L25
- ❏ California Online Test Practice: **ClassZone.com**

RETEACH

- ❏ Reteaching Activity, *IDR Unit 2, p. 34*

Lesson Plans

Muslim Rule in Spain

PE = Pupil's Edition	*IDRS = IDR in Spanish*
TE = Teacher's Edition	*RSG = Reading Study Guide*
IDR = In-Depth Resources	

PLAN AND PREPARE

Lesson Objectives

❑ Trace the rise of the caliphate of Córdoba and the city of Córdoba under Abd al-Rahman III.

❑ Identify the achievements of scholars during the golden age of al-Andalus.

❑ Explain the reasons for the decline of al-Andalus.

❑ **Language Objective:** Formulate statements that compare and contrast details from expository text to identify ways people, characters, events, and ideas are alike and different.

California Standards

7.2.4

7.2.5

7.9.7

How to Teach the Standards, *TE p. 130*

FOCUS AND MOTIVATE

❑ MAIN IDEAS, *PE/TE p. 130*

❑ READING SKILL: Identifying Issues and Problems, *PE/TE p. 130*

❑ TERMS & NAMES, *PE/TE p. 131*

TEACH

Struggling Readers	On-level	Gifted and Talented	English Learners
TE	**PE**	**TE**	**IDRS**
❑ Write Study Notes, p. 135	❑ History Makers: Al-Zahrawi, p. 135	❑ Create Parallel Time Lines, p. 135	❑ Reading Skill, p. 32
IDR Unit 2	**IDR Unit 2**	**Interdisciplinary Projects**	**RSG (Spanish)**
❑ Reading Skill, p. 22	❑ Reading Skill: Identifying Issues and Problems, p. 22	❑ Math, p. 19	❑ Lesson 3, p. 37
❑ Reteaching Activity, p. 35			❑ **California Modified Lesson Plans for English Learners, p. 31**
Reading Study Guide	❑ Vocabulary Cards, p. 28		
❑ Lesson 3, p. 37	❑ Reteaching Activity, p. 35		❑ **Multi-Language Glossary of Social Studies Terms**
❑ RSG Audio CD			
California Reading Toolkit, p. L14			

Lesson Plans

Inclusion

- ❏ **TE:** Use Study Guide Audio, p. 132
- ❏ **California EasyPlanner CD-ROM:** Reading Skill, Vocabulary Study Guide, Reteaching Activity

All Students

- ❏ California Reading Toolkit, p. L14

PE

- ❏ Taking Notes: Identifying Issues and Problems, p. 130
- ❏ **Extend Lesson 3** Connect to Today: The Legacy of the Muslim Golden Age, pp. 138–139

TE

- ❏ More About Abd al-Rahman III, p. 132; Córdoba, p. 133; The Great Mosque, p. 133; Al-Idrisi, p. 134; Al-Zahrawi, p. 135; Al-Zahrawi's Medical Encyclopedia, p. 135; Malmonides, p. 136; Sephardic Jews, p. 136

REVIEW AND ENRICH

Integrate Technology

Transparencies

- ❏ Critical Thinking: CT17 Identifying Issues and Problems
- ❏ Humanities: HT8 Gardens of the Generalife, Granada, Spain
- ❏ Map: MT8 Muslim Expansion

Power Presentations

- ❏ Lesson 3 Lecture Notes

CD-ROMS

- ❏ California EasyPlanner CD-ROM
- ❏ California eEdition CD-ROM
- ❏ California Test Generator CD-ROM

Interdisciplinary Activities

TE

- ❏ Math: Compare Areas, p. 133
- ❏ Language Arts: Trace Muslim Influences, p. 133; Write an Illustrated History, p. 136; Investigate Ladino, p. 136
- ❏ Science: Construct a Planetarium, p. 134; Keep a Nutrition Journal, p. 134

Interdisciplinary Projects

- ❏ Math, p. 19

Transparencies

- ❏ Geography: MT8 Muslim Expansion
- ❏ Art: HT8 Gardens of the Generalife, Granada, Spain

ASSESS

Content Assessment

- ❏ Lesson Review, *PE p. 137*
- ❏ Chapter Review, *PE pp. 140–141*
- ❏ Lesson Quiz, *FA p. 61*
- ❏ California Test Generator CD-ROM: Lesson 3 Quiz
- ❏ Integrated Assessment

Standards Practice

- ❏ California Standards Enrichment Workbook, pp. 43–46, 133–134
- ❏ California Daily Standards Practice Transparencies TT14
- ❏ California Standards Planner and Lesson Plans, p. L27
- ❏ California Online Test Practice: **ClassZone.com**

Struggling Readers	On-Level	Gifted and Talented	English Learners
❏ Test Form A, *FA pp. 62–65*	❏ Test Form B, *FA pp. 66–69*	❏ Test Form C, *FA pp. 70–73*	❏ Test Generator: Forms A, B, and C in Spanish

RETEACH

- ❏ Reteaching Activity, *IDR Unit 2, p. 35*

CHAPTER 5 Lesson 1

West African Culture and Daily Life

INTRODUCE THE UNIT AND CHAPTER

UNIT 3: INTERACT WITH HISTORY: Cairo, Egypt 1324, *PE/TE pp. 144–145*

CHAPTER OBJECTIVE: Summarize how the location of the empires of Ghana, Mali, and Songhai affected their growth.

❑ Before You Read: Anticipation Guide, *PE/TE p. 146*

❑ Big Ideas: Economics, *PE p. 146, TE p. 147*

❑ Time Line Discussion, *TE p. 146*

❑ Map: West African Trade Routes and Empires, A.D. 1000–1500, *PE/TE p. 147*

STARTING WITH A STORY: Trading Gold in Africa, *PE/TE pp. 148–149;* California eEdition CD-ROM

> *PE = Pupil's Edition*
> *TE = Teacher's Edition*
> *IDR = In-Depth Resources*
> *IDRS = IDR in Spanish*
> *RSG = Reading Study Guide*

PLAN AND PREPARE

Lesson Objectives

❑ Analyze the importance of family, labor specialization, and regional commerce in the development of states and cities in West Africa.

❑ Describe the oral tradition in West Africa.

❑ **Language Objective:** Analyze information to effectively illustrate how the trade industry allowed West African empires to grow and prosper.

California Standards

Reading 3.3

Writing 2.4

7.4.1

7.4.2

7.4.5

How to Teach the California Standards, *TE p. 150*

FOCUS AND MOTIVATE

❑ MAIN IDEAS, *PE/TE p. 150*   ❑ READING SKILL: Summarizing, *PE/TE p. 150*   ❑ TERMS & NAMES, *PE/TE p. 151*

TEACH

Struggling Readers	On-level	Gifted and Talented	English Learners
TE	**IDR Unit 3**	**TE**	**TE**
❑ Organize Information, p. 153	❑ Family Newsletter (English and Spanish), pp. 1–2	❑ Tell Traditional Stories, p. 153	❑ Use Pronouns, p. 152
IDR Unit 3	❑ Reading Skill: Summarizing, p. 3	**Interdisciplinary Projects**	**IDRS**
❑ Reading Skill: Summarizing, p. 3	❑ Vocabulary Study Guide, p. 8	❑ Music, p. 28	❑ Reading Skill, p. 40
❑ Vocabulary Study Guide, p. 8	❑ Vocabulary Cards, p. 9		**RSG (Spanish)**
❑ Reteaching Activity, p. 15			❑ Lesson 1, p. 41
Reading Study Guide			❑ **California Modified Lesson Plans for English Learners, p. 31**
❑ Lesson 1, p. 41			❑ **Multi-Language Glossary of Social Studies Terms**
❑ RSG Audio CD			
California Reading Toolkit, p. L15			

Lesson Plans

Inclusion

- ❏ **TE:** Write and Use Definitions, p. 152
- ❏ **California EasyPlanner CD-ROM:** Reading Skill, Vocabulary Study Guide, Reteaching Activity

All Students

- ❏ California Reading Toolkit, p. L15

PE

- ❏ Taking Notes: Summarizing, p. 150
- ❏ **Extend Lesson 1** Activity: Play Mancala, p. 155

TE

- ❏ More About Metalworking, p. 152; West African Trade, p. 153

IDR Unit 3

- ❏ Family Newsletter (English and Spanish), pp. 1–2

REVIEW AND ENRICH

Integrate Technology

Transparencies

- ❏ Critical Thinking: CT19 Summarizing
- ❏ Humanities: HT9 West African Pottery

Power Presentations

- ❏ Lesson 1 Lecture Notes

CD-ROMS

- ❏ California EasyPlanner CD-ROM
- ❏ California eEdition CD-ROM
- ❏ California Test Generator CD-ROM

Interdisciplinary Activities

Interdisciplinary Projects

- ❏ Music, p. 28

Transparencies

- ❏ Humanities: HT9 West African Pottery

ASSESS

Content Assessment

- ❏ Lesson Review, *PE p. 154*
- ❏ Lesson Quiz, *FA p. 78*
- ❏ California Test Generator CD-ROM: Lesson 1 Quiz
- ❏ Integrated Assessment

Standards Practice

- ❏ California Standards Enrichment Workbook, pp. 61–64, 69–70
- ❏ California Daily Standards Practice Transparencies TT15
- ❏ California Standards Planner and Lesson Plans, p. L29
- ❏ California Online Test Practice: **ClassZone.com**

RETEACH

- ❏ Reteaching Activity, *IDR Unit 3, p. 15*

Lesson Plans

CHAPTER 5 Lesson 2

The Empire of Ghana

PE = Pupil's Edition
TE = Teacher's Edition
IDR = In-Depth Resources

IDRS = IDR in Spanish
RSG = Reading Study Guide

PLAN AND PREPARE

Lesson Objectives

❑ Define the vegetation zones in West Africa and analyze how natural resources contributed to success in trade.

❑ Describe how trade brought religious and cultural changes to West Africa.

❑ Analyze the influence of Islam and Ghana.

❑ **Language Objective:** Participate in the dramatization of a scene to describe their experience after being designated as the family trader of goods and services.

California Standards

7.4.1

7.4.3

7.4.4

How to Teach the California Standards, *TE p. 156*

FOCUS AND MOTIVATE

❑ MAIN IDEAS, *PE/TE p. 156*

❑ READING SKILL: Finding Main Ideas, *PE/TE p. 156*

❑ TERMS & NAMES, *PE/TE p. 157*

TEACH

Struggling Readers	On-level	Gifted and Talented	English Learners
TE	**IDR Unit 3**	**TE**	**TE**
❑ Categorize Information, p. 158	❑ Reading Skill: Finding Main Ideas, p. 4	❑ Create a Poster, p. 160	❑ Use a Map, p. 158
IDR Unit 3	❑ Skillbuilder Practice: Using Cost-Benefit Analysis, p. 7	**Interdisciplinary Projects**	**IDRS**
❑ Reading Skill: Finding Main Ideas, p. 4		❑ Science, p. 26	❑ Reading Skill: Finding Main Ideas, p. 41
❑ Reteaching Activity, p. 16	❑ Vocabulary Cards, p. 9		**RSG (Spanish)**
Reading Study Guide	❑ Geography Practice: The Empire of Ghana, p. 11		❑ Lesson 2, p. 43
❑ Lesson 2, p. 43			❑ **California Modified Lesson Plans for English Learners, p. 33**
❑ RSG Audio CD			
California Reading Toolkit, p. L16			❑ **Multi-Language Glossary**

Lesson Plans

Inclusion

- ❑ **TE:** Invent a Quiz, p. 160
- ❑ **California EasyPlanner CD-ROM:** Reading Skill, Vocabulary Study Guide, Vocabulary Cards

All Students

- ❑ California Reading Toolkit, p. L16

PE

- ❑ Taking Notes: Finding Main Ideas, p. 156
- ❑ **Extend Lesson 2** Daily Life: Producing Salt, pp. 162–163

TE

- ❑ More About Desert Travel, p. 158; Salt, p. 163

REVIEW AND ENRICH

Integrate Technology

Transparencies

- ❑ Critical Thinking: CT20 Finding Main Ideas
- ❑ Map: MT9 West African Trade
- ❑ Humanities: HT10 The Niger River

Power Presentations

- ❑ Lesson 2 Lecture Notes

CD-ROMS

- ❑ California EasyPlanner CD-ROM
- ❑ California eEdition CD-ROM
- ❑ California Test Generator CD-ROM

Interdisciplinary Activities

TE

- ❑ Science: Research Gold Mining, p. 159
- ❑ Art: Create a Gallery Exhibit, p. 159
- ❑ Science: Keep a Salt-Use Log, p. 162
- ❑ Language Arts: Create a Salt Web Diagram, p. 162

Interdisciplinary Projects

- ❑ Science, p. 26

Transparencies

- ❑ Geography: MT9 West African Trade

ASSESS

Content Assessment

- ❑ Lesson Review, *PE p. 161*
- ❑ Lesson Quiz, *FA p. 79*
- ❑ California Test Generator CD-ROM: Lesson 2 Quiz
- ❑ Integrated Assessment

Standards Practice

- ❑ California Standards Enrichment Workbook, pp. 37–38, 61–62, 65–68
- ❑ California Daily Standards Practice Transparencies TT16
- ❑ California Standards Planner and Lesson Plans, p. L31
- ❑ California Online Test Practice: **ClassZone.com**

RETEACH

- ❑ Reteaching Activity, *IDR Unit 3, p. 16*

The Empire of Mali

PE = Pupil's Edition	IDRS = IDR in Spanish
TE = Teacher's Edition	RSG = Reading Study Guide
IDR = In-Depth Resources	

PLAN AND PREPARE

Lesson Objectives

❏ Describe the rise and fall of the Mali empire.

❏ Analyze the importance of strong leadership and government organization to the rise of the Songhai empire.

❏ Outline the reasons for the fall of Songhai.

❏ **Language Objective:** Use antonyms to present different sides of a situation or event.

California Standards

7.4.1

7.4.3

7.4.4

Reading 3.3

Writing 2.2

FOCUS AND MOTIVATE

❏ MAIN IDEAS, *PE/TE p. 164*

❏ READING SKILL: Comparing and Contrasting, *PE/TE p. 164*

❏ TERMS & NAMES, *PE/TE p. 165*

TEACH

Struggling Readers

TE

❏ Create an Illustrated Map, p. 166

❏ Make a Cartoon Strip, p. 172

IDR Unit 3

❏ Reading Skill, p. 5

❏ Reteaching Activity, p. 17

Reading Study Guide

❏ Lesson 3, p. 45

❏ RSG Audio CD

California Reading Toolkit, p. L17

On-level

PE

❏ Primary Source: from *Travels in Asia and Africa*, p. 167

❏ History Makers: Askia Muhammad, p. 168

IDR Unit 3

❏ Reading Skill: Comparing and Contrasting, p. 5

❏ Vocabulary Cards, p. 9

Gifted and Talented

TE

❏ Write a Travel Report on Timbuktu, p. 166

❏ Create a Reader's Theater, p. 171

IDR Unit 3

❏ Primary Source: The Court of Mansa Sulayman, p. 13

❏ Literature: Sundiata, the Lion King, p. 14

Interdisciplinary Projects

❏ Math, p. 25

❏ Language Arts, p. 27

English Learners

TE

❏ Use Antonyms, p. 167

❏ Understand Elements of a Story, p. 171

IDRS

❏ Reading Skill, p. 42

RSG (Spanish)

❏ Lesson 3, p. 45

❏ **California Modified Lesson Plans for English Learners, p. 35**

❏ **Multi-Language Glossary**

Lesson Plans

Inclusion

- ❑ **TE:** Take Audio Notes, p. 167
- ❑ **California EasyPlanner CD-ROM:** Reading Skill, Vocabulary Study Guide, Reteaching Activity

All Students

- ❑ California Reading Toolkit, p. L17

PE

- ❑ Taking Notes: Comparing and Contrasting, p. 164
- ❑ **Extend Lesson 3** Literature Connections: from *Sundiata: The Epic of the Lion King,* pp. 170–173

TE

- ❑ More About The Expansion of Mali, p. 166; Sundiata, p. 170; Sumanguru, p. 171; Symbols of Kingship, p. 173

REVIEW AND ENRICH

Integrate Technology

Transparencies

- ❑ Critical Thinking: CT21 Comparing and Contrasting
- ❑ Map: MT10 The Songhai Empire, c. 1540

Power Presentations

- ❑ Lesson 3 Lecture Notes

CD-ROMS

- ❑ California EasyPlanner CD-ROM
- ❑ California eEdition CD-ROM
- ❑ California Test Generator CD-ROM

Interdisciplinary Activities

TE

- ❑ Language Arts: Retell a Story, p. 168
- ❑ Math: Set Up a Tax System, p. 168

Interdisciplinary Projects

- ❑ Math, p. 25
- ❑ Language Arts, p. 27

ASSESS

Content Assessment

- ❑ Lesson Review, *PE p. 169*
- ❑ Chapter Review, *PE pp. 174–175*
- ❑ Lesson Quiz, *FA p. 80*
- ❑ California Test Generator CD-ROM: Lesson 3 Quiz
- ❑ Integrated Assessment

Standards Practice

- ❑ California Standards Enrichment Workbook, pp. 37–38, 61–62, 65–68
- ❑ California Daily Standards Practice Transparencies TT17
- ❑ California Standards Planner and Lesson Plans, p. L33
- ❑ California Online Test Practice: **ClassZone.com**

Struggling Readers	On-Level	Gifted and Talented	English Learners
❑ Test Form A, *FA pp. 81–85*	❑ Test Form B, *FA pp. 86–90*	❑ Test Form C, *FA pp. 91–95*	❑ Test Generator: Forms A, B, and C in Spanish

RETEACH

- ❑ Reteaching Activity, *IDR Unit 3, p. 17*

L34 CHAPTER 5, LESSON 3

Copyright © by McDougal Littell, a division of Houghton Mifflin Company

CHAPTER 6 Lesson 1   Lesson Plan

The Growth of Coastal Trading Cities

INTRODUCE THE CHAPTER

CHAPTER OBJECTIVE: Explore the cultures of southern and central Africa and the influences upon their development.

- ❏ Before You Read: Predicting, *PE/TE p. 176*
- ❏ Big Ideas: Culture, *PE p. 176, TE p. 176*
- ❏ Time Line Discussion, *TE p. 176*
- ❏ Map: African Sub Saharan Kingdoms, 1400s, *PE/TE p. 177*

PE = Pupil's Edition
TE = Teacher's Edition
IDR = In-Depth Resources
IDRS = IDR in Spanish
RSG = Reading Study Guide

STARTING WITH A STORY: An African Tale: The Snake's Daughter, *PE/TE pp. 178–179;* California eEdition CD-ROM

PLAN AND PREPARE

Lesson Objectives

- ❏ Describe the Bantu migrations and their significance.
- ❏ Trace the growth of coastal trading networks and city-states.
- ❏ Explain the impact of Islam on the cultures and governments of East Africa.
- ❏ **Language Objective:** Skim the text to classify details by category to make nonfiction text more comprehensible and meaningful.

California Standards

Reading 2.4
Writing 2.2
7.2.4
7.2.5
CST 3
How to Teach the California Standards, *TE p. 180*

FOCUS AND MOTIVATE

- ❏ MAIN IDEAS, *PE/TE p. 180*
- ❏ READING SKILL: Categorizing, *PE/TE p. 180*
- ❏ TERMS & NAMES, *PE/TE p. 181*

TEACH

Struggling Readers	On-level	Gifted and Talented	English Learners
TE	**IDR Unit 3**	**TE**	**TE**
❏ Summarize Visually, p. 183	❏ Family Newsletter (English and Spanish), pp. 18–19	❏ Create a Dictionary, p. 183	❏ Categorize Information, p. 182
IDR Unit 3	❏ Reading Skill: Categorizing, p. 20	**Interdisciplinary Projects**	**IDRS**
❏ Reading Skill: Categorizing, p. 20	❏ Vocabulary Study Guide, p. 25	❏ Science, p. 32	❏ Reading Skill, p. 67
❏ Vocabulary Study Guide, p. 25	❏ Vocabulary Cards, p. 27	❏ Language Arts, p. 33	**RSG (Spanish)**
❏ Reteaching Activity, p. 33		**History Makers**	❏ Lesson 1, p. 49
Reading Study Guide		❏ Prince Shotoku, p. 15	❏ **California Modified Lesson Plans for English Learners, p. 39**
❏ Lesson 1, p. 49			❏ **Multi-Language Glossary of Social Studies Terms**
❏ RSG Audio CD			
California Reading Toolkit, p. L18			

Lesson Plans

Inclusion

- ❑ **TE:** Read in Pairs, p. 182
- ❑ **California EasyPlanner CD-ROM:** Reading Skill, Vocabulary Study Guide, Reteaching Activity

All Students

- ❑ California Reading Toolkit, p. L18

PE

- ❑ Taking Notes: Categorizing, p. 180
- ❑ **Extend Lesson 1** Activity: Create an African Mask, p. 185

REVIEW AND ENRICH

Integrate Technology

Transparencies

- ❑ Critical Thinking: CT23 Categorizing
- ❑ Map: MT11 East Coast African Trading Cities, c. 1200
- ❑ Humanities: HT11 Kuba Mask

Power Presentations

- ❑ Lesson 1 Lecture Notes

CD-ROMS

- ❑ California EasyPlanner CD-ROM
- ❑ California eEdition CD-ROM
- ❑ California Test Generator CD-ROM

Interdisciplinary Activities

Interdisciplinary Projects

- ❑ Science, p. 32
- ❑ Language Arts, p. 33

Transparencies

- ❑ Geography: MT11 East Coast African Trading Cities, c. 1200
- ❑ Art: HT11 Kurba Mask

ASSESS

Content Assessment

- ❑ Lesson Review, *PE p. 184*
- ❑ Lesson Quiz, *FA p. 96*
- ❑ California Test Generator CD-ROM: Lesson 1 Quiz
- ❑ Integrated Assessment

Standards Practice

- ❑ California Standards Enrichment Workbook, pp. 43–46
- ❑ California Daily Standards Practice Transparencies TT18
- ❑ California Standards Planner and Lesson Plans, p. L35
- ❑ California Online Test Practice: **ClassZone.com**

RETEACH

- ❑ Reteaching Activity, *IDR Unit 3, p. 33*

Lesson Plans

Name _____ Date _____

Empires Built on Gold and Trade

> PE = Pupil's Edition   IDRS = IDR in Spanish
> TE = Teacher's Edition   RSG = Reading Study Guide
> IDR = In-Depth Resources

PLAN AND PREPARE

Lesson Objectives

❑ Trace the development of the Shona Empire.

❑ Explain the relationship between the gold trade and the growth of Great Zimbabwe.

❑ Describe the rise of the Mutapa Empire.

❑ **Language Objective:** Formulate statements that compare and contrast details from expository text to identify ways people, characters, events, and ideas are alike and different.

California Standards

7.2.5

7.4.5

REP 4

How to Teach the California Standards, *TE p. 186*

FOCUS AND MOTIVATE

❑ MAIN IDEAS, *PE/TE p. 186*

❑ READING SKILL: Comparing and Contrasting, *PE/TE p. 186*

❑ TERMS & NAMES, *PE/TE p. 187*

TEACH

Struggling Readers	**On-level**	**Gifted and Talented**	**English Learners**
TE	**PE**	**TE**	**TE**
❑ Develop Fact Sheets, p. 190	❑ Comparisons Across Cultures: Oral Tradition, p. 190	❑ Compare Oral Traditions, p. 190	❑ Compare and Contrast, p. 188
❑ Practice the Skill, p. 192	**IDR Unit 3**	**IDR Unit 3**	❑ Explain Inference, p. 188
IDR Unit 3	❑ Reading Skill: Comparing and Contrasting, p. 21	❑ Geography Practice, p. 29	**IDRS**
❑ Reading Skill: Comparing and Contrasting, p. 21	❑ Skillbuilder Practice: Explaining Historical Patterns, p. 24	❑ Literature: Hymn to Mwari, p. 32	❑ Reading Skill, p. 50
❑ Reteaching Activity, p. 34	❑ Vocabulary Cards, p. 27	**Interdisciplinary Projects**	**RSG (Spanish)**
Reading Study Guide		❑ Math, p. 31	❑ Lesson 2, p. 51
❑ Lesson 2, p. 51			❑ **California Modified Lesson Plans for English Learners, p. 41**
❑ RSG Audio CD			❑ **Multi-Language Glossary of Social Studies Terms**
California Reading Toolkit, p. L19			

Lesson Plans

Inclusion

- ☐ **TE:** Listen to the Lesson, p. 188
- ☐ **California EasyPlanner CD-ROM:** Reading Skill, Vocabulary Study Guide, Reteaching Activity

All Students

- ☐ California Reading Toolkit, p. L19

PE

- ☐ Taking Notes: Comparing and Contrasting, p. 186
- ☐ **Extend Lesson 2** Skillbuilder: Drawing Conclusions from Sources, pp. 192–193

TE

- ☐ More About The Hill Complex, p. 188; The Valley Ruins, p. 188; Gold Trading Networks, p. 189; The Mystery of Great Zimbabwe, p. 193

REVIEW AND ENRICH

Integrate Technology

Transparencies

- ☐ Critical Thinking: CT24 Comparing and Contrasting
- ☐ Map: MT12 Shona Empire, 800–1400
- ☐ Humanities: HT12 Ruins of Great Zimbabwe

Power Presentations

- ☐ Lesson 2 Lecture Notes

CD-ROMS

- ☐ California EasyPlanner CD-ROM
- ☐ California eEdition CD-ROM
- ☐ California Test Generator CD-ROM

Interdisciplinary Activities

TE

- ☐ Math: Calculate the Cost of Gold, p. 189
- ☐ Science: Report on Gold, p. 189

Interdisciplinary Projects

- ☐ Math, p. 31

Transparencies

- ☐ Geography: MT12 Shona Empire, 800–1400
- ☐ Art: HT12 Ruins of Great Zimbabwe

ASSESS

Content Assessment

- ☐ Lesson Review, *PE p. 191*
- ☐ Lesson Quiz, *FA p. 97*
- ☐ California Test Generator CD-ROM: Lesson 2 Quiz
- ☐ Integrated Assessment

Standards Practice

- ☐ California Standards Enrichment Workbook, pp. 45–46, 69–70
- ☐ California Daily Standards Practice Transparencies TT19
- ☐ California Standards Planner and Lesson Plans, p. L37
- ☐ California Online Test Practice: **ClassZone.com**

RETEACH

- ☐ Reteaching Activity, *IDR Unit 3, p. 34*

CHAPTER 6 Lesson 3   **Lesson Plan**

The Kongo Kingdom

> PE = Pupil's Edition   IDRS = IDR in Spanish
> TE = Teacher's Edition   RSG = Reading Study Guide
> IDR = In-Depth Resources

PLAN AND PREPARE

Lesson Objectives	California Standards
❑ Describe the development and organization of the Kongo civilization.	7.11.2
	CST 3
❑ Explain how the Portuguese influenced the religion and government of Kongo.	HI 1
	How to Teach the California Standards, *TE p. 194*
❑ Analyze the impact of the slave trade on relations between Kongo and Portugal.	
❑ **Language Objective:** Complete cause and effect chains to derive the meaning of the text in the lessons.	

FOCUS AND MOTIVATE

❑ MAIN IDEAS, *PE/TE p. 194*

❑ READING SKILL: Understanding Cause and Effect, *PE/TE p. 194*

❑ TERMS & NAMES, *PE/TE p. 195*

TEACH

Struggling Readers	On-level	Gifted and Talented	English Learners
TE	**PE**	**TE**	**TE**
❑ Draw an Organizational Chart, p. 196	❑ History Makers: Afonso I, p. 197	❑ Analyze Afonso's Actions, p. 197	❑ Identify Cause and Effect, p. 196
❑ Answer Questions, p. 200	**IDR Unit 3**	❑ Prepare a Report, p. 200	**IDRS**
IDR Unit 3	❑ Reading Skill: Understanding Cause and Effect, p. 22	**IDR Unit 3**	❑ Reading Skill, p. 51
❑ Reading Skill, p. 22	❑ Skillbuilder Practice, p. 24	❑ Primary Source: Protest to the King of Portugal by Afonso I, p. 31	**RSG (Spanish)**
❑ Vocabulary Cards, p. 27	❑ Vocabulary Study Guide, p. 25	**Interdisciplinary Projects**	❑ Lesson 3, p. 53
❑ Reteaching Activity, p. 35	❑ Vocabulary Cards, p. 27	❑ Art, p. 34	❑ **California Modified Lesson Plans for English Learners, p. 43**
Reading Study Guide		**History Makers**	❑ **Multi-Language Glossary of Social Studies Terms**
❑ Lesson 3, p. 53		❑ Nzinga Mbembay, p. 11	
❑ RSG Audio CD			
California Reading Toolkit, p. L20			

Lesson Plans

Inclusion

☐ **California EasyPlanner CD-ROM:** Reading Skill, Vocabulary Study Guide, Reteaching Activity

All Students

☐ California Reading Toolkit, p. L20

PE

☐ Taking Notes: Understanding Cause and Effect, p. 194

☐ **Extend Lesson 3** Connect to Today: The Timeless Appeal of Gold, pp. 201–201

TE

☐ More About Uses of Gold, p. 201; Gold Mines, p. 201

REVIEW AND ENRICH

Integrate Technology

Transparencies

☐ Critical Thinking: CT25 Understanding Cause and Effect

Power Presentations

☐ Lesson 3 Lecture Notes

CD-ROMS

☐ California EasyPlanner CD-ROM

☐ California eEdition CD-ROM

☐ California Test Generator CD-ROM

Interdisciplinary Activities

TE

☐ Math: Present Statistics, p. 198

☐ Language Arts: Deliver a Persuasive Speech, p. 198

Interdisciplinary Projects

☐ Art, p. 34

ASSESS

Content Assessment

☐ Lesson Review, *PE p. 199*

☐ Chapter Review, *PE pp. 202–203*

☐ Lesson Quiz, *FA p. 98*

☐ California Test Generator CD-ROM: Lesson 3 Quiz

☐ Integrated Assessment

Standards Practice

☐ California Standards Enrichment Workbook, pp. 143–144

☐ California Daily Standards Practice Transparencies TT20

☐ California Standards Planner and Lesson Plans, p. L39

☐ California Online Test Practice: **ClassZone.com**

Struggling Readers	On-Level	Gifted and Talented	English Learners
☐ Test Form A, *FA pp. 99–102*	☐ Test Form B, *FA pp. 103–106*	☐ Test Form C, *FA pp. 107–110*	☐ Test Generator: Forms A, B, and C in Spanish

RETEACH

☐ Reteaching Activity, *IDR Unit 3, p. 35*

Lesson Plans

Reunifying China

INTRODUCE THE UNIT AND CHAPTER

UNIT 4: INTERACT WITH HISTORY: The Great Wall of China, *PE/TE pp. 206–207*

CHAPTER OBJECTIVE: Analyze how philosophy, religion, and technology molded Chinese society and government.

❑   Before You Read: K-W-L, *PE/TE p. 208*
❑   Big Ideas: Belief Systems, *PE p. 208, TE p. 209*
❑   Time Line Discussion, *TE p. 208*
❑   Map: Physical Geography of Present-Day China, *PE/TE p. 209*

> *PE = Pupil's Edition*
> *TE = Teacher's Edition*
> *IDR = In-Depth Resources*
> *IDRS = IDR in Spanish*
> *RSG = Reading Study Guide*

STARTING WITH A STORY: The Fall of Luoyang, *PE/TE pp. 210–211;* California eEdition CD-ROM

PLAN AND PREPARE

Lesson Objectives	California Standards
❑ Explain how the fall of the Han Dynasty affected China.	Reading 3.2
❑ Describe how Buddhism and Confucianism influenced Chinese society.	Writing 2.2
❑ Analyze how the Sui and Tang dynasties reunified China.	7.3.1, 7.3.2, 7.3.3
	HI 1
❑ **Language Objective:** Understand and use terms with the prefix re-, such as *reunify, rebirth,* and *reconquest.*	How to Teach the California Standards, *TE p. 212*

FOCUS AND MOTIVATE

❑   MAIN IDEAS, *PE/TE p. 212*
❑   TERMS & NAMES, *PE/TE p. 213*

❑   READING SKILL: Understanding Cause and Effect, *PE/TE p. 212*

TEACH

Struggling Readers	On-level	Gifted and Talented	English Learners
TE	**IDR Unit 4**	**TE**	**TE**
❑ Focus on Unfamiliar Topics, p. 214	❑ Family Newsletter (English and Spanish), pp. 1–2	❑ Create a Review Game, p. 215	❑ Use the Prefix Re-, p. 214
❑ Identify Key Players, p. 217	❑ Reading Skill: Understanding Cause and Effect, p. 3	❑ Design a Crossword Puzzle, p. 218	❑ Explore Idioms, p. 217
IDR Unit 4		**Interdisciplinary Projects**	**IDRS**
❑ Reading Skill, p. 3	❑ Vocabulary Study Guide, p. 9	❑ Science, p. 38	❑ Reading Skill, p. 58
❑ Vocabulary Study Guide, p. 9	❑ Vocabulary Cards, p. 11	**History Makers**	**RSG (Spanish)**
❑ Reteaching Activity, p. 17		❑ Wu Zhao, p. 13	❑ Lesson 1, p. 67
Reading Study Guide			❑ **California Modified Lesson Plans for English Learners, p. 45**
❑ Lesson 1, p. 67			
❑ RSG Audio CD			❑ **Multi-Language Glossary of Social Studies Terms**
California Reading Toolkit, p. L21			

Lesson Plans

Inclusion

- ❏ **TE:** Make a Graphic Organizer, p. 215; Use Self-Questioning, p. 218
- ❏ **California EasyPlanner CD-ROM:** Reading Skill, Vocabulary Study Guide, Reteaching Activity

All Students

- ❏ California Reading Toolkit, p. L21

PE

- ❏ Taking Notes: Understanding Cause and Effect, p. 212
- ❏ **Extend Lesson 1** Skillbuilder: Identifying Issues and Problems, pp. 220–221

TE

- ❏ More About Daoism and the Tang, p. 215; Wendi, p. 216; The Grand Canal, p. 217; The Reign of Wu Zhao, p. 218

IDR Unit 4

- ❏ Family Newsletter (English and Spanish), pp. 1–2

REVIEW AND ENRICH

Integrate Technology

Transparencies

- ❏ Critical Thinking: CT27 Understanding Cause and Effect
- ❏ Map: MT13 China's Grand Canal System

Power Presentations

- ❏ Lesson 1 Lecture Notes

CD-ROMS

- ❏ California EasyPlanner CD-ROM
- ❏ California eEdition CD-ROM
- ❏ California Test Generator CD-ROM

Interdisciplinary Activities

TE

- ❏ Art: Sculpt a Tang Horse, p. 216
- ❏ Math: Graph Population Changes, p. 216

Interdisciplinary Projects

- ❏ Science, p. 38

Transparencies

- ❏ Geography: MT13 China's Grand Canal System

ASSESS

Content Assessment

- ❏ Lesson Review, *PE p. 219*
- ❏ Lesson Quiz, *FA p. 115*
- ❏ California Test Generator CD-ROM: Lesson 1 Quiz
- ❏ Integrated Assessment

Standards Practice

- ❏ California Standards Enrichment Workbook, pp. 49–54
- ❏ California Daily Standards Practice Transparencies TT21
- ❏ California Standards Planner and Lesson Plans, p. L41
- ❏ California Online Test Practice: **ClassZone.com**

RETEACH

- ❏ Reteaching Activity, *IDR Unit 4, p. 17*

Advances Under the Tang and Song

PE = Pupil's Edition   IDRS = IDR in Spanish
TE = Teacher's Edition   RSG = Reading Study Guide
IDR = In-Depth Resources

PLAN AND PREPARE

Lesson Objectives

❑ Define the vegetation zones in West Africa and analyze how natural resources contributed to success in trade.

❑ Describe how trade brought religious and cultural changes to West Africa.

❑ Analyze the influence of Islam and Ghana.

❑ **Language Objective:** Participate in the dramatization of a scene to describe their experience after being designated as the family trader of goods and services.

California Standards

7.4.1

7.4.3

7.4.4

How to Teach the California Standards, *TE p. 222*

FOCUS AND MOTIVATE

❑ MAIN IDEAS, *PE/TE p. 156*

❑ READING SKILL: Finding Main Ideas, *PE/TE p. 156*

❑ TERMS & NAMES, *PE/TE p. 157*

TEACH

Struggling Readers	On-level	Gifted and Talented	English Learners
TE	**PE**	**TE**	**TE**
❑ Preread and Predict, p. 224	❑ Geography: Terraced Rice Fields, p. 226	❑ Research Tang Law, p. 225	❑ Understand Multiple-Meaning Words, p. 224
❑ List Achievements, p. 227	❑ Primary Source: "On Being Demoted and Sent Away to Qizhou", p. 228	❑ Compare Technologies, p. 227	❑ Find Cognates, p. 226
❑ Make a Commercial, p. 230		**IDR Unit 4**	**IDRS**
IDR Unit 4	**IDR Unit 4**	❑ Primary Source: A Poem by Bo Zhuyi, p. 15	❑ Reading Skill: Finding Main Ideas, p. 59
❑ Reading Skill: Finding Main Ideas, p. 4	❑ Reading Skill: Finding Main Ideas, p. 4	❑ Literature: "A Farm-house on the Wei River" by Wang Wei, p. 16	**RSG (Spanish)**
❑ Reteaching Activity, p. 18	❑ Vocabulary Cards, p. 11		❑ Lesson 2, p. 69
Reading Study Guide	❑ Geography Practice: The City of Ch'ang-an, p. 13	**Interdisciplinary Projects**	❑ **California Modified Lesson Plans for English Learners, p. 47**
❑ Lesson 2, p. 69		❑ Art, p. 40	❑ **Multi-Language Glossary of Social Studies Terms**
❑ RSG Audio CD			
California Reading Toolkit, p. L22			

Lesson Plans

Inclusion

- ❏ **TE:** Answer Questions, p. 225; Track Causes and Effects, p. 226; Trace Problems and Solutions, p. 230
- ❏ **California EasyPlanner CD-ROM:** Reading Skill, Vocabulary Study Guide, Reteaching Activity

All Students

- ❏ California Reading Toolkit, p. L22

PE

- ❏ Taking Notes: Finding Main Ideas, p. 222
- ❏ **Extend Lesson 2** Connect to Today: The Chinese Legacy, pp. 230–231

TE

- ❏ More About Scholar-Officials, p. 224; Confucius, p. 224; The Chinese Postal System, p. 225; Rice, p. 226; Song Trade, p. 226; Porcelain, p. 228; Fireworks, p. 231

REVIEW AND ENRICH

Integrate Technology

Transparencies

- ❏ Critical Thinking: CT28 Finding Main Ideas
- ❏ Map: MT14 The Song Dynasty
- ❏ Humanities: HT13 The Thirteen Emperors
- ❏ Humanities: HT13 Tang Dynasty Horse Sculpture

Power Presentations

- ❏ Lesson 2 Lecture Notes

CD-ROMS

- ❏ California EasyPlanner CD-ROM
- ❏ California eEdition CD-ROM
- ❏ California Test Generator CD-ROM

Interdisciplinary Activities

PE

- ❏ Geography: Terraced Rice Fields, p. 226

TE

- ❏ Language Arts: Discover Chinese Poetry, p. 228
- ❏ Science: Explain Paper-Making, p. 228

Interdisciplinary Projects

- ❏ Art, p. 40

Transparencies

- ❏ Geography: MT14 The Song Dynasty
- ❏ Art: HT13 The Thirteen Emperors

ASSESS

Content Assessment

- ❏ Lesson Review, *PE p. 229*
- ❏ Lesson Quiz, *FA p. 116*
- ❏ California Test Generator CD-ROM: Lesson 2 Quiz
- ❏ Integrated Assessment

Standards Practice

- ❏ California Standards Enrichment Workbook, pp. 51–52, 57–60
- ❏ California Daily Standards Practice Transparencies TT22
- ❏ California Standards Planner and Lesson Plans, p. L37
- ❏ California Online Test Practice: **ClassZone.com**

RETEACH

- ❏ Reteaching Activity, *IDR Unit 4, p. 18*

Lesson Plans

Copyright © by McDougal Littell, a division of Houghton Mifflin Company

CHAPTER (7) Lesson 3 | Lesson Plan

The Mongol Empire

PE = Pupil's Edition	IDRS = IDR in Spanish
TE = Teacher's Edition	RSG = Reading Study Guide
IDR = In-Depth Resources	

PLAN AND PREPARE

Lesson Objectives

❑ Describe how the Mongols created and expanded their empire.

❑ Explain how the Mongols changed Chinese government.

❑ List ways the Mongols expanded trade and foreign contacts.

❑ **Language Objective:** Use context clues to understand new words.

California Standards

7.2.3
7.3.4
CST 2
How to Teach the California Standards, *TE p. 232*

FOCUS AND MOTIVATE

❑ MAIN IDEAS, *PE/TE p. 232*

❑ READING SKILL: Explaining Chronological Order and Sequence, *PE/TE p. 232*

❑ TERMS & NAMES, *PE/TE p. 233*

TEACH

Struggling Readers	**On-level**	**Gifted and Talented**	**English Learners**
TE	**PE**	**TE**	**TE**
❑ Write Newspaper Headlines, p. 234	❑ History Makers: Kublai Khan, p. 236	❑ Put on a Talk Show, p. 235	❑ Examine Word Parts, p. 234
IDR Unit 4	**IDR Unit 4**	**Interdisciplinary Projects**	**IDRS**
❑ Reading Skill, p. 5	❑ Reading Skill: Explaining Chronological Order and Sequence, p. 5	❑ Language Arts, p. 39	❑ Reading Skill, p. 60
❑ Reteaching Activity, p. 19			**RSG (Spanish)**
Reading Study Guide	❑ Vocabulary Study Guide, p. 9		❑ Lesson 3, p. 71
❑ Lesson 3, p. 71	❑ Vocabulary Cards, p. 11		❑ **California Modified Lesson Plans for English Learners, p. 49**
❑ RSG Audio CD			
California Reading Toolkit, p. L23			❑ **Multi-Language Glossary**

Lesson Plans

Inclusion

☐ **TE:** Use a Wall Map or Globe, p. 235

☐ **California EasyPlanner CD-ROM:** Reading Skill, Vocabulary Study Guide, Reteaching Activity

All Students

☐ California Reading Toolkit, p. L23

PE

☐ Taking Notes: Explaining Chronological Order and Sequence, p. 232

TE

☐ More About Mongol Warriors, p. 234; The Mongol Khanates, p. 234; Social Classes in China, p. 236; The Silk Roads, p. 236

REVIEW AND ENRICH

Integrate Technology

Transparencies

☐ Critical Thinking: CT29 Explaining Chronological Order and Sequence

☐ Humanities: HT14 Kublai Khan Hunting

Power Presentations

☐ Lesson 3 Lecture Notes

CD-ROMS

☐ California EasyPlanner CD-ROM

☐ California eEdition CD-ROM

☐ California Test Generator CD-ROM

Interdisciplinary Activities

TE

☐ Language Arts: Write an Acrostic Poem, p. 236

☐ Math: Use an Abacus, p. 236

Interdisciplinary Projects

☐ Language Arts, p. 39

Transparencies

☐ Humanities: HT14 Kublai Khan Hunting

ASSESS

Content Assessment

☐ Lesson Review, *PE p. 237*

☐ Lesson Quiz, *FA p. 117*

☐ California Test Generator CD-ROM: Lesson 3 Quiz

☐ Integrated Assessment

Standards Practice

☐ California Standards Enrichment Workbook, pp. 53–56

☐ California Daily Standards Practice Transparencies TT23

☐ California Standards Planner and Lesson Plans, p. L45

☐ California Online Test Practice: **ClassZone.com**

RETEACH

☐ Reteaching Activity, *IDR Unit 4, p. 19*

Lesson Plans

A Return to Chinese Rule

PE = Pupil's Edition | IDRS = IDR in Spanish
TE = Teacher's Edition | RSG = Reading Study Guide
IDR = In-Depth Resources

PLAN AND PREPARE

Lesson Objectives
❏ Describe the rise and fall of the Mali empire.

❏ Analyze the importance of strong leadership and government organization to the rise of the Songhai empire.

❏ Outline the reasons for the fall of Songhai.

❏ **Language Objective:** Use antonyms to present different sides of a situation or event.

California Standards
7.3
7.3.4
7.3.5
How to Teach the California Standards, *TE p. 238*

FOCUS AND MOTIVATE

❏ MAIN IDEAS, *PE/TE p. 164*

❏ READING SKILL: Comparing and Contrasting, *PE/TE p. 164*

❏ TERMS & NAMES, *PE/TE p. 165*

TEACH

Struggling Readers	On-level	Gifted and Talented	English Learners
TE	**PE**	**TE**	**IDRS**
❏ Do Popcorn Reading, p. 240	❏ Comparison Across Cultures, p. 241	❏ Build a Model, p. 241	❏ Reading Skill: Forming and Supporting Opinions, p. 61
❏ Make Comparisons and Contrasts, p. 241	**IDR Unit 4**	**Interdisciplinary Projects**	**RSG (Spanish)**
IDR Unit 4	❏ Reading Skill: Forming and Supporting Opinions, p. 6	❏ Math, p. 37	❏ Lesson 4, p. 63
❏ Reading Skill, p. 6	❏ Skillbuilder Practice: Reading a Special-Purpose Map, p. 8		❏ **California Modified Lesson Plans for English Learners, p. 51**
❏ Reteaching Activity, p. 20	❏ Vocabulary Cards, p. 11		❏ **Multi-Language Glossary of Social Studies Terms**
Reading Study Guide			
❏ Lesson 4, p. 63			
❏ RSG Audio CD			
California Reading Toolkit, p. L24			

Inclusion

- ❑ **TE:** Use an Interactive Map, p. 240
- ❑ **California EasyPlanner CD-ROM:** Reading Skill, Vocabulary Study Guide, Reteaching Activity

All Students

- ❑ California Reading Toolkit, p. L24

PE

- ❑ Taking Notes: Forming and Supporting Opinions, p. 238
- ❑ **Extend Lesson 4** Activity: Make a Compass, p. 243

TE

- ❑ More About The Forbidden City, p. 240

REVIEW AND ENRICH

Integrate Technology

Transparencies

- ❑ Transparencies
- ❑ Critical Thinking: CT30 Forming and Supporting Opinions

Power Presentations

- ❑ Lesson 4 Lecture Notes

CD-ROMS

- ❑ California EasyPlanner CD-ROM
- ❑ California eEdition CD-ROM
- ❑ California Test Generator CD-ROM

Interdisciplinary Activities

Interdisciplinary Projects

- ❑ Math, p. 37

ASSESS

Content Assessment

- ❑ Lesson Review, *PE p. 242*
- ❑ Chapter Review, *PE pp. 244–245*
- ❑ Lesson Quiz, *FA p. 118*
- ❑ California Test Generator CD-ROM: Lesson 4 Quiz
- ❑ Integrated Assessment

Standards Practice

- ❑ California Standards Enrichment Workbook, pp. 55–58
- ❑ California Daily Standards Practice Transparencies TT24
- ❑ California Standards Planner and Lesson Plans, p. L47
- ❑ California Online Test Practice: **ClassZone.com**

Struggling Readers	On-Level	Gifted and Talented	English Learners
❑ Test Form A, *FA pp. 119–122*	❑ Test Form B, *FA pp. 123–126*	❑ Test Form C, *FA pp. 127–130*	❑ Test Generator: Forms A, B, and C in Spanish

RETEACH

- ❑ Reteaching Activity, *IDR Unit 4, p. 20*

CHAPTER 8 Lesson 1

Land of the Rising Sun

INTRODUCE THE CHAPTER

CHAPTER OBJECTIVE: Trace the development of Japan, Korea, and the kingdoms of Southeast Asia and the influence of China and India upon their cultures.

❏ Before You Read: Predicting, *PE/TE p. 246*

❏ Big Ideas: Geography, *PE p. 246, TE p. 247*

❏ Time Line Discussion, *TE p. 246*

❏ Map: East and Southeast Asia, A.D. 1100, *PE/TE p. 247*

> *PE = Pupil's Edition*
> *TE = Teacher's Edition*
> *IDR = In-Depth Resources*
> *IDRS = IDR in Spanish*
> *RSG = Reading Study Guide*

STARTING WITH A STORY: The Education of a Samurai, *PE/TE pp. 248–249;* California eEdition CD-ROM

PLAN AND PREPARE

Lesson Objectives

❏ Describe the effects of Japan's geography on its culture and economy.

❏ Explain the clan system of early Japan.

❏ Analyze the ways in which Prince Shotoku contributed to the development of Japan.

❏ **Language Objective:** Formulate purpose-setting questions in order to make the text comprehensible and meaningful.

California Standards

7.5.1

7.5.2

HI 2

How to Teach the Standards, *TE p. 250*

FOCUS AND MOTIVATE

❏ MAIN IDEAS, *PE/TE p. 250*   ❏ READING SKILL: Summarizing, *PE/TE p. 250*   ❏ TERMS & NAMES, *PE/TE p. 251*

TEACH

Struggling Readers	On-level	Gifted and Talented	English Learners
TE	**IDR Unit 4**	**TE**	**TE**
❏ Chart Social Scale, p. 252	❏ Family Newsletter (English and Spanish), pp. 21–22	❏ Analyze Influences on American Culture, p. 252	❏ Model How to Preview, p. 253
IDR Unit 4	❏ Reading Skill: Summarizing, p. 23	**Interdisciplinary Projects**	**IDRS**
❏ Reading Skill: Summarizing, p. 23	❏ Vocabulary Study Guide, p. 29	❏ Science, p. 44	❏ Reading Skill, p. 67
❏ Vocabulary Study Guide, p. 29	❏ Vocabulary Cards, p. 31	**History Makers**	**RSG (Spanish)**
❏ Reteaching Activity, p. 37		❏ Prince Shotoku, p. 15	❏ Lesson 1, p. 67
Reading Study Guide			❏ **California Modified Lesson Plans for English Learners, p. 53**
❏ Lesson 1, p. 67			❏ **Multi-Language Glossary of Social Studies Terms**
❏ RSG Audio CD			
California Reading Toolkit, p. L25			

Lesson Plans

Inclusion

- ❏ **TE:** Ask Questions, p. 253
- ❏ **California EasyPlanner CD-ROM:** Reading Skill, Vocabulary Study Guide, Reteaching Activity

All Students

- ❏ California Reading Toolkit, p. L25

PE

- ❏ Taking Notes: Summarizing, p. 250
- ❏ **Extend Lesson 1** Activity: Make a Poster, p. 255

TE

- ❏ More About Japan's Emperors, p. 253

REVIEW AND ENRICH

Integrate Technology

Transparencies

- ❏ Critical Thinking: CT32 Summarizing

Power Presentations

- ❏ Lesson 1 Lecture Notes

CD-ROMS

- ❏ California EasyPlanner CD-ROM
- ❏ California eEdition CD-ROM
- ❏ California Test Generator CD-ROM

Interdisciplinary Activities

Interdisciplinary Projects

- ❏ Science, p. 44

ASSESS

Content Assessment

- ❏ Lesson Review, *PE p. 254*
- ❏ Lesson Quiz, *FA p. 131*
- ❏ California Test Generator CD-ROM: Lesson 1 Quiz
- ❏ Integrated Assessment

Standards Practice

- ❏ California Standards Enrichment Workbook, pp. 71–74
- ❏ California Daily Standards Practice Transparencies TT25
- ❏ California Standards Planner and Lesson Plans, p. L49
- ❏ California Online Test Practice: **ClassZone.com**

RETEACH

- ❏ Reteaching Activity, *IDR Unit 4, p. 37*

Growth of Japanese Culture

> PE = Pupil's Edition
> TE = Teacher's Edition
> IDR = In-Depth Resources
>
> IDRS = IDR in Spanish
> RSG = Reading Study Guide

PLAN AND PREPARE

Lesson Objectives	California Standards
❑ Explain the forms of Buddhism practiced in Japan and their effect on the country's culture.	7.5.4
❑ Examine Japan's literary and dramatic developments.	7.5.5
❑ Describe themes associated with Japanese art forms.	HI 2
❑ **Language Objective:** Categorize information to better understand the Japanese culture.	How to Teach the California Standards, *TE p. 256*

FOCUS AND MOTIVATE

❑ MAIN IDEAS, *PE/TE p. 256*

❑ READING SKILL: Categorizing, *PE/TE p. 256*

❑ TERMS & NAMES, *PE/TE p. 257*

TEACH

Struggling Readers	On-level	Gifted and Talented	English Learners
TE	**PE**	**TE**	**TE**
❑ Create a Time Line, p. 258	❑ Primary Source: from *The Tale of Genji*, p. 259	❑ Make a Mask, p. 258	❑ Categorize, p. 259
❑ Illustrate Scenes, p. 264		❑ Write a Character Sketch, p. 264	❑ Select Words, p. 263
IDR Unit 4	**IDR Unit 4**	**IDR Unit 4**	**IDRS**
❑ Reading Skill: Categorizing, p. 24	❑ Reading Skill: Categorizing, p. 24	❑ Primary Source: Carving of a Buddhist Wisdom King, p. 35	❑ Reading Skill: Categorizing, p. 68
❑ Reteaching Activity, p. 38	❑ Vocabulary Cards, p. 31		**RSG (Spanish)**
Reading Study Guide		**Interdisciplinary Projects**	❑ Lesson 2, p. 69
❑ Lesson 2, p. 69		❑ Art, p. 46	❑ **California Modified Lesson Plans for English Learners, p. 55**
❑ RSG Audio CD			❑ **Multi-Language Glossary of Social Studies Terms**
California Reading Toolkit, p. L26			

Lesson Plans

Inclusion

- ❏ **TE:** Use Flashcards, p. 259; Illustrate the Story, p. 263
- ❏ **California EasyPlanner CD-ROM:** Reading Skill, Vocabulary Study Guide, Vocabulary Cards

All Students

- ❏ California Reading Toolkit, p. L26

PE

- ❏ Taking Notes: Categorizing, p. 256
- ❏ **Extend Lesson 2** Reader's Theater: The Siege of Chihaya Castle, pp. 262–265

TE

- ❏ More About Meditation, p. 258; Kabuki, p. 259; Emperor Go-Daigo, p. 262; Bakufu, p. 264; Kusunoki, p. 265

REVIEW AND ENRICH

Integrate Technology

Transparencies

- ❏ Critical Thinking: CT33 Categorizing
- ❏ Humanities: HT15 Lady Fugitsubo Watching Prince Genji

Power Presentations

- ❏ Lesson 2 Lecture Notes

CD-ROMS

- ❏ California EasyPlanner CD-ROM
- ❏ California eEdition CD-ROM
- ❏ California Test Generator CD-ROM

Interdisciplinary Activities

TE

- ❏ Art: Design a Japanese Garden, p. 260
- ❏ Language Arts: Report on Bonsai, p. 260

Interdisciplinary Projects

- ❏ Art, p. 46

Transparencies

- ❏ Art: HT15 Lady Fugitsubo Watching Prince Genji

ASSESS

Content Assessment

- ❏ Lesson Review, *PE p. 261*
- ❏ Lesson Quiz, *FA p. 132*
- ❏ California Test Generator CD-ROM: Lesson 2 Quiz
- ❏ Integrated Assessment

Standards Practice

- ❏ California Standards Enrichment Workbook, pp. 77–80
- ❏ California Daily Standards Practice Transparencies TT26
- ❏ California Standards Planner and Lesson Plans, p. L51
- ❏ California Online Test Practice: **ClassZone.com**

RETEACH

- ❏ Reteaching Activity, *IDR Unit 4, p. 38*

Samurai and Shoguns

PE = Pupil's Edition	IDRS = IDR in Spanish
TE = Teacher's Edition	RSG = Reading Study Guide
IDR = In-Depth Resources	

PLAN AND PREPARE

Lesson Objectives

❏ Identify reasons for the development of feudalism in Japan.

❏ Describe the hierarchy of Japan's feudalistic society.

❏ Explain the efforts of three powerful leaders to unify Japan.

❏ **Language Objective:** Use antonyms to present different sides of a situation or event.

California Standards

7.5.3

7.5.6

HI 2

How to Teach the California Standards, *TE p. 266*

FOCUS AND MOTIVATE

❏ MAIN IDEAS, *PE/TE p. 266*

❏ READING SKILL: Explaining Chronological Order and Sequence, *PE/TE p. 266*

❏ TERMS & NAMES, *PE/TE p. 267*

TEACH

Struggling Readers

TE

❏ Share Aspects of Culture, p. 269

❏ Perform Skits, p. 272

IDR Unit 4

❏ Reading Skill: Explaining Chronological Order and Sequence, p. 25

❏ Reteaching Activity, p. 39

Reading Study Guide

❏ Lesson 3, p. 71

❏ RSG Audio CD

California Reading Toolkit, p. L27

On-level

PE

❏ History Makers: Tokugawa Ieyasu, p. 270

IDR Unit 4

❏ Reading Skill, p. 25

❏ Skillbuilder Practice: Understanding Cause and Effect, p. 28

❏ Vocabulary Cards, p. 31

Gifted and Talented

TE

❏ Analyze U.S. Class System, p. 269

❏ Identify Musical Instruments, p. 272

Interdisciplinary Projects

❏ Language Arts, p. 45

English Learners

TE

❏ Create a Chart, p. 268

IDRS

❏ Reading Skill: Explaining Chronological Order and Sequence, p. 69

RSG (Spanish)

❏ Lesson 3, p. 71

❏ **California Modified Lesson Plans for English Learners, p. 57**

❏ **Multi-Language Glossary of Social Studies Terms**

Lesson Plans

Inclusion

- **TE:** Answer Questions, p. 268
- **California EasyPlanner CD-ROM:** Reading Skill, Vocabulary Study Guide, Reteaching Activity

All Students

- California Reading Toolkit, p. L27

PE

- Taking Notes: Explaining Chronological Order and Sequence, p. 266
- **Extend Lesson 3** Daily Life: An Inside Look at Himeji Castle, pp. 272–273

TE

- More About Bushido, p. 268; Hierarchy Within the Samurai Class, p. 269; Himeji Castle, p. 273

REVIEW AND ENRICH

Integrate Technology

Transparencies

- Critical Thinking: CT34 Explaining Chronological Order and Sequence
- Map: MT15 Japan: Physical/Political

Power Presentations

- Lesson 3 Lecture Notes

CD-ROMS

- California EasyPlanner CD-ROM
- California eEdition CD-ROM
- California Test Generator CD-ROM

Interdisciplinary Activities

TE

- Language Arts: Write a Script, p. 270; Debate Japan's Closed-Door Policy, p. 270

Interdisciplinary Projects

- Language Arts, p. 45

Transparencies

- Geography: MT15 Japan: Physical/Political

ASSESS

Content Assessment

- Lesson Review, *PE p. 271*
- Lesson Quiz, *FA p. 133*
- California Test Generator CD-ROM: Lesson 3 Quiz
- Integrated Assessment

Standards Practice

- California Standards Enrichment Workbook, pp. 75–76, 81–82
- California Daily Standards Practice Transparencies TT27
- California Standards Planner and Lesson Plans, p. L53
- California Online Test Practice: **ClassZone.com**

RETEACH

- Reteaching Activity, *IDR Unit 4, p. 39*

Korea and Southeast Asia

PE = Pupil's Edition	IDRS = IDR in Spanish
TE = Teacher's Edition	RSG = Reading Study Guide
IDR = In-Depth Resources	

PLAN AND PREPARE

Lesson Objectives

❑ Describe the influence of China upon the development and culture of Korea, Vietnam, and Khmer.

❑ Trace the history of Korea, the Vietnamese kingdoms, and the Khmer Empire through the 15th century.

❑ **Language Objective:** Create a concept cluster of words and terms from the lesson that are related to geography.

California Standards

7.3.1
CST 1
HI 1
Hi 2
How to Teach the California Standards, *TE p. 274*

FOCUS AND MOTIVATE

❑ MAIN IDEAS, *PE/TE p. 274*

❑ READING SKILL: Comparing and Contrasting, *PE/TE p. 274*

❑ TERMS & NAMES, *PE/TE p. 275*

TEACH

Struggling Readers	On-level	Gifted and Talented	English Learners
TE	**IDR Unit 4**	**TE**	**TE**
❑ Retell the Lesson, p. 278	❑ Reading Skill: Comparing and Contrasting, p. 26	❑ Design a Web Site, p. 278	❑ Locate Words, p. 277
IDR Unit 4		**Interdisciplinary Projects**	**IDRS**
❑ Reading Skill: Comparing and Contrasting, p. 26	❑ Vocabulary Cards, p. 31	❑ Math, p. 25	❑ Reading Skill, p. 70
❑ Reteaching Activity, p. 40			**RSG (Spanish)**
Reading Study Guide			❑ Lesson 4, p. 73
❑ Lesson 4, p. 73			❑ **California Modified Lesson Plans for English Learners, p. 59**
❑ RSG Audio CD			❑ **Multi-Language Glossary of Social Studies Terms**
California Reading Toolkit, p. L28			

Lesson Plans

Inclusion

❑ **TE:** Listen to the Lesson, p. 277

❑ **California EasyPlanner CD-ROM:** Reading Skill, Vocabulary Study Guide, Reteaching Activity

All Students

❑ California Reading Toolkit, p. L28

PE

❑ Taking Notes: Comparing and Contrasting, p. 274

TE

❑ More About Celadon, p. 276; Trung Trac and Trung Nhi, p. 277

REVIEW AND ENRICH

Integrate Technology

Transparencies

❑ Critical Thinking: CT35 Comparing and Contrasting

❑ Map: MT16 Southeast Asia, 1200 A.D.

❑ Art: HT16 Angkor Wat, Cambodia

Power Presentations

❑ Lesson 4 Lecture Notes

CD-ROMS

❑ California EasyPlanner CD-ROM

❑ California eEdition CD-ROM

❑ California Test Generator CD-ROM

Interdisciplinary Activities

TE

❑ Art: Explore Korean Art Forms, p. 276

❑ Science: Compare Rice Farming Methods, p. 276

Interdisciplinary Projects

❑ Math, p. 43

Transparencies

❑ Geography: MT16 Southeast Asia, 1200 A.D.

❑ Art: HT16 Angkor Wat, Cambodia

ASSESS

Content Assessment

❑ Lesson Review, *PE p. 279*

❑ Chapter Review, *PE pp. 280–281*

❑ Lesson Quiz, *FA p. 134*

❑ California Test Generator CD-ROM: Lesson 4 Quiz

❑ Integrated Assessment

Standards Practice

❑ California Standards Enrichment Workbook, pp. 49–50

❑ California Daily Standards Practice Transparencies TT28

❑ California Standards Planner and Lesson Plans, p. L55

❑ California Online Test Practice: **ClassZone.com**

Struggling Readers	On-Level	Gifted and Talented	English Learners
❑ Test Form A, *FA pp. 135–139*	❑ Test Form B, *FA pp. 140–144*	❑ Test Form C, *FA pp. 145–149*	❑ Test Generator: Forms A, B, and C in Spanish

RETEACH

❑ Reteaching Activity, *IDR Unit 4, p. 40*

The Development of Feudalism

INTRODUCE THE UNIT AND CHAPTER

UNIT 5: INTERACT WITH HISTORY: Siege of a Castle, A.D. 1000, *PE/TE pp. 284–285*

CHAPTER OBJECTIVE: Examine the rise of feudalism in Europe, the characteristics of European feudalism, and its similarities to Japan's feudal system.

- ❑ Before You Read: Anticipation Guide, *PE/TE p. 146*
- ❑ Big Ideas: Culture, PE p. 286, *TE p. 287*
- ❑ Time Line Discussion, *TE p. 286*
- ❑ Map: Europe, A.D. 1000, *PE/TE p. 287*

> *PE = Pupil's Edition*
> *TE = Teacher's Edition*
> *IDR = In-Depth Resources*
> *IDRS = IDR in Spanish*
> *RSG = Reading Study Guide*

STARTING WITH A STORY: Becoming a Knight, *PE/TE pp. 288–289;* California eEdition CD-ROM

PLAN AND PREPARE

Lesson Objectives	**California Standards**
❑ Describe Europe's geography.	7.6.1
❑ Identify changes in Europe after the fall of the Roman Empire.	7.6.2
❑ Explain the growth of the Frankish empire and the corresponding spread of Christianity.	7.6.3
❑ Analyze causes of feudalism and its structure.	How to Teach the California Standards, *TE p. 290*
❑ **Language Objective:** Use synonyms to present similarities between people, situations, or events.	

FOCUS AND MOTIVATE

❑ MAIN IDEAS, *PE/TE p. 290*   ❑ READING SKILL: Categorizing, *PE/TE p. 290*   ❑ TERMS & NAMES, *PE/TE p. 291*

TEACH

Struggling Readers	**On-level**	**Gifted and Talented**	**English Learners**
TE	**PE**	**TE**	**TE**
❑ Develop Before-and-After Chart, p. 293	❑ History Makers: Charlemagne, p. 294	❑ Write a Biographical Sketch, p. 293	❑ Use Synonyms, p. 292
IDR Unit 5	**IDR Unit 5**	❑ Diagram Roles of Women, p. 296	**IDRS**
❑ Reading Skill: Categorizing, p. 3	❑ Family Newsletter (English and Spanish), pp. 1–2	**Interdisciplinary Projects**	❑ Reading Skill, p. 78
❑ Vocabulary Study Guide, p. 8	❑ Reading Skill: Categorizing, p. 3	❑ Science, p. 50	**RSG (Spanish)**
❑ Reteaching Activity, p. 15	❑ Skillbuilder Practice: Recognizing Changing Interpretations of History, p. 7	**History Makers**	❑ Lesson 1, p. 77
Reading Study Guide		❑ Clovis, p. 17	❑ **California Modified Lesson Plans for English Learners, p. 61**
❑ Lesson 1, p. 77	❑ Vocabulary Study Guide, p. 8		❑ **Multi-Language Glossary of Social Studies Terms**
❑ RSG Audio CD			
California Reading Toolkit, p. L29			

Lesson Plans

Inclusion

- ❑ **TE:** Become Student Teachers, p. 292; Enlarge Images, p. 296
- ❑ **California EasyPlanner CD-ROM:** Reading Skill, Vocabulary Study Guide, Reteaching Activity

All Students

- ❑ California Reading Toolkit, p. L29

PE

- ❑ Taking Notes: Categorizing, p. 290

TE

- ❑ More About Medieval Castles, p. 285; Attacking Castles, p. 285; Farming in the Early Middle Ages, p. 292; The German People, p. 293; Medieval Monasteries, p. 295; Vassals, p. 296

IDR Unit 5

- ❑ Family Newsletter (English and Spanish), pp. 1–2

REVIEW AND ENRICH

Integrate Technology

Transparencies

- ❑ Critical Thinking: CT37 Categorizing
- ❑ Map: MT17 Climates of Europe

Power Presentations

- ❑ Lesson 1 Lecture Notes

CD-ROMS

- ❑ California EasyPlanner CD-ROM
- ❑ California eEdition CD-ROM
- ❑ California Test Generator CD-ROM

Interdisciplinary Activities

TE

- ❑ Language Arts: Write a News Article, p. 294
- ❑ Language Arts: Create a Learning Module, p. 294
- ❑ Art: Practice Illuminating Techniques, p. 295
- ❑ Language Arts: Schedule a Monk's Day, p. 295

Interdisciplinary Projects

- ❑ Science, p. 50

Transparencies

- ❑ Geography: MT17 Climates of Europe

ASSESS

Content Assessment

- ❑ Lesson Review, *PE p. 297*
- ❑ Lesson Quiz, *FA p. 154*
- ❑ California Test Generator CD-ROM: Lesson 1 Quiz
- ❑ Integrated Assessment

Standards Practice

- ❑ California Standards Enrichment Workbook, pp. 83–88
- ❑ California Daily Standards Practice Transparencies TT29
- ❑ California Standards Planner and Lesson Plans, p. L57
- ❑ California Online Test Practice: **ClassZone.com**

RETEACH

- ❑ Reteaching Activity, *IDR Unit 5, p. 15*

Lesson Plans

CHAPTER 9 Lesson 2

Daily Life in Medieval Europe

> PE = Pupil's Edition   IDRS = IDR in Spanish
> TE = Teacher's Edition   RSG = Reading Study Guide
> IDR = In-Depth Resources

PLAN AND PREPARE

Lesson Objectives	California Standards
❑ Describe the way of life on medieval manors. ❑ Explain the role of knights and the code of chivalry that they followed. ❑ Examine medieval towns and guilds. ❑ **Language Objective:** Create a mural to compare and contrast life on a manor and life in a town.	7.6.1 7.6.3 CST 3 How to Teach the California Standards, *TE p. 298*

FOCUS AND MOTIVATE

❑ MAIN IDEAS, *PE/TE p. 298*

❑ READING SKILL: Comparing and Contrasting, *PE/TE p. 298*

❑ TERMS & NAMES, *PE/TE p. 299*

TEACH

Struggling Readers	On-level	Gifted and Talented	English Learners
TE ❑ Develop a Code of Chivalry, p. 301 **IDR Unit 5** ❑ Reading Skill, p. 4 ❑ Vocabulary Cards, p. 9 ❑ Reteaching Activity, p. 16 **Reading Study Guide** ❑ Lesson 2, p. 79 ❑ RSG Audio CD **California Reading Toolkit, p. L30**	**PE** ❑ Geography: Geography and the Manor System, p. 300 ❑ Daily Life: Life on a Medieval Manor, pp. 304–305 **IDR Unit 5** ❑ Reading Skill: Comparing and Contrasting, p. 4 ❑ Vocabulary Study Guide, p. 8 ❑ Vocabulary Cards, p. 9 ❑ Geography Practice: A Medieval Manor, p. 11	**TE** ❑ Read Chaucer's Prologue, p. 301 **IDR Unit 5** ❑ Primary Source: Aquamanile in the Form of a Mounted Knight, p. 13 ❑ Literature: A Legend of Tintagel Castle, p. 14 **Interdisciplinary Projects** ❑ Language Arts, p. 51 ❑ Art, p. 52	**TE** ❑ Create a Mural, p. 300 **IDRS** ❑ Reading Skill: Comparing and Contrasting, p. 79 **RSG (Spanish)** ❑ Lesson 2, p. 79 ❑ **California Modified Lesson Plans for English Learners, p. 63** ❑ **Multi-Language Glossary of Social Studies Terms**

Lesson Plans

Inclusion

- ❏ **TE:** Divide and Conquer, p. 300
- ❏ **California EasyPlanner CD-ROM:** Reading Skill, Vocabulary Study Guide, Vocabulary Cards

All Students

- ❏ California Reading Toolkit, p. L30

PE

- ❏ Taking Notes: Comparing and Contrasting, p. 298
- ❏ **Extend Lesson 2** Activity: Debate the Life of a Knight, p. 303; Life on a Medieval Manor, pp. 304–305

TE

- ❏ More About Chivalry, p. 301

REVIEW AND ENRICH

Integrate Technology

Transparencies

- ❏ Critical Thinking: CT38 Comparing and Contrasting
- ❏ Map: MT18 Trade in Western Europe, 1100 A.D.
- ❏ Humanities: HT17 Fort la Latte on the Breton Coast

Power Presentations

- ❏ Lesson 2 Lecture Notes

CD-ROMS

- ❏ California EasyPlanner CD-ROM
- ❏ California eEdition CD-ROM
- ❏ California Test Generator CD-ROM

Interdisciplinary Activities

PE

- ❏ Geography: Geography and the Manor System, p. 300

Interdisciplinary Projects

- ❏ Language Arts, p. 51
- ❏ Art, p. 52

Transparencies

- ❏ Geography: MT18 Trade in Western Europe, 1100 A.D.
- ❏ Art: HT17 Fort la Latte on the Breton Coast

ASSESS

Content Assessment

- ❏ Lesson Review, *PE p. 302*
- ❏ Lesson Quiz, *FA p. 155*
- ❏ California Test Generator CD-ROM: Lesson 2 Quiz
- ❏ Integrated Assessment

Standards Practice

- ❏ California Standards Enrichment Workbook, pp. 83–86
- ❏ California Daily Standards Practice Transparencies TT30
- ❏ California Standards Planner and Lesson Plans, p. L59
- ❏ California Online Test Practice: **ClassZone.com**

RETEACH

- ❏ Reteaching Activity, *IDR Unit 5, p. 16*

Feudalism in Europe and Japan

PE = Pupil's Edition   IDRS = IDR in Spanish
TE = Teacher's Edition   RSG = Reading Study Guide
IDR = In-Depth Resources

PLAN AND PREPARE

Lesson Objectives	California Standards
❏ Compare and contrast the feudal societies in Europe and Japan.	REP 4
❏ Analyze the impact early feudalism in Europe and Japan had on current cultures.	How to Teach the California Standards, *TE p. 306*
❏ **Language Objective:** Formulate statements that compare and contrast details from expository text to identify ways people, characters, events, and ideas are alike and different.	

FOCUS AND MOTIVATE

❏ MAIN IDEAS, *PE/TE p. 306*

❏ READING SKILL: Comparing and Contrasting, *PE/TE p. 306*

❏ TERMS & NAMES, *PE/TE p. 307*

TEACH

Struggling Readers	On-level	Gifted and Talented	English Learners
TE	**PE**	**TE**	**TE**
❏ Role Play a Conversation Between a Knight and a Samurai, p. 308	❏ Primary Source: from *Beowulf*, p. 309	❏ Read *Beowulf*, p. 309	❏ Compare and Contrast Issues, p. 308
IDR Unit 5	**IDR Unit 5**	**Interdisciplinary Projects**	**IDRS**
❏ Reading Skill, p. 5	❏ Reading Skill: Comparing and Contrasting, p. 5	❏ Math, p. 49	❏ Reading Skill, p. 80
❏ Reteaching Activity, p. 17	❏ Vocabulary Study Guide, p. 8		**RSG (Spanish)**
Reading Study Guide	❏ Vocabulary Cards, p. 9		❏ Lesson 3, p. 81
❏ Lesson 3, p. 81			❏ **California Modified Lesson Plans for English Learners, p. 65**
❏ RSG Audio CD			❏ **Multi-Language Glossary of Social Studies Terms**
California Reading Toolkit, p. L31			

Lesson Plans

Inclusion

- ❏ **TE:** Role Play, p. 309
- ❏ **California EasyPlanner CD-ROM:** Reading Skill, Vocabulary Study Guide, Reteaching Activity

All Students

- ❏ California Reading Toolkit, p. L31

PE

- ❏ Taking Notes: Comparing and Contrasting, p. 306
- ❏ **Extend Lesson 3** Skillbuilder: Comparing and Contrasting, pp. 312–313

TE

- ❏ More About *Beowulf,* p. 309

REVIEW AND ENRICH

Integrate Technology

Transparencies

- ❏ Critical Thinking: CT39 Comparing and Contrasting
- ❏ Humanities: HT18 Knight Carrying Arms of Verona

Power Presentations

- ❏ Lesson 3 Lecture Notes

CD-ROMS

- ❏ California EasyPlanner CD-ROM
- ❏ California eEdition CD-ROM
- ❏ California Test Generator CD-ROM

Interdisciplinary Activities

TE

- ❏ Language Arts: Describe Gothic Features, p. 310
- ❏ Art: Design a Coat of Arms, p. 310

Interdisciplinary Projects

- ❏ Math, p. 49

Transparencies

- ❏ Art: HT18 Knight Carrying Arms of Verona

ASSESS

Content Assessment

- ❏ Lesson Review, *PE p. 311*
- ❏ Chapter Review, *PE pp. 314–315*
- ❏ Lesson Quiz, *FA p. 156*
- ❏ California Test Generator CD-ROM: Lesson 3 Quiz
- ❏ Integrated Assessment

Standards Practice

- ❏ California Standards Enrichment Workbook, pp. 1–16
- ❏ California Daily Standards Practice Transparencies TT31
- ❏ California Standards Planner and Lesson Plans, p. L61
- ❏ California Online Test Practice: **ClassZone.com**

Struggling Readers	**On-Level**	**Gifted and Talented**	**English Learners**
❏ Test Form A, *FA pp. 157–161*	❏ Test Form B, *FA pp. 162–166*	❏ Test Form C, *FA pp. 167–171*	❏ Test Generator: Forms A, B, and C in Spanish

RETEACH

- ❏ Reteaching Activity, *IDR Unit 5, p. 17*

Name _____ Date _____

The Role of the Catholic Church

INTRODUCE THE CHAPTER

CHAPTER OBJECTIVE: Analyze the religious, political, and social institutions of the later medieval period and the circumstances that led to the emergence of modern states in Europe and the Ottoman Empire.

❏ Before You Read: Predicting, *PE/TE p.316*

❏ Big Ideas: Belief Systems, *PE p. 316, TE p. 317*

❏ Time Line Discussion, *TE p. 316*

❏ Map: Europe and the Ottoman Empire, c. 1500, *PE/TE p. 317*

PE = Pupil's Edition
TE = Teacher's Edition
IDR = In-Depth Resources
IDRS = IDR in Spanish
RSG = Reading Study Guide

STARTING WITH A STORY: The Plague, *PE/TE pp. 318–319;* California eEdition CD-ROM

PLAN AND PREPARE

Lesson Objectives

❏ Analyze the reasons the Church was so powerful in medieval Europe.

❏ Identify causes of conflict between the Church and monarchs.

❏ Describe the contributions of the Church to education.

❏ **Language Objective:** Use the SQ3R strategy to preview the text, formulate purpose-setting questions, and retain information.

California Standards

Reading 2.3

Writing 2.1

7.6.4

7.6.8

How to Teach the California Standards, *TE p. 320*

FOCUS AND MOTIVATE

❏ MAIN IDEAS, *PE/TE p. 320*   ❏ READING SKILL: Summarizing, *PE/TE p. 320*   ❏ TERMS & NAMES, *PE/TE p. 321*

TEACH

Struggling Readers	**On-level**	**Gifted and Talented**	**English Learners**
TE	**PE**	**TE**	**TE**
❏ Identify Topic Sentences, p. 322	❏ Clergy in the Roman Catholic Church, p. 322	❏ Perform a Skit, p. 323	❏ Make Predictions, p. 322
IDR Unit 5	**IDR Unit 5**	**IDR Unit 5**	**IDRS**
❏ Reading Skill: Summarizing, p. 20	❏ Family Newsletter (English and Spanish), pp. 18–19	❏ Primary Source: Lay Investitures by Gregory VII, p. 33	❏ Reading Skill, p. 87
❏ Reteaching Activity, p. 35	❏ Reading Skill: Summarizing, p. 20	**Interdisciplinary Projects**	**RSG (Spanish)**
Reading Study Guide	❏ Vocabulary Study Guide, p. 27	❏ Math, p. 55	❏ Lesson 1, p. 85
❏ Lesson 1, p. 85	❏ Vocabulary Cards, p. 29		❏ **California Modified Lesson Plans for English Learners, p. 67**
❏ RSG Audio CD			❏ **Multi-Language Glossary of Social Studies Terms**
California Reading Toolkit, p. L32			

Inclusion

- ❏ **TE:** Ask and Answer Questions, p. 323

- ❏ **California EasyPlanner CD-ROM:** Reading Skill, Vocabulary Study Guide, Reteaching Activity

All Students

- ❏ California Reading Toolkit, p. L32

PE

- ❏ Taking Notes: Summarizing, p. 320

TE

- ❏ More About Cardinals, p. 322; St. Francis of Assisi, p. 324

REVIEW AND ENRICH

Integrate Technology

Transparencies

- ❏ Critical Thinking: CT41 Summarizing

- ❏ Humanities: HT19 Notre Dame

Power Presentations

- ❏ Lesson 1 Lecture Notes

CD-ROMS

- ❏ California EasyPlanner CD-ROM

- ❏ California eEdition CD-ROM

- ❏ California Test Generator CD-ROM

Interdisciplinary Activities

TE

- ❏ Language Arts: Investigate Religious Orders, p. 324; Create a Catalog, p. 324

Interdisciplinary Projects

- ❏ Math, p. 55

Transparencies

- ❏ Art: HT19 Notre Dame

ASSESS

Content Assessment

- ❏ Lesson Review, *PE p. 325*

- ❏ Lesson Quiz, *FA p. 172*

- ❏ California Test Generator CD-ROM: Lesson 1 Quiz

- ❏ Integrated Assessment

Standards Practice

- ❏ California Standards Enrichment Workbook, pp. 89–90, 97–98

- ❏ California Daily Standards Practice Transparencies TT32

- ❏ California Standards Planner and Lesson Plans, p. L63

- ❏ California Online Test Practice: **ClassZone.com**

RETEACH

- ❏ Reteaching Activity, *IDR Unit 5, p. 35*

CHAPTER **10** Lesson 2   Lesson Plan

The Crusades

PE = Pupil's Edition   IDRS = IDR in Spanish
TE = Teacher's Edition   RSG = Reading Study Guide
IDR = In-Depth Resources

PLAN AND PREPARE

Lesson Objectives	California Standards
❑ Explain the reasons for the Crusades.	7.6.6
❑ Describe the results of each Crusade.	7.6.9
❑ Examine the effects of the Crusades on the economies and societies of Europe and Palestine.	How to Teach the California Standards, *TE p. 326*
❑ **Language Objective:** Construct a time line to depict the sequence of historical events.	

FOCUS AND MOTIVATE

❑ MAIN IDEAS, *PE/TE p. 326*

❑ READING SKILL: Explaining Chronological Order and Sequence, *PE/TE p. 326*

❑ TERMS & NAMES, *PE/TE p. 327*

TEACH

Struggling Readers	On-level	Gifted and Talented	English Learners
TE	**IDR Unit 5**	**TE**	**TE**
❑ Construct a Cause-and-Effect Chart, p. 330	❑ Reading Skill: Explaining Chronological Order and Sequence, p. 21	❑ Analyze Literature, p. 330	❑ Create a Time Line, p. 328
IDR Unit 5	❑ Skillbuilder Practice: Determining Historical Content, p. 26	**Interdisciplinary Projects**	**IDRS**
❑ Reading Skill, 21		❑ Language Arts, p. 57	❑ Reading Skill, p. 88
❑ Reteaching Activity, p. 36	❑ Vocabulary Study Guide, p. 27		**RSG (Spanish)**
Reading Study Guide	❑ Vocabulary Cards, p. 29		❑ Lesson 2, p. 87
❑ Lesson 2, p. 87			❑ **California Modified Lesson Plans for English Learners, p. 64**
❑ RSG Audio CD			❑ **Multi-Language Glossary of Social Studies Terms**
California Reading Toolkit, p. L33			

Lesson Plans

Inclusion

- ❏ **TE:** Illustrate Important Points, p. 328
- ❏ **California EasyPlanner CD-ROM:** Reading Skill, Vocabulary Study Guide, Reteaching Activity

All Students

- ❏ California Reading Toolkit, p. L33

PE

- ❏ Taking Notes: Explaining Chronological Order and Sequence, p. 326

TE

- ❏ More About Saladin and Richard the Lion-Hearted, p. 329; The Spanish Inquisition, p. 330; The Auto-Da-Fé, p. 330

REVIEW AND ENRICH

Integrate Technology

Transparencies

- ❏ Critical Thinking: CT42 Explaining Chronological Order and Sequence
- ❏ Map: MT19 Christian and Muslim Lands, A.D. 1000

Power Presentations

- ❏ Lesson 2 Lecture Notes

CD-ROMS

- ❏ California EasyPlanner CD-ROM
- ❏ California eEdition CD-ROM
- ❏ California Test Generator CD-ROM

Interdisciplinary Activities

TE

- ❏ Art: Create a Brochure, p. 329
- ❏ Language Arts: Write an Article, p. 329

Interdisciplinary Projects

- ❏ Language Arts, p. 57

Transparencies

- ❏ Geography: MT19 Christian and Muslim Lands, A.D. 1000

ASSESS

Content Assessment

- ❏ Lesson Review, *PE p. 331*
- ❏ Lesson Quiz, *FA p. 173*
- ❏ California Test Generator CD-ROM: Lesson 2 Quiz
- ❏ Integrated Assessment

Standards Practice

- ❏ California Standards Enrichment Workbook, pp. 93–94, 99–100
- ❏ California Daily Standards Practice Transparencies TT33
- ❏ California Standards Planner and Lesson Plans, p. L65
- ❏ California Online Test Practice: **ClassZone.com**

RETEACH

- ❏ Reteaching Activity, *IDR Unit 5, p. 36*

CHAPTER 10 Lesson 3

Plague and the Hundred Years' War

PE = Pupil's Edition   IDRS = IDR in Spanish
TE = Teacher's Edition   RSG = Reading Study Guide
IDR = In-Depth Resources

PLAN AND PREPARE

Lesson Objectives

❏ Describe the effects of the plague on European society.

❏ Identify the causes and outcome of the Hundred Years' War.

❏ Explain the significance of new warfare technologies developed during the Hundred Years' War.

❏ Trace the emergence of modern European nations.

❏ **Language Objective:** Create a concept cluster of words and terms from the lesson that are related to *bubonic plague*.

California Standards

7.6

7.6.7

HI 2

How to Teach the California Standards, *TE p. 332*

FOCUS AND MOTIVATE

❏ MAIN IDEAS, *PE/TE p. 332*

❏ READING SKILL: Finding Main Ideas, *PE/TE p. 332*

❏ TERMS & NAMES, *PE/TE p. 333*

TEACH

Struggling Readers	On-level	Gifted and Talented	English Learners
TE	**PE**	**TE**	**TE**
❏ Broadcast the News, p. 335	❏ History Makers: Joan of Arc, p. 335	❏ Read Primary Sources, p. 334	❏ Create Word Webs, p. 334
❏ Report on Germs, p. 338	**IDR Unit 5**	❏ Compare Treatment Methods, p. 338	**IDRS**
IDR Unit 5	❏ Reading Skill: Finding Main Ideas, p. 22	**IDR Unit 5**	❏ Reading Skill, p. 89
❏ Reading Skill, p. 22	❏ Vocabulary Study Guide, p. 27	❏ Primary Source: Decameron by Boccaccio, p. 34	**RSG (Spanish)**
❏ Reteaching Activity, p. 37	❏ Vocabulary Cards, p. 29	**Interdisciplinary Projects**	❏ Lesson 3, p. 89
Reading Study Guide	❏ Geography Practice: The Norman Conquest, p. 32	❏ Science, p. 56	❏ **California Modified Lesson Plans for English Learners, p. 71**
❏ Lesson 3, p. 89		**History Makers**	❏ **Multi-Language Glossary of Social Studies Terms**
❏ RSG Audio CD		❏ Joan of Arc, p. 19	
California Reading Toolkit, p. L34			

Inclusion

- [ ] **TE:** Make a Collage, p. 335

- [ ] **California EasyPlanner CD-ROM:** Reading Skill, Vocabulary Study Guide, Reteaching Activity

All Students

- [ ] California Reading Toolkit, p. L34

PE

- [ ] Taking Notes: Finding Main Ideas, p. 332

- [ ] **Extend Lesson 3** Connect to Today: Epidemics, pp. 338–339

TE

- [ ] More About Warding Off the Plague, p. 334

REVIEW AND ENRICH

Integrate Technology

Transparencies

- [ ] Critical Thinking: CT43 Finding Main Ideas

Power Presentations

- [ ] Lesson 3 Lecture Notes

CD-ROMS

- [ ] California EasyPlanner CD-ROM

- [ ] California eEdition CD-ROM

- [ ] California Test Generator CD-ROM

Interdisciplinary Activities

TE

- [ ] Math: Compare Epidemics, p. 336

- [ ] Science: Hold a Debate, p. 336

Interdisciplinary Projects

- [ ] Science, p. 56

ASSESS

Content Assessment

- [ ] Lesson Review, *PE p. 337*

- [ ] Lesson Quiz, *FA p. 174*

- [ ] California Test Generator CD-ROM: Lesson 3 Quiz

- [ ] Integrated Assessment

Standards Practice

- [ ] California Standards Enrichment Workbook, pp. 95–96

- [ ] California Daily Standards Practice Transparencies TT34

- [ ] California Standards Planner and Lesson Plans, p. L67

- [ ] California Online Test Practice: **ClassZone.com**

RETEACH

- [ ] Reteaching Activity, *IDR Unit 5, p. 37*

Lesson Plans

Changes in Government and Economics

PE = *Pupil's Edition*   IDRS = *IDR in Spanish*
TE = *Teacher's Edition*   RSG = *Reading Study Guide*
IDR = *In-Depth Resources*

PLAN AND PREPARE

Lesson Objectives

❑ Describe changes in England's legal system in the 12th and 13th centuries.

❑ Explain the growth of representative government in England.

❑ Identify the influence of English legal and political innovations on later governments.

❑ **Language Objective:** Compare legal practices of medieval England and legal practices today.

California Standards

7.6

7.6.5

HI 3

How to Teach the California Standards, *TE p. 340*

FOCUS AND MOTIVATE

❑ MAIN IDEAS, *PE/TE p. 340*

❑ READING SKILL: Making Generalizations, *PE/TE p. 340*

❑ TERMS & NAMES, *PE/TE p. 341*

TEACH

Struggling Readers	**On-level**	**Gifted and Talented**	**English Learners**
TE	**PE**	**TE**	**TE**
❑ Answer Essential Questions, p. 344	❑ Primary Source: from the Magna Carta, p. 342	❑ Chart Similarities, p. 344	❑ Make Comparisons, p. 342
❑ Map the Plot, p. 348		❑ Write a Sequel, p. 348	❑ Analyze Story Structure, p. 347
IDR Unit 5	**IDR Unit 5**	**Interdisciplinary Projects**	**IDRS**
❑ Reading Skill, p. 23	❑ Reading Skill: Making Generalizations, p. 23	❑ Art, p. 58	❑ Reading Skill, p. 90
❑ Reteaching Activity, p. 38	❑ Vocabulary Study Guide, p. 27		**RSG (Spanish)**
Reading Study Guide	❑ Vocabulary Cards, p. 29		❑ Lesson 4, p. 91
❑ Lesson 4, p. 91			❑ **California Modified Lesson Plans for English Learners, p. 73**
❑ RSG Audio CD			
California Reading Toolkit, p. L35			❑ **Multi-Language Glossary**

Lesson Plans

Inclusion

- ❏ **TE:** Use Self-Questioning, p. 342; Paraphrase, p. 347

- ❏ **California EasyPlanner CD-ROM:** Reading Skill, Vocabulary Study Guide, Reteaching Activity

All Students

- ❏ California Reading Toolkit, p. L35

PE

- ❏ Taking Notes: Understanding Cause and Effect, p. 58

- ❏ **Extend Lesson 4** Reader's Theater: The Barons Confront King John, pp. 346–349

TE

- ❏ More About The Magna Carta, p. 342; Habeas Corpus, p. 344; King John, p. 346; The Rebellious Barons, p. 348; Events after Runnymeade, p. 349

REVIEW AND ENRICH

Integrate Technology

Transparencies

- ❏ Critical Thinking: CT44 Making Generalizations

Power Presentations

- ❏ Lesson 4 Lecture Notes

CD-ROMS

- ❏ California EasyPlanner CD-ROM

- ❏ California eEdition CD-ROM

- ❏ California Test Generator CD-ROM

Interdisciplinary Activities

TE

- ❏ Language Arts: Interview a Historical Figure, p. 343; Collect Facts, p. 343

Interdisciplinary Projects

- ❏ Art, p. 58

ASSESS

Content Assessment

- ❏ Lesson Review, *PE p. 345*

- ❏ Lesson Quiz, *FA p. 175*

- ❏ California Test Generator CD-ROM: Lesson 4 Quiz

- ❏ Integrated Assessment

Standards Practice

- ❏ California Standards Enrichment Workbook, pp. 91–92

- ❏ California Daily Standards Practice Transparencies TT35

- ❏ California Standards Planner and Lesson Plans, p. L69

- ❏ California Online Test Practice: **ClassZone.com**

RETEACH

- ❏ Reteaching Activity, *IDR Unit 5, p. 38*

Lesson Plans

The Ottoman Empire

PE = Pupil's Edition	IDRS = IDR in Spanish
TE = Teacher's Edition	RSG = Reading Study Guide
IDR = In-Depth Resources	

PLAN AND PREPARE

Lesson Objectives

❑ Explain the structure of the Ottoman Empire and its legal system.

❑ Trace the expansion of the Ottoman Empire.

❑ Describe the status of various religious groups, enslaved people, and women in the Ottoman Empire.

❑ **Language Objective:** Use structural and context clues to define words to gain a deeper understanding of the information read.

California Standards

HI 1
How to Teach the California Standards, *TE p. 350*

FOCUS AND MOTIVATE

❑ MAIN IDEAS, *PE/TE p. 350*

❑ READING SKILL: Finding Main Ideas, *PE/TE p. 350*

❑ TERMS & NAMES, *PE/TE p. 351*

TEACH

Struggling Readers	On-level	Gifted and Talented	English Learners
TE	**IDR Unit 5**	**TE**	**TE**
❑ Find Significant Details, p. 353	❑ Reading Skill: Finding Main Ideas, p. 24	❑ Design a Review Board Game, p. 353	❑ Make Comparisons, p. 352
IDR Unit 5	❑ Vocabulary Study Guide, p. 27	**Humanities Transparencies**	**IDRS**
❑ Reading Skill, p. 24	❑ Vocabulary Cards, p. 29	❑ HT20 Ottoman Tile	❑ Reading Skill, p. 91
❑ Reteaching Activity, p. 39			**RSG (Spanish)**
Reading Study Guide			❑ Lesson 5, p. 93
❑ Lesson 5, p. 93			❑ **California Modified Lesson Plans for English Learners, p. 75**
❑ RSG Audio CD			❑ **Multi-Language Glossary of Social Studies Terms**
California Reading Toolkit, p. L36			

Lesson Plans

Inclusion

- ☐ **TE:** Take Audio Notes, p. 352
- ☐ **California EasyPlanner CD-ROM:** Reading Skill, Vocabulary Study Guide, Reteaching Activity

All Students

- ☐ California Reading Toolkit, p. L36

PE

- ☐ Taking Notes: Finding Main Ideas, p. 350
- ☐ **Extend Lesson 5** Activity: Trade with Your Neighbor, p. 355

TE

- ☐ More About Suleyman's Law Code, p. 352

REVIEW AND ENRICH

Integrate Technology

Transparencies

- ☐ Critical Thinking: CT45 Finding Main Ideas
- ☐ Map: MT20 The Ottoman Empire in Europe
- ☐ Humanities: HT20 Ottoman Tile

Power Presentations

- ☐ Lesson 5 Lecture Notes

CD-ROMS

- ☐ California EasyPlanner CD-ROM
- ☐ California eEdition CD-ROM
- ☐ California Test Generator CD-ROM

Interdisciplinary Activities

Transparencies

- ☐ Geography: MT20 The Ottoman Empire in Europe
- ☐ Art: HT20 Ottoman Tile

ASSESS

Content Assessment

- ☐ Lesson Review, *PE p. 354*
- ☐ Chapter Review, *PE pp. 356–357*
- ☐ Lesson Quiz, *FA p. 176*
- ☐ California Test Generator CD-ROM: Lesson 5 Quiz
- ☐ Integrated Assessment

Standards Practice

- ☐ California Standards Enrichment Workbook, pp. 1–16
- ☐ California Daily Standards Practice Transparencies TT36
- ☐ California Standards Planner and Lesson Plans, p. L71
- ☐ California Online Test Practice: **ClassZone.com**

Struggling Readers	On-Level	Gifted and Talented	English Learners
☐ Test Form A, *FA pp. 177–180*	☐ Test Form B, *FA pp. 181–184*	☐ Test Form C, *FA pp. 185–188*	☐ Test Generator: Forms A, B, and C in Spanish

RETEACH

- ☐ Reteaching Activity, *IDR Unit 5, p. 39*

Lesson Plans

CHAPTER 11 Lesson 1   **Lesson Plan**

Geography and Agriculture in Meso-America

INTRODUCE THE UNIT AND CHAPTER

UNIT 6: INTERACT WITH HISTORY: The Caracol Observatory, Chickén Itzá, about 1000 A.D., *PE/TE pp. 360–361*

CHAPTER OBJECTIVE: Analyze how geography and culture influenced civilization in Meso-America.

☐ Before You Read: K-W-L, *PE/TE p.362*
☐ Big Ideas: Culture, *PE p. 362, TE p. 363*
☐ Time Line Discussion, *TE p. 362*
☐ Map: Present-Day Mexico and Central America: Physical, *PE/TE p. 363*

> *PE = Pupil's Edition*
> *TE = Teacher's Edition*
> *IDR = In-Depth Resources*
> *IDRS = IDR in Spanish*
> *RSG = Reading Study Guide*

STARTING WITH A STORY: Take Me Out to the Ball Game!, *PE/TE pp. 364–365;* California eEdition CD-ROM

PLAN AND PREPARE

Lesson Objectives

☐ Describe the geographic landforms of Meso-America.

☐ Explain the different climates of Meso-America.

☐ Analyze how the geographic diversity of Meso-America produced a variety of natural resources and crops.

☐ **Language Objective:** Create a concept cluster of words and terms from the lesson that are related to the geography of Meso-America.

California Standards

Reading 3.2

Writing 2.1

7.7.1

CST 3

REP 3

How to Teach the California Standards, *TE p. 366*

FOCUS AND MOTIVATE

☐ MAIN IDEAS, *PE/TE p. 366*	☐ READING SKILL: Finding Main Ideas, *PE/TE p. 366*
☐ TERMS & NAMES, *PE/TE p. 367*	

TEACH

Struggling Readers	**On-level**	**Gifted and Talented**	**English Learners**
TE	**PE**	**TE**	**TE**
☐ Map the Climate Zones, p. 368	☐ Geography: Elevation and Climate in Central America, p. 369	☐ Create a Maize Exhibit, p. 370	☐ Make Word Webs, p. 368
IDR Unit 6		**Interdisciplinary Projects**	**IDRS**
☐ Reading Skill: Finding Main Ideas, p. 3	**IDR Unit 6**	☐ Science, p. 62	☐ Reading Skill, p. 98
☐ Reteaching Activity, p. 15	☐ Family Newsletter (English and Spanish), pp. 1–2		**RSG (Spanish)**
Reading Study Guide	☐ Reading Skill: Finding Main Ideas, p. 3		☐ Lesson 1, p. 105
☐ Lesson 1, p. 105	☐ Vocabulary Study Guide, p. 8		☐ **California Modified Lesson Plans for English Learners, p. 77**
☐ RSG Audio CD	☐ Vocabulary Cards, p. 9		☐ **Multi-Language Glossary of Social Studies Terms**
California Reading Toolkit, p. L37			

Lesson Plans

Inclusion

- ☐ **TE:** Make a Climate Collage, p. 370
- ☐ **California EasyPlanner CD-ROM:** Reading Skill, Vocabulary Study Guide, Reteaching Activity

All Students

- ☐ California Reading Toolkit, p. L37

PE

- ☐ Taking Notes: Finding Main Ideas, p. 366

TE

- ☐ More About Average Annual Precipitation, p. 368; Cacao, p. 370

REVIEW AND ENRICH

Integrate Technology

Transparencies

- ☐ Critical Thinking: CT47 Finding Main Ideas
- ☐ Map: MT21 Volcanoes of Middle America

Power Presentations

- ☐ Lesson 1 Lecture Notes

CD-ROMS

- ☐ California EasyPlanner CD-ROM
- ☐ California eEdition CD-ROM
- ☐ California Test Generator CD-ROM

Interdisciplinary Activities

PE

- ☐ Geography: Elevation and Climate in Central America, p. 369

TE

- ☐ Science: Research the Quetzal, p. 369
- ☐ Science: Create a Meso-American Menu, p. 369

Interdisciplinary Projects

- ☐ Science, p. 62

Transparencies

- ☐ Geography: MT21 Volcanoes of Middle America

ASSESS

Content Assessment

- ☐ Lesson Review, *PE p. 371*
- ☐ Lesson Quiz, *FA p. 193*
- ☐ California Test Generator CD-ROM: Lesson 1 Quiz
- ☐ Integrated Assessment

Standards Practice

- ☐ California Standards Enrichment Workbook, pp. 101–102
- ☐ California Daily Standards Practice Transparencies TT37
- ☐ California Standards Planner and Lesson Plans, p. L73
- ☐ California Online Test Practice: **ClassZone.com**

RETEACH

- ☐ Reteaching Activity, *IDR Unit 6, p. 15*

The Olmec Civilization

PE = Pupil's Edition   IDRS = IDR in Spanish
TE = Teacher's Edition   RSG = Reading Study Guide
IDR = In-Depth Resources

PLAN AND PREPARE

Lesson Objectives

❑ Trace the role of agriculture in the development of the Olmec culture.

❑ Examine historical evidence relating to Olmec culture.

❑ Analyze the effects of Olmec beliefs and practices on other cultures.

❑ **Language Objective:** Create a mural to show how the Olmec were able to develop as the first major civilization in Meso-America.

California Standards

7.7
HI 2
CST 2
How to Teach the California Standards, *TE p. 372*

FOCUS AND MOTIVATE

❑   MAIN IDEAS, *PE/TE p. 372*

❑   READING SKILL: Summarizing, *PE/TE p. 372*

❑   TERMS & NAMES, *PE/TE p. 373*

TEACH

Struggling Readers	**On-level**	**Gifted and Talented**	**English Learners**
TE	**PE**	**TE**	**TE**
❑ Produce a News Report, p. 374	❑ Primary Source: Olmec Glyph, p. 375	❑ Advertise Olmec Wares, p. 376	❑ Draw a Mural, p. 374
IDR Unit 6	**IDR Unit 6**	❑ Write a Summary Paragraph, p. 378	**IDRS**
❑ Reading Skill: Summarizing, p. 4	❑ Reading Skill: Summarizing, p. 4	**IDR Unit 6**	❑ Reading Skill, p. 12
❑ Reteaching Activity, p. 16	❑ Vocabulary Study Guide, p. 8	❑ Geography Practice: Zapotec Sites in Oaxaca, Mexico, p. 11	**RSG (Spanish)**
Reading Study Guide	❑ Vocabulary Cards, p. 9	**Interdisciplinary Projects**	❑ Lesson 2, p. 99
❑ Lesson 2, p. 99		❑ Physical Education, p. 64	❑ **California Modified Lesson Plans for English Learners, p. 79**
❑ RSG Audio CD			❑ **Multi-Language Glossary of Social Studies Terms**
California Reading Toolkit, p. L38			

Lesson Plans

Inclusion

- ❏ **TE:** Create a Graphic Organizer, p. 376; Create a Human Time Line, p. 378
- ❏ **California EasyPlanner CD-ROM:** Reading Skill, Vocabulary Study Guide, Reteaching Activity

All Students

- ❏ California Reading Toolkit, p. L38

PE

- ❏ Taking Notes: Summarizing, p. 372
- ❏ **Extend Lesson 2** Skillbuilder: Explaining Chronological Order and Sequence, pp. 378–379

TE

- ❏ More About Olmec Jewelry, p. 374; Olmec Monuments, p. 375; La Venta, p. 379

REVIEW AND ENRICH

Integrate Technology

Transparencies

- ❏ Critical Thinking: CT48 Summarizing
- ❏ Humanities: HT21 Head of Quetzalcoatl, Teotihuacán

Power Presentations

- ❏ Lesson 2 Lecture Notes

CD-ROMS

- ❏ California EasyPlanner CD-ROM
- ❏ California eEdition CD-ROM
- ❏ California Test Generator CD-ROM

Interdisciplinary Activities

TE

- ❏ Physical Education: Play Pok-a-Tok, p. 375
- ❏ Language Arts: Create a Glyph Message, p. 375

Interdisciplinary Projects

- ❏ Physical Education, p. 64

Transparencies

- ❏ Art: HT21 Head of Quetzalcoatl, Teotihuacán

ASSESS

Content Assessment

- ❏ Lesson Review, *PE p. 377*
- ❏ Lesson Quiz, *FA p. 194*
- ❏ California Test Generator CD-ROM: Lesson 2 Quiz
- ❏ Integrated Assessment

Standards Practice

- ❏ California Standards Enrichment Workbook, pp. 1–16
- ❏ California Daily Standards Practice Transparencies TT38
- ❏ California Standards Planner and Lesson Plans, p. L75
- ❏ California Online Test Practice: **ClassZone.com**

RETEACH

- ❏ Reteaching Activity, *IDR Unit 6, p. 16*

The Mayan Civilization

PE = Pupil's Edition   IDRS = IDR in Spanish
TE = Teacher's Edition   RSG = Reading Study Guide
IDR = In-Depth Resources

PLAN AND PREPARE

Lesson Objectives

❏ Describe the rise and fall of the Mayan civilization.

❏ Analyze the Mayan way of life and Mayan accomplishments.

❏ **Language Objective:** Classify details by category to make nonfiction text more comprehensible and meaningful.

California Standards

7.7.2
7.7.3
7.7.4
7.7.5
How to Teach the California Standards, *TE p. 380*

FOCUS AND MOTIVATE

❏ MAIN IDEAS, *PE/TE p. 380*

❏ READING SKILL: Framing Historical Questions, *PE/TE p. 380*

❏ TERMS & NAMES, *PE/TE p. 381*

TEACH

Struggling Readers	**On-level**	**Gifted and Talented**	**English Learners**
TE	**PE**	**TE**	**IDRS**
❏ Outline a Passage, p. 385	❏ History Makers: Pacal II of Palenque, p. 384	❏ Make a Storyboard, p. 388	❏ Reading Skill, p. 24
IDR Unit 6	**IDR Unit 6**	**IDR Unit 6**	**RSG (Spanish)**
❏ Reading Skill, p. 5	❏ Reading Skill: Framing Historical Questions, p. 5	❏ Primary Source, p. 13	❏ Lesson 3, p. 101
❏ Reteaching Activity, p. 17		❏ Literature: *Popol Vuh*, p. 14	❏ **California Modified Lesson Plans for English Learners, p. 81**
Reading Study Guide	❏ Vocabulary Study Guide, p. 8	**Interdisciplinary Projects**	❏ **Multi-Language Glossary of Social Studies Terms**
❏ Lesson 3, p. 101	❏ Vocabulary Cards, p. 9	❏ Math, p. 61	
❏ RSG Audio CD		❏ Language Arts, p. 63	
California Reading Toolkit, p. L39			

Lesson Plans

Inclusion

- ❑ **TE:** Create a List, p. 388
- ❑ **California EasyPlanner CD-ROM:** Reading Skill, Vocabulary Study Guide, Reteaching Activity

All Students

- ❑ California Reading Toolkit, p. L39

PE
- ❑ Taking Notes: Framing Historical Questions, p. 380
- ❑ **Extend Lesson 3** Activity: Count the Mayan Way, p. 387; Connect to Today: The Mayan Legacy, pp. 388–389

TE
- ❑ More About Mayan Books, p. 385

REVIEW AND ENRICH

Integrate Technology

Transparencies
- ❑ Critical Thinking: CT49 Framing Historical Questions
- ❑ Map: MT22 Chichén Itzá
- ❑ Humanities: HT22 Caracol Observatory, Chichén Itzá

Power Presentations
- ❑ Lesson 3 Lecture Notes

CD-ROMS
- ❑ California EasyPlanner CD-ROM
- ❑ California eEdition CD-ROM
- ❑ California Test Generator CD-ROM

Interdisciplinary Activities

TE
- ❑ Language Arts: Plan a Travel Brochure, p. 384
- ❑ Science: Investigate Mayan Astronomy, p. 384

Transparencies
- ❑ Geography: MT22 Chichén Itzá
- ❑ Art: HT22 Caracol Observatory, Chichén Itzá

ASSESS

Content Assessment

- ❑ Lesson Review, *PE p. 386*
- ❑ Chapter Review, *PE pp. 390–391*
- ❑ Lesson Quiz, *FA p. 195*
- ❑ California Test Generator CD-ROM: Lesson 3 Quiz
- ❑ Integrated Assessment

Standards Practice

- ❑ California Standards Enrichment Workbook, pp. 103–110
- ❑ California Daily Standards Practice Transparencies TT39
- ❑ California Standards Planner and Lesson Plans, p. L77
- ❑ California Online Test Practice: **ClassZone.com**

Struggling Readers	On-Level	Gifted and Talented	English Learners
❑ Test Form A, *FA pp. 196–200*	❑ Test Form B, *FA pp. 201–205*	❑ Test Form C, *FA pp. 206–210*	❑ Test Generator: Forms A, B, and C in Spanish

RETEACH

- ❑ Reteaching Activity, *IDR Unit 6, p. 17*

Lesson Plans

The Aztecs

INTRODUCE THE CHAPTER

CHAPTER OBJECTIVE: Describe the cultures, beliefs, and legacies of the Aztec and Inca empires.

❑ Before You Read: Preview Map, *PE/TE p. 392*
❑ Big Ideas: Belief Systems, *PE p.392, TE p. 393*
❑ Time Line Discussion, *TE p. 392*
❑ Map: The Americas, A.D. 1200–1500, *PE/TE p. 393*

> *PE = Pupil's Edition*
> *TE = Teacher's Edition*
> *IDR = In-Depth Resources*
> *IDRS = IDR in Spanish*
> *RSG = Reading Study Guide*

STARTING WITH A STORY: Turning Swamps into Floating Gardens, *PE/TE pp. 394–395;* California eEdition CD-ROM

PLAN AND PREPARE

Lesson Objectives

❑ Trace the development of the Aztec empire.
❑ Analyze the Aztec government.
❑ Describe achievements the Aztecs made in art, architecture, and astronomy.
❑ **Language Objective:** Create a concept cluster of words and terms from the lesson that are related to the geography of the Valley of Mexico.

California Standards

Reading 2.3
Writing 2.4
7.7.1, 7.7.2, 7.7.3, 7.7.4, 7.7.5
How to Teach the California Standards, *TE p. 396*

FOCUS AND MOTIVATE

❑ MAIN IDEAS, *PE/TE p. 396*
❑ TERMS & NAMES, *PE/TE p. 397*
❑ READING SKILL: Explaining Chronological Order and Sequence, *PE/TE p. 396*

TEACH

Struggling Readers	On-level	Gifted and Talented	English Learners
TE	**PE**	**TE**	**TE**
❑ Make a Plan for Tenochtitlán, p. 398	❑ Primary Source: Aztec Codices, p. 401	❑ Draw Aztec Warriors, p. 400	❑ Locate Geography Words, p. 398
❑ Ask Questions, p. 405	**IDR Unit 6**	**Interdisciplinary Projects**	❑ Create a Story Structure Organizer, p. 405
IDR Unit 6	❑ Family Newsletter (English and Spanish), pp. 18–19	❑ Science, p. 68	**IDRS**
❑ Reading Skill: Explaining Chronological Order and Sequence, p. 20	❑ Reading Skill: Explaining Chronological Order and Sequence, p. 20	❑ Art, p. 70	❑ Reading Skill, p. 11
❑ Reteaching Activity, p. 31	❑ Skillbuilder Practice, p. 23		RSG (Spanish)
Reading Study Guide	❑ Vocabulary Cards, p. 25		❑ Lesson 1, p. 105
❑ Lesson 1, p. 105	❑ Geography Practice: Aztec Empire, 1520, p. 27		❑ **California Modified Lesson Plans for English Learners, p. 83**
❑ RSG Audio CD			❑ **Multi-Language Glossary of Social Studies Terms**
California Reading Toolkit, p. L40			

Lesson Plans

Inclusion

❑ **TE:** Take Audio Notes, p. 400

❑ **California EasyPlanner CD-ROM:** Reading Skill, Vocabulary Study Guide, Reteaching Activity

All Students

❑ California Reading Toolkit, p. L40

PE

❑ Taking Notes: Explaining Chronological Order and Sequence, p. 396

❑ **Extend Lesson 1** Activity: Create a Picture Story, p. 403; Literature Connections: The Eagle on the Prickly Pear, pp. 404–407

TE

❑ More About Tenochtitlán, p. 398; Aztec Trade, p. 398; Aztec Religion, p. 399; Montezuma II, p. 400; Huitzilopochtli, p. 404; Aztec Beliefs, p. 405; Copil and Huitzilopochtli, p. 406; Names, p. 406

REVIEW AND ENRICH

Integrate Technology

Transparencies

❑ Critical Thinking: CT51 Explaining Chronological Order and Sequence

Power Presentations

❑ Lesson 1 Lecture Notes

CD-ROMS

❑ California EasyPlanner CD-ROM

❑ California eEdition CD-ROM

❑ California Test Generator CD-ROM

Interdisciplinary Activities

TE

❑ Art: Design an Aztec Mural, p. 399

❑ Science: Plan *Chinampas,* p. 399

❑ Language Arts: Plan an Archaeology Tour, p. 401; Montezuma's Capture, p. 401; Retell the Story, p. 406

❑ Art: Create a Picture Dictionary of Aztec Gods, p. 406

Interdisciplinary Projects

❑ Science, p. 68

❑ Art, p. 70

ASSESS

Content Assessment

❑ Lesson Review, *PE p. 402*

❑ Lesson Quiz, *FA p. 211*

❑ California Test Generator CD-ROM: Lesson 1 Quiz

❑ Integrated Assessment

Standards Practice

❑ California Standards Enrichment Workbook, pp. 101–110

❑ California Daily Standards Practice Transparencies TT40

❑ California Standards Planner and Lesson Plans, p. L79

❑ California Online Test Practice: **ClassZone.com**

RETEACH

❑ Reteaching Activity, *IDR Unit 6, p. 31*

Lesson Plans

The Inca

PE = Pupil's Edition	IDRS = IDR in Spanish
TE = Teacher's Edition	RSG = Reading Study Guide
IDR = In-Depth Resources	

PLAN AND PREPARE

Lesson Objectives

- ❑ Analyze the rise and fall of the Inca empire.
- ❑ Explore the cultural legacy of the Inca empire.
- ❑ **Language Objective:** Create a concept cluster of words and terms from the lesson that are related to the geography of the Andes Mountains.

California Standards

7.7.1
7.7.2
7.7.3
7.7.4
7.7.5

How to Teach the California Standards, *TE p. 408*

FOCUS AND MOTIVATE

- ❑ MAIN IDEAS, *PE/TE p. 408*
- ❑ READING SKILL: Categorizing, *PE/TE p. 408*
- ❑ TERMS & NAMES, *PE/TE p. 409*

TEACH

Struggling Readers

TE

- ❑ Illustrate Incan Class Structure, p. 412
- ❑ Connect Captions to Illustrations, p. 414

IDR Unit 6

- ❑ Reading Skill, p. 21
- ❑ Reteaching Activity, p. 32

Reading Study Guide

- ❑ Lesson 2, p. 109
- ❑ RSG Audio CD

California Reading Toolkit, p. L41

On-level

PE

- ❑ History Makers: Pachacuti, p. 410

IDR Unit 6

- ❑ Reading Skill: Categorizing, p. 21
- ❑ Vocabulary Study Guide, p. 24
- ❑ Vocabulary Cards, p. 25

Gifted and Talented

TE

- ❑ Design a Crossword Puzzle, p. 412

History Makers

- ❑ Pachacuti, p. 23

English Learners

TE

- ❑ Create an Andes Word Web, p. 410

IDRS

- ❑ Reading Skill, p. 108

RSG (Spanish)

- ❑ Lesson 2, p. 109
- ❑ **California Modified Lesson Plans for English Learners, p. 85**
- ❑ **Multi-Language Glossary of Social Studies Terms**

Lesson Plans

Inclusion

- ❏ **TE:** Divide and Conquer, p. 410; Student Teachers, p. 414
- ❏ **California EasyPlanner CD-ROM:** Reading Skill, Vocabulary Study Guide, Reteaching Activity

All Students

- ❏ California Reading Toolkit, p. L41

PE

- ❏ Taking Notes: Categorizing, p. 408
- ❏ **Extend Lesson 2** Daily Life: Runners on the Royal Road, pp. 416–417

TE

- ❏ More About Machu Picchu, p. 410; Pachacuti, p. 410; Incan Agriculture, p. 411; Incan Society, p. 412; Francisco Pizarro, p. 413; Incan Roads and Bridges, p. 417

REVIEW AND ENRICH

Integrate Technology

Transparencies

- ❏ Critical Thinking: CT52 Categorizing

Power Presentations

- ❏ Lesson 2 Lecture Notes

CD-ROMS

- ❏ California EasyPlanner CD-ROM
- ❏ California eEdition CD-ROM
- ❏ California Test Generator CD-ROM

Interdisciplinary Activities

TE

- ❏ Science: Create Fact Cards about Llamas and Alpacas, p. 411
- ❏ Math: Calculate Fleece Yield, p. 411
- ❏ Language Arts: Have a Debate, p. 413; Give a News Report on the Fall of the Inca Empire, p. 413; Write an Acrostic Poem, p. 416
- ❏ Physical Education: Plan a Relay Race, p. 416

ASSESS

Content Assessment

- ❏ Lesson Review, *PE p. 415*
- ❏ Chapter Review, *PE pp. 418–419*
- ❏ Lesson Quiz, *FA p. 212*
- ❏ California Test Generator CD-ROM: Lesson 2 Quiz
- ❏ Integrated Assessment

Standards Practice

- ❏ California Standards Enrichment Workbook, pp. 101–110
- ❏ California Daily Standards Practice Transparencies TT41
- ❏ California Standards Planner and Lesson Plans, p. L81
- ❏ California Online Test Practice: **ClassZone.com**

Struggling Readers	**On-Level**	**Gifted and Talented**	**English Learners**
❏ Test Form A, *FA pp. 213–216*	❏ Test Form B, *FA pp. 217–220*	❏ Test Form C, *FA pp. 221–224*	❏ Test Generator: Forms A, B, and C in Spanish

RETEACH

- ❏ Reteaching Activity, *IDR Unit 6, p. 32*

Lesson Plans

Origins of the Renaissance

INTRODUCE THE UNIT AND CHAPTER

UNIT 7: INTERACT WITH HISTORY: Building the Duomo, c. 1420, *PE/TE pp. 422–423*

CHAPTER OBJECTIVE: Analyze Renaissance ideas and the period's artistic, literary, intellectual, and technological advances.

❏   Before You Read: Predicting, *PE/TE p. 424*

❏   Big Ideas: Science and Technology, *PE p. 424, TE p. 425*

❏   Time Line Discussion, *TE p. 424*

❏   Map: Renaissance Europe, c. 1500, *PE/TE p. 425*

> *PE = Pupil's Edition*
> *TE = Teacher's Edition*
> *IDR = In-Depth Resources*
> *IDRS = IDR in Spanish*
> *RSG = Reading Study Guide*

STARTING WITH A STORY: A Fierce Competition, *PE/TE pp. 426–427;* California eEdition CD-ROM

PLAN AND PREPARE

Lesson Objectives	California Standards
❏ Review the events that led to the demise of feudalism.	Reading 3.3
❏ Analyze the reasons for the growth of trade.	Writing 2.5
❏ Describe humanism and its relationship to the emergence of the Renaissance.	7.8.1
	7.8.3
❏ **Language Objective:** Sort terms in the lesson into categories to make the text more meaningful and comprehensible.	CST 3
	How to Teach the Standards, *TE p. 428*

FOCUS AND MOTIVATE

❏ MAIN IDEAS, *PE/TE p. 428*   ❏ READING SKILL: Categorizing, *PE/TE p. 428*   ❏ TERMS & NAMES, *PE/TE p. 429*

TEACH

Struggling Readers	On-level	Gifted and Talented	English Learners
TE	**IDR Unit 7**	**TE**	**TE**
❏ Read in Pairs, p. 432	❏ Family Newsletter (English and Spanish), pp. 1–2	❏ Write Dialogue, p. 432	❏ Categorize Ideas, p. 430
IDR Unit 7		**IDR Unit 7**	**IDRS**
❏ Reading Skill, p. 3	❏ Reading Skill: Categorizing, p. 3	❏ Primary Source: The English Ordinance of Laborers of 1349, p. 13	❏ Reading Skill, p. 116
❏ Vocabulary Study Guide, p. 8	❏ Vocabulary Study Guide, p. 8	**Interdisciplinary Projects**	❏ Geography Practice, p. 123
❏ Reteaching Activity, p. 15	❏ Vocabulary Cards, p. 9	❏ Language Arts, p. 75	**RSG (Spanish)**
Reading Study Guide	❏ Geography Practice: Earliest Universities in Europe, p. 11		❏ Lesson 1, p. 111
❏ Lesson 1, p. 111			❏ **California Modified Lesson Plans for English Learners, p. 87**
❏ RSG Audio CD			
California Reading Toolkit, p. L42			❏ **Multi-Language Glossary**

Inclusion

☐ **TE**: Role-Play a Trader, p. 430

☐ **California EasyPlanner CD-ROM:** Reading Skill, Vocabulary Study Guide, Reteaching Activity

All Students

☐ California Reading Toolkit, p. L42

PE

☐ Taking Notes: Categorizing, p. 428

TE

☐ More About TheDuomo, p. 423; Brunelleschi, p. 423; Marco Polo, p. 430; Humanism, p. 432; Francesco Petrarch, p. 432

IDR Unit 7

☐ Family Newsletter (English and Spanish), pp. 1–2

REVIEW AND ENRICH

Integrate Technology

Transparencies

☐ Critical Thinking: CT54 Categorizing

Power Presentations

☐ Lesson 1 Lecture Notes

CD-ROMS

☐ California EasyPlanner CD-ROM

☐ California eEdition CD-ROM

☐ California Test Generator CD-ROM

Interdisciplinary Activities

TE

☐ Art: Design a Promotional Poster, p. 431

☐ Language Arts: Join the Controversy, p. 431

Interdisciplinary Projects

☐ Language Arts, p. 75

ASSESS

Content Assessment

☐ Lesson Review, *PE p. 433*

☐ Lesson Quiz, *FA p. 229*

☐ California Test Generator CD-ROM: Lesson 1 Quiz

☐ Integrated Assessment

Standards Practice

☐ California Standards Enrichment Workbook, pp. 111–112, 115–116

☐ California Daily Standards Practice Transparencies TT42

☐ California Standards Planner and Lesson Plans, p. L83

☐ California Online Test Practice: **ClassZone.com**

RETEACH

☐ Reteaching Activity, *IDR Unit 7, p. 15*

The Italian Renaissance

PE = Pupil's Edition   IDRS = IDR in Spanish
TE = Teacher's Edition   RSG = Reading Study Guide
IDR = In-Depth Resources

PLAN AND PREPARE

Lesson Objectives

❏ Explain why the Renaissance began in Italy.

❏ Describe advances in the arts, literature, architecture, and engineering.

❏ Examine the effects of the Renaissance on society.

❏ **Language Objective:** Preview the text to formulate purpose-setting questions that will help make the text comprehensible and meaningful.

California Standards

7.8.2

7.8.5

Writing 2.4

How to Teach the Standards, *TE p. 434*

FOCUS AND MOTIVATE

❏ MAIN IDEAS, *PE/TE p. 434*

❏ READING SKILL: Finding Main Ideas, *PE/TE p. 434*

❏ TERMS & NAMES, *PE/TE p. 435*

TEACH

Struggling Readers	**On-level**	**Gifted and Talented**	**English Learners**
TE	**PE**	**TE**	**TE**
❏ Identify Characteristics of Renaissance Art, p. 439	❏ History Makers: Leonardo da Vinci, Michelangelo, p. 438	❏ Present an Oral Report, p. 439	❏ Use Headings in Text, p. 436
❏ Analyze Photographs, p. 442	**IDR Unit 7**	❏ Record Observations, p. 442	**IDRS**
IDR Unit 7	❏ Reading Skill: Finding Main Ideas, p. 4	**IDR Unit 7**	❏ Reading Skill, p. 117
❏ Reading Skill, p. 4	❏ Skillbuilder Practice: Framing Historical Questions, p. 7	❏ Literature: Dante's *Inferno*, p. 14	**RSG (Spanish)**
❏ Reteaching Activity, p. 16		**Interdisciplinary Projects**	❏ Lesson 2, p. 113
Reading Study Guide	❏ Vocabulary Cards, p. 9	❏ Math, p. 73	❏ **California Modified Lesson Plans for English Learners, p. 89**
❏ Lesson 2, p. 113		❏ Art, p. 76	❏ **Multi-Language Glossary of Social Studies Terms**
❏ RSG Audio CD			
California Reading Toolkit, p. L43			

Inclusion

- ❑ **TE:** Write and Administer Renaissance Quizzes, p. 436
- ❑ **California EasyPlanner CD-ROM:** Reading Skill, Vocabulary Study Guide, Reteaching Activity

All Students

- ❑ California Reading Toolkit, p. L43

PE

- ❑ Taking Notes: Finding Main Ideas, p. 434
- ❑ **Extend Lesson 2** Connect to Today: Renaissance Advances, pp. 442–443

TE

- ❑ More About Renaissance Florence, p. 436; The Medici, p. 436; The Mona Lisa, p. 438; Raphael, p. 439; Dante, p. 439

REVIEW AND ENRICH

Integrate Technology

Transparencies

- ❑ Critical Thinking: CT55 Finding Main Ideas
- ❑ Map: MT25 Renaissance Italy
- ❑ Humanities: HT25 *The Last Supper,* HT26 A Lute Player

Power Presentations

- ❑ Lesson 2 Lecture Notes

CD-ROMS

- ❑ California EasyPlanner CD-ROM
- ❑ California eEdition CD-ROM
- ❑ California Test Generator CD-ROM

Interdisciplinary Activities

TE

- ❑ Art: Develop an Art Lesson, p. 437; Organize a Museum Display, p. 438
- ❑ Math: Report on the Fibonacci Sequence, p. 437
- ❑ Science: Study Engineering Advances, p. 438
- ❑ Language Arts: Choose a Renaissance Person, p. 440; Report on Renaissance Pursuits, p. 440

Interdisciplinary Projects

- ❑ Math, p. 73
- ❑ Art, p. 76

Transparencies

- ❑ Geography: MT25 Renaissance Italy
- ❑ Art: HT25 *The Last Supper,* HT26 A Lute Player

ASSESS

Content Assessment

- ❑ Lesson Review, *PE p. 441*
- ❑ Lesson Quiz, *FA p. 230*
- ❑ California Test Generator CD-ROM: Lesson 2 Quiz
- ❑ Integrated Assessment

Standards Practice

- ❑ California Standards Enrichment Workbook, pp. 113–114, 119–120
- ❑ California Daily Standards Practice Transparencies TT43
- ❑ California Standards Planner and Lesson Plans, p. L85
- ❑ California Online Test Practice: **ClassZone.com**

RETEACH

- ❑ Reteaching Activity, *IDR Unit 7, p. 16*

CHAPTER **13** *Lesson 3*   **Lesson Plan**

The Renaissance Spreads

PE = Pupil's Edition	IDRS = IDR in Spanish
TE = Teacher's Edition	RSG = Reading Study Guide
IDR = In-Depth Resources	

PLAN AND PREPARE

Lesson Objectives

❑ Identify reasons for the spread of the Renaissance to northern Europe.

❑ Examine the styles and accomplishments of significant artists and writers of the Northern Renaissance.

❑ Explain the impact of the scientific and technological advances of the Renaissance.

❑ **Language Objective:** Demonstrate an understanding of the difference between a fact and an opinion.

California Standards

7.8.4

7.8.5

REP 4

Writing 2.4

How to Teach the Standards, *TE p. 444*

FOCUS AND MOTIVATE

❑ MAIN IDEAS, *PE/TE p. 444*

❑ READING SKILL: Evaluating Information, *PE/TE p. 444*

❑ TERMS & NAMES, *PE/TE p. 445*

TEACH

Struggling Readers	On-level	Gifted and Talented	English Learners
TE	**PE**	**TE**	**TE**
❑ Watch Shakespeare's Plays, p. 452	❑ Primary Source: from *Romeo and Juliet*, p. 448	❑ Analyze Poetry, p. 448	❑ Use Context Clues, p. 446
IDR Unit 7		❑ Build a Model, p. 452	**IDRS**
❑ Reading Skill, p. 5	**IDR Unit 7**	**Interdisciplinary Projects**	❑ Reading Skill, p. 13
❑ Reteaching Activity, p. 17	❑ Reading Skill: Evaluating Information, p. 5	❑ Science, p. 74	**RSG (Spanish)**
Reading Study Guide	❑ Vocabulary Study Guide, p. 8	**History Makers**	❑ Lesson 3, p. 115
❑ Lesson 3, p. 115	❑ Vocabulary Cards, p. 9	❑ Albrecht Dürer, p. 25	❑ **California Modified Lesson Plans for English Learners, p. 91**
❑ RSG Audio CD	❑ Reteaching Activity, p. 17		❑ **Multi-Language Glossary of Social Studies Terms**
California Reading Toolkit, p. L44			

Lesson Plans

Inclusion

- ❏ **TE:** Practice Remembering, p. 446
- ❏ **California EasyPlanner CD-ROM:** Reading Skill, Vocabulary Study Guide, Reteaching Activity

All Students

- ❏ California Reading Toolkit, p. L44

PE

- ❏ Taking Notes: Evaluating Information, p. 444
- ❏ **Extend Lesson 3** Activity: Create a Quiz Show, p. 451; Daily Life: Life at the Globe Theater, pp. 452–453

TE

- ❏ More About Woodcuts, p. 447; The Printing Press, p. 449; The Globe Theater, p. 453

REVIEW AND ENRICH

Integrate Technology

Transparencies

- ❏ Critical Thinking: CT56 Evaluating Information
- ❏ Map: MT26 The Growth of Towns Post-1453

Power Presentations

- ❏ Lesson 3 Lecture Notes

CD-ROMS

- ❏ California EasyPlanner CD-ROM
- ❏ California eEdition CD-ROM
- ❏ California Test Generator CD-ROM

Interdisciplinary Activities

TE

- ❏ Art: Produce Woodcuts, p. 447
- ❏ Language Arts: Compare Sonnets, p. 447
- ❏ Math: Create Word Problems, p. 449
- ❏ Science: Make a Printing-Press Time Line, p. 449

Interdisciplinary Projects

- ❏ Science, p. 74

Transparencies

- ❏ Geography: MT26 The Growth of Towns Post-1453

ASSESS

Content Assessment

- ❏ Lesson Review, *PE p. 450*
- ❏ Chapter Review, *PE pp. 454–455*
- ❏ Lesson Quiz, *FA p. 231*
- ❏ California Test Generator CD-ROM: Lesson 3 Quiz
- ❏ Integrated Assessment

Standards Practice

- ❏ California Standards Enrichment Workbook, pp. 117–120
- ❏ California Daily Standards Practice Transparencies TT44
- ❏ California Standards Planner and Lesson Plans, p. L87
- ❏ California Online Test Practice: **ClassZone.com**

Struggling Readers	On-Level	Gifted and Talented	English Learners
❏ Test Form A, *FA pp. 232–236*	❏ Test Form B, *FA pp. 237–241*	❏ Test Form C, *FA pp. 242–246*	❏ Test Generator: Forms A, B, and C in Spanish

RETEACH

- ❏ Reteaching Activity, *IDR Unit 7, p. 17*

Name _____ Date _____

Trouble for the Catholic Church

INTRODUCE THE CHAPTER

CHAPTER OBJECTIVE: Analyze the causes and effects of the religious movements known as the Reformation and Counter Reformation.

❏ Before You Read: Previewing Key Concepts, *PE/TE p. 456*
❏ Big Ideas: Government, *PE p. 456, TE p. 457*
❏ Time Line Discussion, *TE p. 456*
❏ Map: Christianity in Europe, A.D. 1600, *PE/TE p. 457*

> *PE = Pupil's Edition*
> *TE = Teacher's Edition*
> *IDR = In-Depth Resources*
> *IDRS = IDR in Spanish*
> *RSG = Reading Study Guide*

STARTING WITH A STORY: Printing Challenging Ideas, *PE/TE pp. 458–459;* California eEdition CD-ROM

PLAN AND PREPARE

Lesson Objectives	California Standards
❏ Describe the factors influencing the settlement of Rome.	Reading 2.3
❏ Identify the characteristics of the Roman Republic.	Writing 2.4
❏ Explain reasons for the growth of the Roman Empire and the emergence of Christianity.	7.9.1
❏ **Language Objective:** Use note-taking skills to organize the key information in the lesson.	7.9.2
	CST 1
	How to Teach the California Standards, *TE p. 460*

FOCUS AND MOTIVATE

❏ MAIN IDEAS, *PE/TE p. 460*   ❏ READING SKILL: Summarizing, *PE/TE p. 460*   ❏ TERMS & NAMES, *PE/TE p. 461*

TEACH

Struggling Readers	On-level	Gifted and Talented	English Learners
TE	**PE**	**TE**	**TE**
❏ List Grievances, p. 462	❏ Primary Source, p. 464	❏ Write an Analytical Essay, p. 464	❏ Summarize Information, p. 462
❏ Dramatize Scene, p. 468	**IDR Unit 7**	❏ Review Books, p. 468	❏ Use Context Clues, p. 467
IDR Unit 7	❏ Family Newsletter (English and Spanish), pp. 18–19	**IDR Unit 7**	**IDRS**
❏ Reading Skill, p. 20	❏ Reading Skill: Summarizing, p. 20	❏ Primary Source: Appeal to the Ruling Class, p. 31	❏ Reading Skill, p. 125
❏ Reteaching Activity, p. 33	❏ Vocabulary Study Guide, p. 25	**Interdisciplinary Projects**	**RSG (Spanish)**
Reading Study Guide	❏ Vocabulary Cards, p. 27	❏ Science, p. 80	❏ Lesson 1, p. 119
❏ Lesson 1, p. 119		**History Makers**	❏ **California Modified Lesson Plans for English Learners, p. 93**
❏ RSG Audio CD		❏ Martin Luther, p. 27	❏ **Multi-Language Glossary**
California Reading Toolkit, p. L45			

Lesson Plans

Inclusion

- ❏ **TE:** Identify Causes and Effects, p. 464; Record Answers, p. 467
- ❏ **California EasyPlanner CD-ROM:** Reading Skill, Vocabulary Study Guide, Reteaching Activity

All Students

- ❏ California Reading Toolkit, p. L45

PE

- ❏ Taking Notes: Summarizing, p. 460
- ❏ **Extend Lesson 1** Literature Connections: from Martin Luther, pp. 466–469

TE

- ❏ More About Erasmus and Luther, p. 463; The Ninety-Five Theses, p. 464; The Meeting in Worms, p. 466; Frederick III, p. 467; Martin Luther's Year at the Wartburg, p. 468; Luther's Return to Wittenberg, p. 469

REVIEW AND ENRICH

Integrate Technology

Transparencies

- ❏ Critical Thinking: CT58 Summarizing
- ❏ Humanities: HT27 Martin Luther's Study at Wartburg Castle
- ❏ Humanities: HT28 The Council of Constance

Power Presentations

- ❏ Lesson 1 Lecture Notes

CD-ROMS

- ❏ California EasyPlanner CD-ROM
- ❏ California eEdition CD-ROM
- ❏ California Test Generator CD-ROM

Interdisciplinary Activities

TE

- ❏ Language Arts: Explore Ninety-Five Theses, p. 463
- ❏ Art: Organize Picture Gallery, p. 463

Interdisciplinary Projects

- ❏ Science, p. 80

Transparencies

- ❏ Art: HT27 Martin Luther's Study at Wartburg Castle
- ❏ Art: HT28 The Council of Constance

ASSESS

Content Assessment

- ❏ Lesson Review, *PE p. 465*
- ❏ Lesson Quiz, *FA p. 247*
- ❏ California Test Generator CD-ROM: Lesson 1 Quiz
- ❏ Integrated Assessment

Standards Practice

- ❏ California Standards Enrichment Workbook, pp. 121–124
- ❏ California Daily Standards Practice Transparencies TT45
- ❏ California Standards Planner and Lesson Plans, p. L89
- ❏ California Online Test Practice: **ClassZone.com**

RETEACH

- ❏ Reteaching Activity, *IDR Unit 7, p. 33*

Reform and Reaction

> PE = Pupil's Edition
> TE = Teacher's Edition
> IDR = In-Depth Resources
>
> IDRS = IDR in Spanish
> RSG = Reading Study Guide

PLAN AND PREPARE

Lesson Objectives

❑ Describe how Luther's message spread and how it affected Europe.

❑ Explain the development of other Protestant religions in Europe.

❑ Analyze the methods used by the Catholic Church in the Counter Reformation.

❑ **Language Objective:** Preview the text to formulate purpose-setting questions in order to make the text comprehensible and meaningful.

California Standards

7.9.2

7.9.5

HI 2

How to Teach the California Standards, *TE p. 470*

FOCUS AND MOTIVATE

❑ MAIN IDEAS, *PE/TE p. 470*

❑ READING SKILL: Finding Main Ideas, *PE/TE p. 470*

❑ TERMS & NAMES, *PE/TE p. 471*

TEACH

Struggling Readers	**On-level**	**Gifted and Talented**	**English Learners**
TE	**PE**	**TE**	**TE**
❑ Formulate Questions, p. 473	❑ History Makers: St. Ignatius of Loyola, p. 474	❑ Write a Royal Press Release, p. 473	❑ Preview the Lesson, p. 472
❑ Practice the Skill, p. 476		**IDR Unit 7**	❑ Use Cause and Effect, p. 476
IDR Unit 7	**IDR Unit 7**	❑ Literature: Holy Sonnet 10, p. 32	**IDRS**
❑ Reading Skill, p. 21	❑ Reading Skill: Finding Main Ideas, p. 21	**Interdisciplinary Projects**	❑ Reading Skill, p. 126
❑ Vocabulary Cards, p. 27	❑ Skillbuilder Practice: Explaining Geographic Patterns, p. 24	❑ Language Arts, p. 81	**RSG (Spanish)**
❑ Reteaching Activity, p. 34			❑ Lesson 2, p. 121
Reading Study Guide	❑ Vocabulary Cards, p. 27		❑ **California Modified Lesson Plans for English Learners, p. 95**
❑ Lesson 2, p. 121			
❑ RSG Audio CD			❑ **Multi-Language Glossary**
California Reading Toolkit, p. L46			

Inclusion

- ❏ **TE:** Use Study Guide, p. 472

- ❏ **California EasyPlanner CD-ROM:** Reading Skill, Vocabulary Study Guide, Reteaching Activity

All Students

- ❏ California Reading Toolkit, p. L46

PE

- ❏ Taking Notes: Finding Main Ideas, p. 470

- ❏ **Extend Lesson 2** Skillbuilder: Understanding Cause and Effect, pp. 476–477

TE

- ❏ More About King Henry VIII, p. 472; The Counter-Reformatin Pope, p. 474; John Calvin's Beliefs, p. 477

REVIEW AND ENRICH

Integrate Technology

Transparencies

- ❏ Critical Thinking: CT59 Finding Main Ideas

- ❏ Map: MT27 The First Printing Presses

Power Presentations

- ❏ Lesson 2 Lecture Notes

CD-ROMS

- ❏ California EasyPlanner CD-ROM

- ❏ California eEdition CD-ROM

- ❏ California Test Generator CD-ROM

Interdisciplinary Activities

TE

- ❏ Language Arts: Write an Encyclopedia Article, p. 474

- ❏ Art: Explore Baroque Art, p. 474

Interdisciplinary Projects

- ❏ Language Arts, p. 81

Transparencies

- ❏ Geography: MT27 The First Printing Presses

ASSESS

Content Assessment

- ❏ Lesson Review, *PE p. 475*

- ❏ Lesson Quiz, *FA p. 248*

- ❏ California Test Generator CD-ROM: Lesson 2 Quiz

- ❏ Integrated Assessment

Standards Practice

- ❏ California Standards Enrichment Workbook, pp. 123–124

- ❏ California Daily Standards Practice Transparencies TT46

- ❏ California Standards Planner and Lesson Plans, p. L91

- ❏ California Online Test Practice: **ClassZone.com**

RETEACH

- ❏ Reteaching Activity, *IDR Unit 7, p. 34*

Lesson Plans

Name _____ Date _____

Expansion of Christianity

PE = Pupil's Edition
TE = Teacher's Edition
IDR = In-Depth Resources
IDRS = IDR in Spanish
RSG = Reading Study Guide

PLAN AND PREPARE

Lesson Objectives
- ❑ Examine the religious orders involved in the Catholic missionary movement.
- ❑ Explain the efforts of Catholic and Protestant missionaries in the Americas and other areas.
- ❑ Analyze the short-term and long-term effects of the Reformation.
- ❑ **Language Objective:** Compare and contrast details by identifying how people, characters, events, and ideas are alike and different.

California Standards
7.9.3
7.9.4
7.9.6
How to Teach the California Standards, *TE p. 478*

FOCUS AND MOTIVATE

- ❑ MAIN IDEAS, *PE/TE p. 478*
- ❑ READING SKILL: Comparing and Contrasting, *PE/TE p. 478*
- ❑ TERMS & NAMES, *PE/TE p. 479*

TEACH

Struggling Readers	On-level	Gifted and Talented	English Learners
TE ❑ Identify Important Ideas, p. 483 **IDR Unit 7** ❑ Reading Skill, p. 22 ❑ Reteaching Activity, p. 35 **Reading Study Guide** ❑ Lesson 3, p. 123 ❑ RSG Audio CD **California Reading Toolkit, p. L47**	**PE** ❑ Geography: Distribution of Religions in the Americas, p. 482 **IDR Unit 7** ❑ Reading Skill: Comparing and Contrasting, p. 22 ❑ Vocabulary Cards, p. 27 ❑ Geography Practice: Countries with the Largest Christian Populations, p. 29	**TE** ❑ Draw Map of Europe, p. 483 **Interdisciplinary Projects** ❑ Math, p. 79	**TE** ❑ Use Compare and Contrast, p. 481 **IDRS** ❑ Reading Skill, p. 127 **RSG (Spanish)** ❑ Lesson 3, p. 123 ❑ **California Modified Lesson Plans for English Learners, p. 97** ❑ **Multi-Language Glossary of Social Studies Terms**

Lesson Plans

Copyright © by McDougal Littell, a division of Houghton Mifflin Company

Inclusion

- ❑ **TE:** Create Vocabulary Cards, p. 481
- ❑ **California EasyPlanner CD-ROM:** Reading Skill, Vocabulary Study Guide, Reteaching Activity

All Students

- ❑ California Reading Toolkit, p. L47

PE
- ❑ Taking Notes: Comparing and Contrasting, p. 478
- ❑ **Extend Lesson 3** Activity: Communication Across Cultures, p. 485

TE
- ❑ More About St. Dominic, p. 480; Christianity in Japan, p. 481; Peace of Westphalia, p. 483

REVIEW AND ENRICH

Integrate Technology

Transparencies
- ❑ Critical Thinking: CT60 Comparing and Contrasting
- ❑ Map: MT28 Europe After the Peace of Westphalia, 1648

Power Presentations
- ❑ Lesson 3 Lecture Notes

CD-ROMS
- ❑ California EasyPlanner CD-ROM
- ❑ California eEdition CD-ROM
- ❑ California Test Generator CD-ROM

Interdisciplinary Activities

PE
- ❑ Geography: Distribution of Religions in the Americas, p. 482

TE
- ❑ Science: Describe Jesuit Achievements, p. 480
- ❑ Language Arts: Write Journal Entries, p. 480; Design a Crossword Puzzle, p. 482
- ❑ Math: Create Pie Charts, p. 482

Transparencies
- ❑ Geography: MT28 Europe After the Peace of Westphalia, 1648

ASSESS

Content Assessment

- ❑ Lesson Review, *PE p. 484*
- ❑ Chapter Review, *PE pp. 486–487*
- ❑ Lesson Quiz, *FA p. 249*
- ❑ California Test Generator CD-ROM: Lesson 3 Quiz
- ❑ Integrated Assessment

Standards Practice

- ❑ California Standards Enrichment Workbook, pp. 125–128, 131–132
- ❑ California Daily Standards Practice Transparencies TT47
- ❑ California Standards Planner and Lesson Plans, p. L93
- ❑ California Online Test Practice: **ClassZone.com**

Struggling Readers	On-Level	Gifted and Talented	English Learners
❑ Test Form A, *FA pp. 250–253*	❑ Test Form B, *FA pp. 254–257*	❑ Test Form C, *FA pp. 258–261*	❑ Test Generator: Forms A, B, and C in Spanish

RETEACH

- ❑ Reteaching Activity, *IDR Unit 7, p. 35*

Lesson Plans

History of Scientific Thought

INTRODUCE THE UNIT AND CHAPTER

UNIT 8: INTERACT WITH HISTORY: The Waterfront of Lisbon, Portugal, late 1500s, *PE/TE pp. 490–491*

CHAPTER OBJECTIVE: Examine causes and effects of the Scientific Revolution and the increased exploration undertaken during this period.

❑ Before You Read: Anticipation Guide, *PE/TE p. 492*

❑ Big Ideas: Science and Technology, *PE p. 492, TE p. 493*

❑ Time Line Discussion, *TE p. 492*

❑ Map: Great voyages of Discovery, A.D. 1492–1610, *PE/TE p. 493*

> *PE = Pupil's Edition*
> *TE = Teacher's Edition*
> *IDR = In-Depth Resources*
> *IDRS = IDR in Spanish*
> *RSG = Reading Study Guide*

STARTING WITH A STORY: Conducting an Experiment, *PE/TE pp. 494–495;* California eEdition CD-ROM

PLAN AND PREPARE

Lesson Objectives	California Standards
❑ Identify important theories advanced by Greek scientists.	Reading 3.2
❑ Examine contributions to scientific and mathematical knowledge by Muslim, Christian, and Jewish scholars in the Middle Ages.	Writing 2.1 7.10.1 7.10.3
❑ Explain how humanism and global exploration led to the Scientific Revolution.	HI 2 How to Teach the Standards, *TE p. 496*
❑ **Language Objective:** Classify details by category to make nonfiction text more comprehensible and meaningful.	

FOCUS AND MOTIVATE

❑ MAIN IDEAS, *PE/TE p. 496*   ❑ READING SKILL: Explaining Chronological Order and Sequence, *PE/TE p. 496*

❑ TERMS & NAMES, *PE/TE p. 497*

TEACH

Struggling Readers	On-level	Gifted and Talented	English Learners
TE	**IDR Unit 8**	**TE**	**TE**
❑ Chart Contributions, p. 498	❑ Family Newsletter (English and Spanish), pp. 1–2	❑ Present Syllogisms, p. 499	❑ Create a Chart, p. 498
IDR Unit 8	❑ Reading Skill: Explaining Chronological Order and Sequence, p. 3	**Interdisciplinary Projects**	**IDRS**
❑ Reading Skill, p. 3		❑ Math, p. 85	❑ Reading Skill, p. 134
❑ Reteaching Activity, p. 17			**RSG (Spanish)**
Reading Study Guide	❑ Vocabulary Cards, p. 11		❑ Lesson 1, p. 127
❑ Lesson 1, p. 127			❑ **California Modified Lesson Plans for English Learners, p. 99**
❑ RSG Audio CD			❑ **Multi-Language Glossary of Social Studies Terms**
California Reading Toolkit, p. L48			

Lesson Plans

Inclusion

❑ Organize a Collage, p. 499

❑ **California EasyPlanner CD-ROM:** Reading Skill, Vocabulary Study Guide, Reteaching Activity

All Students

❑ California Reading Toolkit, p. L48

PE

❑ Taking Notes: Explaining Chronological Order and Sequence, p. 496

TE

❑ More About Gersonidea, p. 499

IDR Unit 8

❑ Family Newsletter (English and Spanish), pp. 1–2

REVIEW AND ENRICH

Integrate Technology

Transparencies

❑ Critical Thinking: CT62 Explaining Chronological Order and Sequence

Power Presentations

❑ Lesson 1 Lecture Notes

CD-ROMS

❑ California EasyPlanner CD-ROM

❑ California eEdition CD-ROM

❑ California Test Generator CD-ROM

Interdisciplinary Activities

TE

❑ Art: Draw Sketches, p. 500

❑ Science: Present a Plant Study, p. 500

Interdisciplinary Projects

❑ Math, p. 85

ASSESS

Content Assessment

❑ Lesson Review, *PE p. 501*

❑ Lesson Quiz, *FA p. 266*

❑ California Test Generator CD-ROM: Lesson 1 Quiz

❑ Integrated Assessment

Standards Practice

❑ California Standards Enrichment Workbook, pp. 135–136, 139–140

❑ California Daily Standards Practice Transparencies TT48

❑ California Standards Planner and Lesson Plans, p. L95

❑ California Online Test Practice: **ClassZone.com**

RETEACH

❑ Reteaching Activity, *IDR Unit 8, p. 17*

CHAPTER 15 Lesson 2   **Lesson Plan**

The Scientific Revolution

PE = Pupil's Edition	IDRS = IDR in Spanish
TE = Teacher's Edition	RSG = Reading Study Guide
IDR = In-Depth Resources	

PLAN AND PREPARE

Lesson Objectives

❏ Examine new scientific theories and discoveries of the 17th century.

❏ Describe inventions of the 17th and 18th centuries.

❏ Explain the development of scientific rationalism and its effect on the Church and political thinking.

❏ **Language Objective:** Formulate purpose-setting questions in order to make the text comprehensible and meaningful.

California Standards

7.10.2

7.10.3

REP 2

How to Teach the Standards, *TE p. 502*

FOCUS AND MOTIVATE

❏ MAIN IDEAS, *PE/TE p. 502*

❏ READING SKILL: Categorizing, *PE/TE p. 502*

❏ TERMS & NAMES, *PE/TE p. 503*

TEACH

Struggling Readers	On-level	Gifted and Talented	English Learners
TE	**PE**	**TE**	**TE**
❏ Support an Opinion, p. 504	❏ History Makers: Sir Francis Bacon, p. 506	❏ Design a T-Shirt, p. 506	❏ Formulate Questions and Answers, p. 504
❏ Practice the Skill, p. 508	**IDR Unit 8**	**IDR Unit 8**	❏ Formulate Facts and Opinions, p. 508
IDR Unit 8	❏ Reading Skill: Categorizing, p. 4	❏ Primary Source, p. 15	**IDRS**
❏ Reading Skill, p. 4	❏ Vocabulary Cards, p. 11	**Interdisciplinary Projects**	❏ Reading Skill, p. 135
❏ Reteaching Activity, p. 18		❏ Science, p. 86	**RSG (Spanish)**
Reading Study Guide			❏ Lesson 2, p. 129
❏ Lesson 2, p. 129			❏ **California Modified Lesson Plans for English Learners, p. 101**
❏ RSG Audio CD			
California Reading Toolkit, p. L49			❏ **Multi-Language Glossary**

Lesson Plans

Inclusion

- ❑ **TE:** Follow the Scientific Method, p. 506

- ❑ **California EasyPlanner CD-ROM:** Reading Skill, Vocabulary Study Guide, Reteaching Activity

All Students

- ❑ California Reading Toolkit, p. L49

PE

- ❑ Taking Notes: Categorizing, p. 502

- ❑ **Extend Lesson 2** Skillbuilder: Distinguishing Fact from Opinion, pp. 508–509

TE

- ❑ More About Isaac Newton, p. 504; Women Astronomers, p. 509

REVIEW AND ENRICH

Integrate Technology

Transparencies

- ❑ Critical Thinking: CT63 Categorizing

- ❑ Humanities: HT29 The Trial of Galileo

Power Presentations

- ❑ Lesson 2 Lecture Notes

CD-ROMS

- ❑ California EasyPlanner CD-ROM

- ❑ California eEdition CD-ROM

- ❑ California Test Generator CD-ROM

Interdisciplinary Activities

TE

- ❑ Science: Design an Invention, p. 505

- ❑ Language Arts: Explain Steps, p. 505

Interdisciplinary Projects

- ❑ Science, p. 86

Transparencies

- ❑ Art: HT29 The Trial of Galileo

ASSESS

Content Assessment

- ❑ Lesson Review, *PE p. 507*

- ❑ Lesson Quiz, *FA p. 267*

- ❑ California Test Generator CD-ROM: Lesson 2 Quiz

- ❑ Integrated Assessment

Standards Practice

- ❑ California Standards Enrichment Workbook, pp. 137–140

- ❑ California Daily Standards Practice Transparencies TT49

- ❑ California Standards Planner and Lesson Plans, p. L97

- ❑ California Online Test Practice: **ClassZone.com**

RETEACH

- ❑ Reteaching Activity, *IDR Unit 8, p. 18*

Lesson Plans

The Age of Exploration

PE = Pupil's Edition	IDRS = IDR in Spanish
TE = Teacher's Edition	RSG = Reading Study Guide
IDR = In-Depth Resources	

PLAN AND PREPARE

Lesson Objectives

❏ Trace the establishment of Portugal's trading network in Africa and India.

❏ Explain the results of Columbus' voyages.

❏ Identify later European explorations of the Americas and their effect on Europe's worldview.

❏ **Language Objective:** Summarize information from the text to make the content more comprehensible.

California Standards

7.11.1
CST 2
How to Teach the Standards, *TE p. 510*

FOCUS AND MOTIVATE

❏ MAIN IDEAS, *PE/TE p. 510*

❏ READING SKILL: Summarizing, *PE/TE p. 510*

❏ TERMS & NAMES, *PE/TE p. 511*

TEACH

Struggling Readers	**On-level**	**Gifted and Talented**	**English Learners**
TE	**PE**	**TE**	**TE**
❏ Present a Pageant, p. 516	❏ Primary Source, p. 514	❏ Write a Short Story or Play, p. 516	❏ Create a Cluster Web, p. 513
❏ Role-Play, p. 518	**IDR Unit 8**	❏ Find Accounts of Life on a Ship, p. 518	**IDRS**
IDR Unit 8	❏ Reading Skill: Summarizing, p. 5	**Interdisciplinary Projects**	❏ Reading Skill, p. 136
❏ Reading Skill, p. 5	❏ Skillbuilder Practice: Creating a Map, p. 8	❏ Language Arts, p. 87	**RSG (Spanish)**
❏ Reteaching Activity, p. 19	❏ Vocabulary Study Guide, p. 9		❏ Lesson 3, p. 131
Reading Study Guide	❏ Vocabulary Cards, p. 11		❏ **California Modified Lesson Plans for English Learners, p. 103**
❏ Lesson 3, p. 131			❏ **Multi-Language Glossary of Social Studies Terms**
❏ RSG Audio CD			
California Reading Toolkit, p. L50			

Lesson Plans

Inclusion

- ☐ **TE:** Study a World Map, p. 513
- ☐ **California EasyPlanner CD-ROM:** Reading Skill, Vocabulary Study Guide, Reteaching Activity

All Students

- ☐ California Reading Toolkit, p. L50

PE

- ☐ Taking Notes: Summarizing, p. 510
- ☐ **Extend Lesson 3** Daily Life: Life on a Ship, pp. 518–519

TE

- ☐ More About Prince Henry, p. 512; The Treaty of Tordesillas, p. 514; The Northwest Passage, p. 516; Diet Aboard Ship, p. 519

REVIEW AND ENRICH

Integrate Technology

Transparencies

- ☐ Critical Thinking: CT64 Summarizing
- ☐ Map: MT29 Columbus' Voyages to the Americas

Power Presentations

- ☐ Lesson 3 Lecture Notes

CD-ROMS

- ☐ California EasyPlanner CD-ROM
- ☐ California eEdition CD-ROM
- ☐ California Test Generator CD-ROM

Interdisciplinary Activities

TE

- ☐ Science: Make an Astrolabe, p. 512; Match Animals, p. 514
- ☐ Art: Build a Model Caravel, p. 512; Compare Maps, p. 515
- ☐ Language Arts: Write Descriptive Letters, p. 514
- ☐ Math: Calculate Distance, p. 515

Interdisciplinary Projects

- ☐ Language Arts, p. 87

Transparencies

- ☐ Geography: MT29 Columbus' Voyages to the Americas

ASSESS

Content Assessment

- ☐ Lesson Review, *PE p. 517*
- ☐ Lesson Quiz, *FA p. 268*
- ☐ California Test Generator CD-ROM: Lesson 3 Quiz
- ☐ Integrated Assessment

Standards Practice

- ☐ California Standards Enrichment Workbook, pp. 141–142
- ☐ California Daily Standards Practice Transparencies TT50
- ☐ California Standards Planner and Lesson Plans, p. L99
- ☐ California Online Test Practice: **ClassZone.com**

RETEACH

- ☐ Reteaching Activity, *IDR Unit 8, p. 19*

CHAPTER 15 *Lesson 4*   **Lesson Plan**

Impact of Exploration

PE = Pupil's Edition   IDRS = IDR in Spanish
TE = Teacher's Edition   RSG = Reading Study Guide
IDR = In-Depth Resources

PLAN AND PREPARE

Lesson Objectives

❑ Describe the Columbian Exchange and its effects on the populations and trading patterns of the Americas, Europe, Africa, and Asia.

❑ Explain the competition between European countries to establish colonies in the Americas and elsewhere.

❑ Identify the factors that led to the growth of capitalism and the adoption of mercantilist policies by European countries.

❑ **Language Objective:** Formulate statements from cause-and-effect chains to derive the meaning of the text in the lesson.

California Standards

7.11.2
7.11.3
How to Teach the Standards, *TE p. 520*

FOCUS AND MOTIVATE

❑ MAIN IDEAS, *PE/TE p. 520*

❑ READING SKILL: Understanding Cause and Effect, *PE/TE p. 520*

❑ TERMS & NAMES, *PE/TE p. 521*

TEACH

Struggling Readers	**On-level**	**Gifted and Talented**	**English Learners**
TE	**PE**	**TE**	**TE**
❑ Write Summaries, p. 522	❑ Mercantilism, p. 525	❑ Describe Economic Systems, p. 525	❑ Complete a Chart, p. 522
IDR Unit 8	**IDR Unit 8**	**IDR Unit 8**	**IDRS**
❑ Reading Skill, p. 6	❑ Reading Skill: Understanding Cause and Effect, p. 6	❑ Literature, p. 16	❑ Reading Skill, p. 137
❑ Reteaching Activity, p. 20		**Interdisciplinary Projects**	**RSG (Spanish)**
Reading Study Guide	❑ Vocabulary Cards, p. 11	❑ Art, p. 88	❑ Lesson 4, p. 133
❑ Lesson 4, p. 133	❑ Reteaching Activity, p. 20		❑ **California Modified Lesson Plans for English Learners, p. 105**
❑ RSG Audio CD			
California Reading Toolkit, p. L51			❑ **Multi-Language Glossary**

Lesson Plans

Inclusion

- ❑ **TE:** Devise a Business Plan, p. 525
- ❑ **California EasyPlanner CD-ROM:** Reading Skill, Vocabulary Study Guide, Reteaching Activity

All Students

- ❑ California Reading Toolkit, p. L51

PE
- ❑ Taking Notes: Understanding Cause and Effect, p. 520
- ❑ **Extend Lesson 4** Activity: Hold a Debate, p. 527

TE
- ❑ More About The Slave Trade, p. 522; Chartered Companies, p. 525

REVIEW AND ENRICH

Integrate Technology

Transparencies
- ❑ Critical Thinking: CT65 Understanding Cause and Effect
- ❑ Map: MT30 European Claims in the Americas, c. 1700
- ❑ Humanities: HT30 Map of New Amsterdam, 1661

Power Presentations
- ❑ Lesson 4 Lecture Notes

CD-ROMS
- ❑ California EasyPlanner CD-ROM
- ❑ California eEdition CD-ROM
- ❑ California Test Generator CD-ROM

Interdisciplinary Activities

TE
- ❑ Science: Research Effects of Exchange, p. 523
- ❑ Art: Report on Spanish Art, p. 523; Depict Battle, p. 524
- ❑ Math: Illustrate Principles, p. 524

Interdisciplinary Projects
- ❑ Art, p. 88

Transparencies
- ❑ Geography: MT30 European Claims in the Americas, c. 1700
- ❑ Art: HT30 Map of New Amsterdam, 1661

ASSESS

Content Assessment

- ❑ Lesson Review, *PE p. 526*
- ❑ Chapter Review, *PE pp. 528–529*
- ❑ Lesson Quiz, *FA p. 269*
- ❑ California Test Generator CD-ROM: Lesson 4 Quiz
- ❑ Integrated Assessment

Standards Practice

- ❑ California Standards Enrichment Workbook, pp. 143–146
- ❑ California Daily Standards Practice Transparencies TT51
- ❑ California Standards Planner and Lesson Plans, p. L101
- ❑ California Online Test Practice: **ClassZone.com**

Struggling Readers	On-Level	Gifted and Talented	English Learners
❑ Test Form A, *FA pp. 270–274*	❑ Test Form B, *FA pp. 275–279*	❑ Test Form C, *FA pp. 280–284*	❑ Test Generator: Forms A, B, and C in Spanish

RETEACH

- ❑ Reteaching Activity, *IDR Unit 8, p. 20*

CHAPTER 16 Lesson 1 **Lesson Plan**

The Enlightenment

INTRODUCE THE CHAPTER

CHAPTER OBJECTIVE: Identify important Enlightenment philosophers and explain the influence of their ideas on society and systems of government.

- ❏ Before You Read: Predicting, *PE/TE p. 530*
- ❏ Big Ideas: Government, *PE p. 530, TE p. 531*
- ❏ Time Line Discussion, *TE p. 530*
- ❏ Map: Cultural Centers, 1700, *PE/TE p. 531*

> *PE = Pupil's Edition*
> *TE = Teacher's Edition*
> *IDR = In-Depth Resources*
> *IDRS = IDR in Spanish*
> *RSG = Reading Study Guide*

STARTING WITH A STORY: Challenging Old Ideas, *PE/TE pp. 532–533;* California eEdition CD-ROM

PLAN AND PREPARE

Lesson Objectives

- ❏ Trace the origins of the Enlightenment.
- ❏ Examine the philosophies of major thinkers of this time period.
- ❏ Examine the views of some Enlightenment women.
- ❏ **Language Objective:** Classify details by category to make nonfiction text more comprehensible and meaningful.

California Standards

Reading 3.3
Writing 2.4
7.11.4
7.11.5
HI 2
How to Teach the Standards, *TE p. 534*

FOCUS AND MOTIVATE

- ❏ MAIN IDEAS, *PE/TE p. 534*
- ❏ TERMS & NAMES, *PE/TE p. 535*
- ❏ READING SKILL: Finding Main Ideas, *PE/TE p. 534*

TEACH

Struggling Readers	On-level	Gifted and Talented	English Learners
TE	**PE**	**TE**	**TE**
❏ Make Flashcards, p. 536	❏ History Makers: John Locke, p. 536	❏ Prepare Time Line of Philosophies, p. 537	❏ Work with Categories, p. 536
IDR Unit 8	**IDR Unit 8**	❏ Write Editorials, p. 540	❏ Discuss Women's Rights, p. 540
❏ Reading Skill: Finding Main Ideas, p. 23	❏ Family Newsletter (English and Spanish), pp. 21–22	**IDR Unit 8**	**IDRS**
❏ Vocabulary Cards, p. 29		❏ Primary Source, p. 33	❏ Reading Skill, p. 143
❏ Reteaching Activity, p. 35	❏ Reading Skill: Finding Main Ideas, p. 23	❏ Literature, p. 34	**RSG (Spanish)**
Reading Study Guide	❏ Vocabulary Cards, p. 29	**Interdisciplinary Projects**	❏ Lesson 1, p. 137
❏ Lesson 1, p. 137		❏ Math, p. 91	❏ **California Modified Lesson Plans for English Learners, p. 107**
❏ RSG Audio CD		❏ Science, p. 92	
California Reading Toolkit, p. L52		**History Makers**	❏ **Multi-Language Glossary**
		❏ Mary Wollstonecraft, p. 31	

Lesson Plans

Inclusion

- ❑ **TE:** Write Captions, p. 537
- ❑ **California EasyPlanner CD-ROM:** Reading Skill, Vocabulary Study Guide, Reteaching Activity

All Students

- ❑ California Reading Toolkit, p. L52

PE

- ❑ Taking Notes: Finding Main Ideas, p. 534
- ❑ **Extend Lesson 1** Connect to Today: Democracy for Women, pp. 540–541

TE

- ❑ More About Voltaire, p. 537; Montesquieu, p. 537; Mary Wollstonecraft, p. 538; Olympe de Gouges, p. 541; Women in the Enlightenment, p. 541

IDR Unit 8

- ❑ Family Newsletter (English and Spanish), pp. 21–22

REVIEW AND ENRICH

Integrate Technology

Transparencies

- ❑ Critical Thinking: CT67 Finding Main Ideas
- ❑ Humanities: HT31 View of London
- ❑ Map: MT31 World Literacy

Power Presentations

- ❑ Lesson 1 Lecture Notes

CD-ROMS

- ❑ California EasyPlanner CD-ROM
- ❑ California eEdition CD-ROM
- ❑ California Test Generator CD-ROM

Interdisciplinary Activities

TE

- ❑ Language Arts: Read Primary Sources, p. 538
- ❑ Art: Investigate the Arts, p. 538

Interdisciplinary Projects

- ❑ Math, p. 91
- ❑ Science, p. 92

Transparencies

- ❑ Art: HT31 View of London
- ❑ Geography: MT31 World Literacy

ASSESS

Content Assessment

- ❑ Lesson Review, *PE p. 539*
- ❑ Lesson Quiz, *FA p. 285*
- ❑ California Test Generator CD-ROM: Lesson 1 Quiz
- ❑ Integrated Assessment

Standards Practice

- ❑ California Standards Enrichment Workbook, pp. 147–150
- ❑ California Daily Standards Practice Transparencies TT52
- ❑ California Standards Planner and Lesson Plans, p. L103
- ❑ California Online Test Practice: **ClassZone.com**

RETEACH

- ❑ Reteaching Activity, *IDR Unit 8, p. 35*

Lesson Plans

Copyright © by McDougal Littell, a division of Houghton Mifflin Company

Democratic Ideas Develop

PE = Pupil's Edition   IDRS = IDR in Spanish
TE = Teacher's Edition   RSG = Reading Study Guide
IDR = In-Depth Resources

PLAN AND PREPARE

Lesson Objectives

❑ Describe the reforms instituted by some European monarchs.

❑ Trace the effect of Enlightenment ideas on the American Revolution.

❑ Explain the development of democracy in North America and the global spread of democratic ideals.

❑ **Language Objective:** Preview the text to formulate purpose-setting questions in order to make the text comprehensible and meaningful.

California Standards

7.11.5
7.11.6
HI 3
How to Teach the Standards, *TE p. 542*

FOCUS AND MOTIVATE

❑ MAIN IDEAS, *PE/TE p. 542*

❑ READING SKILL: Summarizing, *PE/TE p. 542*

❑ TERMS & NAMES, *PE/TE p. 543*

TEACH

Struggling Readers	**On-level**	**Gifted and Talented**	**English Learners**
TE	**PE**	**TE**	**TE**
❑ Write Headlines, p. 544	❑ Primary Source: from the Declaration of Independence, p. 546	❑ Annotate the Declaration, p. 546	❑ Preview the Text, p. 544
❑ Prepare Commentaries, p. 552		❑ Write a Character Sketch, p. 552	❑ Understand Story Structure, p. 551
IDR Unit 8	**IDR Unit 8**	**Interdisciplinary Projects**	**IDRS**
❑ Reading Skill, p. 24	❑ Reading Skill: Summarizing, p. 24	❑ Language Arts, p. 93	❑ Reading Skill, p. 144
❑ Reteaching Activity, p. 36	❑ Skillbuilder Practice: Analyzing Economic and Political Issues, p. 26	❑ Art, p. 94	**RSG (Spanish)**
Reading Study Guide			❑ Lesson 2, p. 139
❑ Lesson 2, p. 139	❑ Vocabulary Cards, p. 29		❑ **California Modified Lesson Plans for English Learners, p. 109**
❑ RSG Audio CD			
California Reading Toolkit, p. L53			❑ **Multi-Language Glossary of Social Studies Terms**

Lesson Plans

Inclusion

- ❑ **TE:** Paraphrase a Passage, p. 546; Answere Essential Questions, p. 551
- ❑ **California EasyPlanner CD-ROM:** Reading Skill, Vocabulary Study Guide, Reteaching Activity

All Students

- ❑ California Reading Toolkit, p. L53

PE

- ❑ Taking Notes: Summarizing, p. 542
- ❑ **Extend Lesson 2** Activity: Design a Museum Exhibit, p. 549; Adopting a Bill of Rights, pp. 550–553

TE

- ❑ More About Joseph II, p. 544; Thomas Jefferson and the Declaration of Independence, p. 546; King James II, p. 550; William, p. 552; English Bill of Rights, p. 553

REVIEW AND ENRICH

Integrate Technology

Transparencies

- ❑ Critical Thinking: CT68 Summarizing
- ❑ Map: MT32 The United States in 1795
- ❑ Humanities: HT32 Drafting the Declaration of Independence

Power Presentations

- ❑ Lesson 2 Lecture Notes

CD-ROMS

- ❑ California EasyPlanner CD-ROM
- ❑ California eEdition CD-ROM
- ❑ California Test Generator CD-ROM

Interdisciplinary Activities

TE

- ❑ Science: Display Inventions, p. 545
- ❑ Art: Illustrate Poor Richard's Sayings, p. 545
- ❑ Language Arts: Report on the Convention, p. 547; Write a Song About the American Revolution, p. 547

Interdisciplinary Projects

- ❑ Language Arts, p. 93
- ❑ Art, p. 94

Transparencies

- ❑ Geography: MT32 The United States in 1795
- ❑ Art: HT32 Drafting the Declaration of Independence

ASSESS

Content Assessment

- ❑ Lesson Review, *PE p. 548*
- ❑ Chapter Review, *PE pp. 554–555*
- ❑ Lesson Quiz, *FA p. 286*
- ❑ California Test Generator CD-ROM: Lesson 2 Quiz
- ❑ Integrated Assessment

Standards Practice

- ❑ California Standards Enrichment Workbook, pp. 149–152
- ❑ California Daily Standards Practice Transparencies TT53
- ❑ California Standards Planner and Lesson Plans, p. L105
- ❑ California Online Test Practice: **ClassZone.com**

Struggling Readers	**On-Level**	**Gifted and Talented**	**English Learners**
❑ Test Form A, *FA pp. 287–290*	❑ Test Form B, *FA pp. 291–294*	❑ Test Form C, *FA pp. 295–298*	❑ Test Generator: Forms A, B, and C in Spanish

RETEACH

- ❑ Reteaching Activity, *IDR Unit 8, p. 36*